Nadine
After the Darkness Comes Light

Nadine
After the Darkness Comes Light

PATRICIA ERWIN CALL

Mountain Memories Books
Charleston, West Virginia

Mountain Memories Books
Charleston, WV

First Edition

10 9 8 7 6 5 4 3 2 1

Printed in the United States of America

Library of Congress Control Number: 2012000000
ISBN-13: 978-0-938985-31-0
ISBN-10: 0-938985-31-0
Book & cover design: Mark S. Phillips

Distributed by:

West Virginia Book Company
1125 Central Avenue
Charleston, WV 25302
www.wvbookco.com

Dedication

The source of *Nadine: After the Darkness Comes Light* is love. The love shared between the people written about in this book, the love they showered upon me, and the love of my many friends who encouraged me to write this reminiscence. It is written to rekindle the warmth of a wonderful person for those who had the privilege of knowing her, for those who did not and especially for Nadine and Vinson's grandchildren, Mark, Rochelle and Patrick and great-grandchildren, Sophie, Haleigh, and MacKenzie. I am particularly grateful to my husband, Doug, who has been uncommonly dedicated in helping me with *Nadine: After the Darkness Comes Light*.

HE WILL GIVE HIS ANGELS CHARGE OF YOU
TO GUARD YOU IN ALL YOUR WAYS.
(PSALM 91: 11, RSV).

DO NOT FORGET TO ENTERTAIN STRANGERS, FOR BY
DOING SO SOME PEOPLE HAVE ENTERTAINED ANGELS
WITHOUT KNOWING IT.
(ROMANS 13:2, NIV)

You will be captivated by Nadine's story. She is orphaned at birth. She lives with three families before moving to the Taylor's. Here she meets fascinating characters and hears stories of slavery, romance, murders, ghosts, gypsies, the Civil War, the Great Depression and the 1918 Flu Epidemic. Some of these she experiences personally. When evil creeps into the Taylor's home, Nadine's life there begins to crumble. She must leave.

Finding herself now in a harsh world, her goals are to find her father, love and security. Nadine's memory of a fateful encounter with a kind young woman who promises to pray for her enables her to endure the tough times and to persevere. You will be entertained, inspired, and grow to love Nadine.

Nadine's conversations with me when I was a youngster into adulthood are the basis for *Nadine: After the Darkness Comes Light*. Facts were also gained through interviews, newspaper articles, regional nonfiction books, letters, audio tapes and her diary. The book is a historical fiction that is mostly factual.

You are welcomed into Nadine's personal world from 1908–1941 and into St. Albans, West Virginia, a small Appalachian Village.

NADINE: AFTER THE DARKNESS COMES LIGHT

The only light came from an oil lamp, flickering from the raw March wind which could be heard and felt as it sent a draft through the room. Dr. Dan Miller shrugged into his coat, folded his stethoscope, and placed it into his sagging, brown leather bag where bottles of red, blue, and yellow powders and pills were visible. None of these could help the twenty-six year old dying woman.

Hazel's eyes were closed. The paleness of her face exaggerated the blueness of her lips. A few strands of strawberry blonde hair stuck to her forehead beaded with perspiration. The sheets were saturated with blood, and its source still flowed.

Nanna tiptoed into the room with clean linens and a bowl of water with the steam still rising from it. "Now I know what labor is," she said softly, moving toward the bed. "My babies just popped out."

Dr. Dan cleared his throat, "She'll not make it through the night," he whispered. "She's lost too much blood, and her infected wisdom tooth has shot poison all through her body." Still gazing into the gaping medical bag, unable to look his dying sister-in-law in the face, he asked Nanna, "Where is my brother?"

Nanna stared at Hazel as though mesmerized. "After seeing the baby, Phil just bolted out of the front door."

Dan's face turned crimson as he finally closed the bag, gripping its handle tightly. Phil never could face responsibility. Now he is going to let his wife die without him, Dan wanted to say but restrained himself. "Just clean Hazel as best you can and keep swabbing her down to see if her fever will break. I'll speak to Hazel's mother. Where is she?"

"Trying to put Carl to bed. He can't understand his mother's screams. He's just four himself," Nanna answered, reaching up to wipe a tear away before its saltiness reached her mouth.

An hour later, Nanna saw Hazel's eyelids slightly flicker, but not

HAZEL MILLER

enough to expose the pupils of her eyes. "Nadine," Hazel's lips formed the words.

Nanna, without hesitation, brought the baby, placing her cautiously into Hazel's awaiting arms.

Hazel's lips quivered into a smile as she pulled back the blanket and gazed at Nadine. Her lips began to shape the words to the prayer she had chanted as a child.

Angel of God my guardian dear
because of God's love He sent you here
From this day stay by my (children's) side
to light, to guard, to rule and to guide

With the last word, Hazel's body relaxed and her breathing stopped.

* * *

The little girl stood on her tiptoes with muscles taut in the calves of her legs, so her elbows could reach the windowsill. She cradled her chin in her hands. With her auburn hair cascading down her back, she tilted her head just slightly to the right to study the mother cat and her three kittens on the front porch. The child winced as the mother cat hissed and slapped her kittens away as they attempted to nuzzle close to nurse her warm milk. The mother hissed, struck out once more then turned and ran into the front lawn. One of the kittens pursued her as the others stood watching her disappear into the dense gray early morning fog.

Suddenly there was a loud snap and hissing sounds, and the room was momentarily illuminated with a red glow, making shadows on the walls. The child turned to see a chunk of coal break open in the fireplace. The sudden light drew the child's attention to two figures silhouetted against the fireplace which was the room's only source of light in the early morning of October, 1912.

Her Aunt Vonzine and Vonzine's neighbor, Nanna Rimmer, sat in rocking chairs facing each other. Their silver needles driven by their expert hands whipped quickly through what the child recognized as her clothes being mended.

The child had been listening to their quiet whispers as she watched the kittens. Her question cut through the room, "Why is the momma cat being so mean to her babies? She won't feed them."

Vonzine weighed her words. "The momma is trying to wean her kittens, so they can go out into the world and take care of themselves."

"But she's being mean," the small girl of about four said, stamping her foot.

Nanna Rimmer took up the conversation. "No, she's being good. It just appears mean."

"She's smacking them," persisted the child.

"The kittens have depended on their momma for everything. It would be mean not to teach them to fend for themselves. If she didn't, they would starve. Mommas can't always be with their small ones," continued Nanna Rimmer.

"You mean like Momma and Grandmomma Dunlap, leaving me and going to heaven?" the child questioned. Aunt Vonzine and Nanna nodded in agreement.

"But I miss Grandmomma," the child responded, turning back to the window.

The women resumed rocking in sync, not responding but with their heads bent, continuing their chore of mending the child's floral feed sack dresses, faded from wear.

Vonzine was small, frail, and her square shaped face showed fatigue. In contrast, Nanna's plumpness and sagging breasts bore witness to a woman who had born several children.

Their whispers continued as the child's attention returned to the kittens. The child blew vapor onto the window and letter by letter wrote, "Nadine Ruth."

Vonzine's voice now rose above a whisper, "Nadine." The child made a half turn toward the voice. "Nadine, don't write on the windows, I just washed them yesterday. Lord knows I've enough to do around here with your uncle upstairs dying. I can't be redoing windows." Nadine obediently erased her name with her small pudgy fist.

Rocking in sync again with Nanna, Vonzine swept back a few strands of strawberry-blonde hair from her forehead. With this sudden movement, Nanna glanced up, noting once more the resemblance between Vonzine and Vonzine's dead sister, Hazel, who had been Nadine's mother.

Vonzine spoke in a strained whisper as tears began to form in her eyes. "I feel like a failure, sending Nadine to live with somebody outside of the family. This will be her fourth home since Hazel died: Hazel and Phil's, Mom's, mine and now Mrs. Taylor's. I promised Momma when she was dying that I would care for Nadine."

"You've done the best you can, Vonzine." Dr. Cunningham says that Nadine cannot stay here with a TB patient, and none of her family will take her. You're lucky to have found good homes for both Carl and Nadine," consoled Nanna.

"Seems unfair that Uncle John and Aunt Nona were quick to volunteer to take Carl but not Nadine; girls just aren't wanted," Vonzine retorted.

Nanna lowered her gaze to her mending, not wanting to show emotion, "I'm sorry I can't raise Nadine. She is such a sweet child, but I do well to care for my own nine."

Vonzine quickly took her turn as consoler, "It was good of you to wet nurse Nadine after Hazel died. You have done your share. Just look how healthy she is."

"Since my Howard was born about the same time as Nadine, it was easy. Lord knows I had enough milk for both. Now quit your worrying and accept God's gift of Mrs. Taylor who is willing to raise Nadine."

After a brief pause, Vonzine added, "If Phil hadn't been so heartbroken after Hazel's death and taken off for God knows where, we wouldn't have this situation."

*   *   *

Nadine sat on a long wooden bench. Beneath the bench was her child-sized camelback trunk, containing all of her belongings. Clutching her cloth doll, Miss Betsy, to her chest, Nadine crossed her ankles, which dangled several inches from the boat's deck, and swung them rhythmically. Her hazel eyes darted back and forth, taking in all the sights as people boarded the sternwheeler at Swann's landing, Saint Albans, West Virginia.

There were people carrying bushels of Silver Queen corn, freshly dug potatoes, and cages with chickens whose auburn red feathers shone in the bright sun much as did Nadine's long red curls that Aunt Vonzine had curled on rags the night before.

Nadine had fidgeted in her seat, not a child to sit still long, as Vonzine quarreled, "Now sit still. We want Mrs. Taylor to know right off what a pretty little girl is coming to live with her. Don't we?"

As Aunt Vonzine's nimble fingers curled Nadine's hair, she explained the upcoming adventure which would unfold tomorrow afternoon. "We'll walk down to Swann's Lane to the landing where you will get on a sternwheeler which will take you to Institute. There you will be met by Mrs. Taylor's handyman." She stopped combing long enough to pull from her apron pocket a wrinkled letter and reread the handyman's name aloud just to be sure, "Henry. Now remember, his name is Henry. Oh, I'll tell the captain too, in case you forget. Plus I'll hang this note around your neck. It says, Institute, West Virginia," Vonzine pointed.

Swann's Lane sounded nice, Nadine thought. Grandmomma Dunlap had once read her *Ugly Duckling* where the duck had turned into a beautiful swan. Nadine remembered the graceful white bird as the picture showed it gliding across the water.

"You're a mighty lucky young lady," Aunt Vonzine rushed on. "My, at your age, you have ridden on a train. Remember? That's where you met Mrs. Taylor, and she agreed you could come live on her big farm. Now you're going to ride a boat on the Kanawha River."

Nadine nodded her head in agreement as she recalled the lady with the kind blue eyes.

"Stop wiggling," Vonzine directed again as she continued to unfold the pluses of going to Mrs. Taylor's to live. "There will be animals. You love animals: horses, pigs, cows, chickens. Doesn't that sound grand?"

"Will there be other children?" inquired Nadine hopefully. She would miss Nanna's son, Howard. Nadine called him Howie. He was her favorite playmate.

"Mr. and Mrs. Taylor don't have any children. That's why they want you. You are very lucky and special," Vonzine said in a rising tone which she always used to impart a positive.

Nadine, leaning her head back against the boat's cabin, closed her eyes as she continued to recall last night's conversation with Aunt Vonzine. She thought of how disappointed she had been this morning in the pretty sounding Swann's Lane. It was in reality a narrow, rutted, dirt road with barely enough room for one wagon and a few people to pass and which held the pungent smell of horse poop. Nadine hoped Mrs. Taylor's farm would not be a disappointment. As Nadine almost dozed off, she felt the boat slow down and heard two quick toots as the boat changed course, heading toward the riverbank. Nadine straightened in alarm and looked toward the great turning wheel which churned the river water, changing its mirror like surface into bubbly white foam.

Nadine shyly tugged at the dress sleeve of the lady seated beside her and questioned. "Are we at Institute?"

"No child, we're stopping at Sattes Landing to pick up more passengers and freight. There are a lot of people traveling on this fine Indian Summer day. Institute is our next stop. Just relax, dear". She noted the sign about Nadine's neck. "I'll tell you when we arrive," said the smiling young blonde woman.

Nadine scooted back and closed her eyes. Indian Summer, she remembered that phrase. She had asked Grandmomma Dunlap what it meant. "It is the warm days after a brief cold snap as winter is approaching. The leaves put on their brilliant dress—the yellow and orange maples, yellow poplar and sycamores and red oak and sumac." Grandmomma Dunlap had patted Nadine's hand as she held the child on her lap. In a whisper she added, "It's the time of the year when the Indians used to come into these parts to pillage, raid and harass the white folks and to get supplies before winter set in." This memory sent a shiver up Nadine's spine as she peeked between her eyelashes to see if any Indians wearing war paint moved along the banks of the river. She didn't see any, but that didn't mean they weren't there, thought Nadine.

Nadine's attention shifted from the river bank, and out of the corner of her eye she noticed the lady beside her with the soft friendly voice watching her. So when she fully opened her eyes, conversation naturally ensued as the lady commented, "That is a beautiful dress you are wearing with the pink rosebuds and that lace around the collar."

Nadine scooted a little closer to the lady, breathing in the sweet smell of her talcum powder. "My Aunt Vonzine made this from a feed sack," Nadine said proudly.

"You're very young to be riding on a boat alone. Are you visiting a relative?"

Nadine hesitated before answering. She knew Aunt Vonzine did not want some things told. This, however, was a nice lady, and Nadine was glad to have someone to talk to. Besides, Grandmomma Dunlap had said, "Respect your elders, Child."

"No, I'm going to live on Mrs. Taylor's farm where there will be all kinds of animals."

"Who is Mrs. Taylor? Oh, excuse me, I never introduced myself. My name is Angela." She extended her hand.

"Mine is Nadine." The two very formally shook hands.

"My Aunt Vonzine was taking me to the Davis Child Shelter after Grandmomma Dunlap died, and my aunt's husband got TB. On the train, we met Mrs. Taylor, and she said that she would like to have me. You see, the Taylors don't have any children."

"And your parents?"

"Momma died when I was born. Grandmomma Dunlap took care of me until she died. Aunt Vonzine said the Taylor's are a gift from God."

"I do say," Angela shook her head positively.

Their conversation ceased but in the background could be heard the sounds of chickens' clucking, voices gossiping and the stern wheel swishing. These sounds were once again interrupted by two toots as the boat slowed, moving toward the bank.

Nadine saw the captain in his white billed cap coming toward her. "Well, young lady, we're at Institute. You get off here."

"I'll assist her," volunteered Angela.

As they walked down the rough plank, the captain carried all of Nadine's worldly possessions in her small humpbacked trunk except for Miss Betsy. Nadine clutched the doll close to her body with one hand while holding tightly to Angela's soft hand with her other. Nadine spied a wagon with a stout looking man seated in the driver's seat. "That must be Henry," she cried.

"Must be," the captain agreed since it was the only wagon about. "Your aunt's note says Henry will pick you up in a wagon. Henry?" the captain called.

The man's dark hair had been slicked back, probably with lard, and laid flat except for an unruly cowlick, which shot straight up like a horn. His skin was reddish brown and leathery from working in the fields. He flashed a simple smile in response while avoiding eye contact. "That's me," he waved.

After loading the wagon, Henry leaned over and lifted Nadine up onto the seat. With a gentle touch, which seemed out of character for this rough looking man, Henry situated Nadine in her seat, and patted the doll with his large callused hand. He then gave a tug at the horse's reins, and they were off.

In the distance, Nadine heard Angela call, "I'll be praying for you, Nadine." With these words, Angela folded her arms across her chest giving them the appearance of wings.

Nadine turned and waved until she lost sight of Angela as the horse-driven wagon was drawn into a cornfield. Its brownish stalks shot up above Nadine's head, cutting off much of the light of a sunny afternoon that, due to the slant of the sun, was drawing to a close.

"What's your dolly's name?" Henry asked, punctuating the question by clearing his throat. Nadine looked up at Henry, but he stared straight ahead.

"Miss Betsy. What is your horse's name?"

"This here is Big Red, but I just call him Red." Again he punctuated his answer by clearing his throat.

Nadine eyed Red who was chestnut red—true to his name. She noted his wide back. Indeed, with her short legs, she would have to do a split to sit astride him. The horse's flesh and ears twitched as black horseflies zeroed in on their target, drawing blood. Big Red, in defense, swished his tail as he plodded along with a clip-clop, clip-clop.

Suddenly, with a bump, they pulled into a clearing where they saw a white house with high pillars. It had been a grand house for this area, but now the paint peeled and the out buildings sagged. In the yard children played hide and seek. Nadine was thrilled because they had red hair like hers. But unlike her fair skin, peppered with freckles, their skin was the color of toast.

Nadine's voice rose with excitement. "Is this the Taylor's house?" She did not care about the condition of the house but only about the children with red hair because she loved children, and especially redheaded children because she knew so few.

"Nope! Them's a Mulatto family." Henry cleared his throat.

Nadine assumed Mulatto was the family's last name. "How much farther is it then?"

"Just a hop and a jump." Again he cleared his throat.

Nadine giggled at the thought of a hop and a jump as if Red could do either, and the realization that Henry's clearing his throat did not mean he had a "frog in his throat" as Grandmomma Dunlap would say. That was just the funny way Henry talked. Or, perhaps he had a frog in his throat, and it just hopped and jumped out, and Henry had not realized it.

Henry and Nadine rode in silence as she took in the sights along the rutted dirt road. They had not traveled far when Nadine noticed the land was cleared to till and for pasture. She watched the honey colored Jersey cattle peacefully munch the sweet grass in a green meadow that stopped at the edge of the barbed wire fence. Beyond, laid the freshly plowed, black, river bottom land, plowed no doubt with the help of Red.

Wooden outbuildings seasoned to a soft silver gray by the sun with silver tin roofs spotted here and there by caramel colored rust came into view. "This here is the Taylor's place," said Henry with a nod.

Red began pulling toward the left of the road as he neared the first building, the barn. Henry flicked the reins, "Gitty up, we ain't done," he directed Red.

"Soon as we deliver our goods, I'll give you some hay and cool water, not till," Henry punctuated this by clearing his throat. Red obediently centered himself in the road with a whinny, sensing by Henry's tone that he had to postpone his rewards.

"Is this where Red lives?" questioned Nadine.

"Yep, him, other horses, cows, and a big black snake."

Nadine's voice raised an octave, "A black snake?"

"Sure thing. He keeps the mice out of the potato bin and root cellar inside the barn."

The green of Nadine's eyes seemed intensified when contrasted against the whites which were more visible with the thought of a snake living in the barn.

Seeing her reaction, Henry quickly added, "That snake is a friend."

"Not my friend," Nadine said enunciating each word. Henry's lips curled up into a smile at her reaction.

Behind Red's barn was a larger barn with golden tobacco hanging from its ceiling, curing in preparation for the tobacco auction. The pigpen where the fat hogs either rooted or rolled in the mud came next. Nadine held her nose at the stench as Red pulled their wagon along. The clucking chickens seemed to have the run of the area in front of the chicken house as they scratched in the dirt and sauntered in and out of the road.

Nadine's attention was distracted from the chickens by squeaking hinges and then a sharp slam of the screen door as Mrs. Taylor stepped out on the large porch of the two-story white frame house. Wiping her hands on the corner of her white apron, she walked down the steps and proceeded down the path sheltered by a row of golden sugar maple trees, forming a canopy overhead. She was a stout looking woman and wore her brown chestnut hair pulled back in a bun.

"I saw you a coming," she said. Opening the gate of the white picket fence, she stooped and shooed the chickens as they tried to enter into unexplored territory. Mrs. Taylor wore a blue cotton dress which came to her ankles and ended under her chin with a neatly starched white collar. From her breast pocket, she pulled a gold watch which hung from a gold chain around her neck. "The boat must have been late. It's past suppertime—almost bedtime," she stated factually. The chirping of the katydids verified the lateness of the day as did the sinking sun.

Henry's only response was a nod and a verbal, "Yep," followed, as always, by that guttural sound in his throat. He pulled Red to a stop, gently lifted Nadine to the ground, and proceeded to carry her trunk into the house.

Mrs. Taylor clapped her hands with joy at seeing Nadine, "And here is our little girl that we've been waiting for all afternoon." Mrs. Taylor stooped to be on Nadine's eye level, holding her arms wide for a hug.

"Mind your manners when you're living at the Taylor's," Aunt Vonzine directed Nadine upon her departure from Swann's Landing that morning. Nevertheless, Nadine felt her body tense as Mrs. Taylor's arms began to encircle her. But the little girl was unable to avoid looking into Mrs. Taylor's blue eyes, glowing with liveliness. This lady was younger than Granmamma Dunlap but older than Aunt Vonzine, and Nanna had said that she was a gift from God. With these thoughts, she allowed her body to fold into Mrs. Taylor's as she was hugged.

"I bet you're hungry," said Mrs. Taylor, releasing Nadine.

Nadine nodded as she pulled Miss Betsy close with one hand while giving Mrs. Taylor her other hand. "What a pretty doll," Mrs. Taylor chattered on as they approached the house.

Nadine smiled at the approval of Miss Betsy because Aunt Vonzine had said she was worn and dirty and should be thrown away. This thought made Nadine clutch Miss Betsy closer.

"You'll have to tell Mr. Taylor about your boat ride and introduce him to Miss Betsy."

Nadine agreed and abruptly said, "You sure smell nice."

"That must be the lavender which I grow right over there,"

Mrs. Taylor pointed to a patch of spent flowers, growing along the vegetable garden beside of the house. "I dry it and line my dresser drawers with it. Maybe you'd like some in a sachet bag to make your clothes smell sweet.

"Miss Betsy's too," suggested Nadine.

"Sounds good to me," Mrs. Taylor agreed as she swung open the screen door while waving away the flies.

Nadine now stood in the hallway where the pine floors had been painted a deep gold. After Nadine's eyes adjusted to the dimly lit hall, her gaze shifted to the parlor whose door was left ajar, allowing a cold musty smelling draft to drift into the hall. Even though evening was closing in, the three windows with tassel-trimmed antique satin drapes afforded enough light to see the black horse hair stuffed settee and two side chairs trimmed in walnut decorated with spoon carving. Beside each chair and the settee, sat pink marble topped tables, hosting matching hurricane lamps painted with pink rose buds.

Nadine remembered when Grandmomma Dunlap died that she was placed in a casket in her parlor for viewing. Oh, yes, and when Preacher Davis visited, he was received in the parlor. Other than that the parlor was unused. By the smell and perfection of the room, this must be true here also.

Mrs. Taylor led Nadine into a combination master bedroom and sitting room where the white starched lace curtains allowed in more light. The room smelled of sulfur from the dying coal fire in the fireplace. In front of the fire sat a heavy set gentleman, resembling pictures of Santa with his bushy white beard.

Mrs. Taylor crossed her arms at her waist and cleared her throat. With a start, the man dropped the newspaper he had been reading before dozing, and with an exaggerated gesture of opening his eyes wide, making his eyebrows arch, stuttered, "I was just, just resting my eyes." He turned toward Nadine, and with the smile lines that ran from the corners of his blue eyes to below his mouth deepening, he said, "This must be Nadine. I fought in the Civil War as did your Grandfather Colonel William Miller. I fought under Stonewall." With no recognition on Nadine's part, he rambled on, "Why your grandpa and I were just young boys when we joined up. He later became Mayor of St. Albans, you know! I hated to hear of him dying last year."

Mrs. Taylor cleared her throat again and interrupted the monologue. "This is Mr. Taylor, Nadine."

"Yes, yes and I have something here." Mr. Taylor reached into his bib overall pocket and pulled out a stick of horehound candy.

With a tilt of her head Nadine reached out and grabbed the candy, remembering to say, "Thank you."

"Ok, now you must eat your supper before the candy," instructed Mrs. Taylor as she led Nadine into a large kitchen with a long wooden table on which an oil lamp glowed, making the oil cloth tablecloth shine. "Mr. Taylor is very rigid in his eating habits. Eats at 5:00 p.m. sharp, so he and I ate earlier. I'm keeping Henry's warm while he finishes his chores." Mrs. Taylor set a bowl of potato soup with bits of potatoes, celery, carrots and transparent onions floating in a buttery milk sauce in front of Nadine. Beside the bowl, she placed a hunk of fresh cornbread, oozing with butter. Nadine ate with relish, licking the butter from her finger tips and gulping down the glass of cool milk. She had not eaten for hours, and Mrs. Taylor was a good cook. Besides when she cleaned her bowl she could have that stick of candy.

Nadine sat at the end of the table slowly licking her candy as Mrs. Taylor quickly tidied up the kitchen, scraping the scraps into the slop bucket for feeding the hogs. Afterwards she washed the dishes. "Is that Henry's room?" Nadine asked pointing to a door in the rear of the kitchen.

"No, that's the pantry. Henry sleeps out back in his own room." "You and Mr. Taylor sleep in there?" Nadine pointed toward the sitting room from where Mr. Taylor's snoring came.

"That's right, and I'll show you your room now. You've had a long day, and it's time to go to bed." With that, Mrs. Taylor picked up the oil lamp and led Nadine out of the kitchen and up a steep stairway that creaked with each step. From the second floor hallway, Mrs. Taylor opened a door and set the lamp on the dresser. A white painted iron bed dominated the room. The room was cool as there was no source of heat on the second floor.

Mrs. Taylor walked over to the corner where Nadine's trunk sat and rummaged through it, pulling out her night gown. After shaking the wrinkles out, she pulled Nadine's dress over her head with these words, "Daddy's gone a huntin' to make the baby a buntin'...Let's skin the bunny."

Nadine giggled at this verse as she wiggled into her night gown with Mrs. Taylor's help. "I'll leave the lamp here till you get used to the room," Mrs. Taylor said. After she tucked Nadine in, she left, closing the door behind her.

Nadine heard the stairs creak as Mrs. Taylor descended them. She got up to place her candy on the dresser, having carefully re-wrapped it for tomorrow. She quickly jumped back into bed where she was swallowed by a soft feathertick mattress. She lay on her back, watching the shadows formed by the oil lamp. Then she heard a scratching sound. Lifting herself upon her elbow, she looked for its source, but it stopped. Pulling the cover over her head so she no longer could see the ominous shadows moving across the ceiling and walls, she heard the noise again. At times the scratching would be hard and long in duration and at others soft and short.

The wind began a low howling sound. Peeping from beneath the covers, she saw the shadows dance faster, and the scratching increased. Nadine bit her lip, and with all the nerve she could gain, slowly got out of bed and went to the window. There, rubbing against the side of the house, she saw the tip of a tree branch.

With relief, Nadine climbed back into bed, and pulled the covers over her head again. She was dozing off when she thought she heard a low moaning and a soft knocking on the wall behind the head of her bed. Her body stiffened and her fingernails cut into her palms. Listening intently, she recognized that the moan was actually someone singing. Henry sleeps out back and Mr. and Mrs. Taylor are asleep downstairs, she remembered. There was someone else in the next room.

The singing was mournful. The tears of fear seeped down Nadine's cheeks and soaked into the collar of her nightgown. Pulling Mrs. Betsy up under her chin, Nadine glanced at the wall opposite the dresser, and she saw for the first time a picture of an angel hovering protectively over a little girl and boy crossing a wooden bridge suspended above a raging creek. Because the mournful singing ceased, Nadine dared not look away from the picture. That is Carl, the pretty lady on the boat, Angela, and me, Nadine thought as her eyes began to close, and she sank deeper into the warm womb of the feathertick.

Nadine awoke to the chirping of many birds. The sun had risen up over the hills, and the shadows of the night danced no more. Nadine listened for the sad song she had heard earlier, but it too had been silenced. Perhaps it had been a dream. Enjoying the warmth of the feathertick, she lay in bed smelling the ham, eggs and biscuits cooking downstairs.

*   *   *

"It's about time you got up sleepy head," Mrs. Taylor greeted. "Do you like blackberry jelly on your biscuits?" Nadine's shrug sent Mrs. Taylor into the pantry, returning with a jar of the deep purple delicacy.

"You'll like that on a hot biscuit. Mrs. Taylor picked those blackberries herself," Mr. Taylor greeted as he finished his coffee, got up and began filling a clean plate with food. He carried the food out of the room, and Nadine could hear his footsteps on the bare wooden steps.

Nadine would again observe Mr. Taylor fill a plate at both lunch and supper. This would be followed by the sound of those squeaking stairs.

After supper, Nadine sat at the end of the table, savoring jelly on the last biscuit as Mrs. Taylor heated water drawn from a well. Next to the kitchen was a screened porch, with red and yellow peppers hanging from the ceiling. Right outside was the well. "Mr. Taylor must be real hungry, he eats here and then takes another full plate upstairs."

Mrs. Taylor smiled, "So he does," was her reply.

Chores finished, Mrs. Taylor took Nadine's hand and instructed, "Come with me." Again they mounted the steps. This time Mrs. Taylor headed toward a closed door from which a low humming sound came.

Slowly she opened the door, and Nadine was startled by a sudden movement from inside. When Mrs. Taylor entered the room, a human form jumped behind her and clung to her shoulders, hiding. "Frances, do not act like that. I've brought Nadine to meet you. She'll think you're silly." These words brought no reaction from Frances. "I'm going to stand here until you say hello to Nadine and make her feel welcome." There was no sound in the room except for Nadine's heart which seemed to beat in her ears. Not knowing what the next sudden move by Frances might be, Nadine stood close to the open door.

"Frances," Mrs. Taylor's voice raised with a note of authority. Nadine saw a pair of blue eyes peering at her. Quickly Frances' face disappeared as she shifted her body to hide. Again the blue eyes peeped from over Mrs. Taylor's shoulder.

Nadine's heart beat a little slower as she realized that Frances, although a grown woman, was playing peek-a-boo with her. So she covered her face with her hands and slowly parted her index fingers, showing only her eyes.

Frances giggled and stepped from behind Mrs. Taylor. Placing her hand to her mouth, Frances looked at the floor. She wore a cotton dress much like Mrs. Taylor's, and her salt and pepper hair was pulled back into a single braid that hung down her back.

"Frances, I would like you to meet Nadine who has come to live with us." Frances removed her hand from her mouth and did a quick curtsey, "Nadine, this is my sister, Frances."

"You have a matching set of eyes," Nadine responded.

"Indeed we do. Frances is not only my sister but my buddy," continued Mrs. Taylor. Frances shyly smiled. "You see, Frances ran a high temperature when she had Chicken Pox at age six and still thinks somewhat as a six year old. So, she also lives with us. This is who Mr. Taylor brings meals to." Frances shook her head in agreement. A plate with remnants of supper sitting on the night stand attested to this.

"Nadine, you might enjoy getting to know Frances while I do my chores." Frances hesitantly reached out and took Nadine's hand, pulling her further into the room, as Mrs. Taylor's dress could be heard sweeping the stairs as she went down.

"We can play," said Frances.

Looking around the room, Nadine did not see much to play with. "What would you like to do?" Nadine asked. Frances shrugged. "Was that you I heard singing last night?" Frances nodded eagerly. "My friend Howie and I liked to play church. I can be the preacher and you can be the congregation."

"What do I do?" Frances asked.

"Sing! Haven't you been to church?"

Frances shook her head from side to side, making her braid bounce back and forth."

"Then I'll show you." This is going to be more fun than with Howie, Nadine thought. Frances will do anything I ask. Nadine stood on a chair and began her imitation of Preacher Davis at the Baptist Church where she had gone with Grandmomma Dunlap every Sunday morning.

"Let me tell you, Brother! Let me tell you, Sister!" Nadine began her monologue, jabbing her finger into the air and acquiring a singsong chant as her voice grew louder and louder, and Frances' eyes got wider and wider. "You've all sinned! There is a coming judgement day!" Nadine punctuated this by raising her small fist into the air to emphasize her words. With all her inhibitions lost in the message, Nadine's face turned red with enthusiasm as she added, "And you'll burn in fire if you don't change your ways!" Frances' wide eyes blinked as she nodded her head saying, "Yes, yes," but the last statement, "burn in fire!" brought a loud gasp, signaling Nadine that maybe she had gone too far. She quickly added, "Now let's sing a hymn." "Jesus loves me..." sang Nadine, and Frances enthusiastically joined in.

This is how Nadine and Frances spent many a rainy afternoon.

When Nadine heard Frances singing at bedtime, it no longer frightened her because she and Frances were now friends.

*   *   *

"Mornin' Mrs. Taylor. It sure is a beautiful day for a makin' apple butter, and the apple crop has been plentiful. Why, we had to stake our apple trees limbs to keep them from a draggin' on the ground." Melinda said, fanning her face with her handkerchief to keep the flies and sweat bees away. "Lord's done been good to us. Yes, Mamm." Melinda had initiated the conversation as soon as she saw Mrs. Taylor, sitting on the front porch, leaning over in the oak swing peeling apples. There were already a variety of containers—bowls, milking pails and crocks—brimming over with milky white apples, now turning brown around the edges.

Melinda was a heavy set woman with kinky red hair and toast brown skin. Her face was beginning to take on the features of a dried apple doll, but her bright brown eyes reflected a youthful spirit. She turned and put her hands on her hips. "Get up out of that dusty road, Sassy, and put them dirty rocks down. I swan, it doesn't do a bit of good to wash you up."

Sassy reluctantly stood and dusted herself off. "But this is a pretty pebble." she answered, sliding it into her dress pocket with one eye on her grandmother to see if she was going to object. Sassy ran along side of Melinda and whispered "Where is the little girl?" She gave a tug at Melinda's full skirt.

"I brung Sassy to play with your little girl while we make the apple butter," Melinda said glancing toward the corn crib at the big copper kettle hanging above the crackling fire.

"Nadine, Sassy is here," Mrs. Taylor called. "Nadine has been asking over and over when you would be coming. She is so excited about having somebody to play with."

Hearing her name, Nadine bounded out onto the porch, letting the screen door bang behind her. Being held by one arm, Miss Betsy dangled at her side.

"My, you sure are a pretty little thing," Melinda said.

"This is Nadine," Mrs. Taylor nodded in her direction, "and this is Melinda and her daughter, Sassy," Mrs. Taylor nodded in their direction. "Now you two go play while the apple butter cooks."

Nadine recognized Sassy as being one of the mulatto children she had seen playing hide-and-seek down the road on her way to the Taylor's. "You have red hair just like I do," Nadine said with pleasure.

"And freckles too," Sassy answered as she walked over and placed her fingers on Nadine's nose and cheeks, pointing to the sprinkling of freckles. Then she let her hand slide down to touch the doll.

"This is Miss Betsy." Nadine offered the doll to Sassy.

Sassy examined the doll with some of its stuffing sticking out, smiled and handed it back. Then she reached into her pocket, pulled out the pretty white pebble, wiped it on her dress, and handed it to Nadine.

Nadine slowly rolled it between her fingers feeling its smoothness and warmth. "Look how white it is. Where did you get this?"

"There are lots out along the road. You can keep it if you want."

Nadine wrapped the stone in her handkerchief and dropped it in her pocket. "Let's go find some more." The two redheads, holding hands, headed toward the gate.

"You two don't go wandering off." Mrs. Taylor warned, "and do not go near the pig pen. Those big hogs could eat two little girls like you for breakfast."

Melinda, bending over to pick up another apple to peel, added, "Don't go near the beehive neither, or down where them Gypsies are along the creek. They steal children you know." With this last sentence, Melinda stood up and yelled her warning louder as Nadine and Sassy wandered down the road digging their toes into the dusty road in pursuit of the treasured smooth white pebbles, causing fine dust particles to float up and settle on their bare feet.

* * *

With their pockets sagging from their collection of stones, Nadine asked, "What can we do now?"

Sassy shrugged her shoulders and with little hesitation, said, "Want to see the Gypsies?"

Nadine's eyes widened, "But your grandma said they steal children."

"Can't steal what they can't see, so we'll just spy on them."

This made sense to Nadine. But just in case they had to run fast, to escape, they emptied their pockets of their treasures, placing them at the base of an oak tree beside the creek.

With Sassy as their guide, they followed the creek until they heard voices. Nadine tried to understand what was being said, but a different language was spoken. Topping a knoll, Sassy jerked Nadine behind a clump of bushes where they squatted and looked between the limbs into a clearing where covered wagons were situated along the creek bank. Nadine's breathing became shallow with fear. There were ragged children splashing in the water. Nadine wondered if these children had been stolen from their families. Her attention shifted to the center of camp, to men wearing bandanas that covered their heads and gold hooped earrings hanging from their ear lobes. They moved about the camp with ease, feeding cracked corn to the few chickens and horses. Some of the women cooked over the fire, while others washed clothes in the creek water. A wrinkled old woman, squatting beside the fire, smiled as another woman spoke to her. The old woman's front teeth were stained brown and worn almost into the gums. A young woman, wearing a low-cut dress, carried wet clothes up from the creek to a bush where she began draping them over limbs to dry in the soft autumn breeze. Nadine's attention now focused on this woman. She had long black hair the color of a black bird's wing shining in the sun, and smooth skin the color of a copper penny. As she gracefully sauntered along, there was a tinkling sound made by the many gold bracelets that adorned her arms. "She is beautiful," Nadine whispered.

Sassy placed her fingers across her lips, "Shhh." Then seeing one of the older boys walking toward their hiding place, Sassy grabbed Nadine by her dress sleeve, tearing it at the shoulder seam. Nadine jumped and ran, trying to catch up with Sassy as they weaved through withered raspberry and blackberry bushes that scratched their arms, legs and faces as they ran.

Once out of hearing distance of the camp, Sassy panting and looking over her shoulder warned, "Watch out for snakes. They lie around in the raspberry and blackberry bushes." Nadine began running faster even though her feet were being pricked by the undergrowth, and her heart was thumping hard against her ribs.

Sassy abruptly stopped and listened. Hearing nothing, she dropped to her knees and began laughing, "Wasn't that fun?"

Nadine slumped beside her friend to catch her breath. "Do you think we're safe now?"

"We're okay except for that snake right behind you."

Nadine jumped up with a yelp, dancing around screaming, "Where, Where!"

Sassy bent over laughing again. "You sure are easy to spook, Girl."

Nadine, not to be outdone, sat down beside of her and said, "Sassy, I knew you were just kidding."

"Uh Huh," Sassy replied.

Thirsty from running and fright, Nadine worked her tongue around the inside of her mouth, trying to moisten it, but to no avail. The scratches made by the slaps of the blackberry bushes also stung.

Looking up, she saw Sassy ambling toward the creek. Midway, she turned and yelled at Nadine, "You better get cleaned up. You look a sight." Sassy fell to her knees and began scooping handfuls of water to her mouth.

Nadine quickly joined her. The water was so cold it made her teeth ache just like they did when she ate the ice cream Grandmomma Dunlap used to make. She felt the coldness in her throat as she swallowed. Seeing her reflection, she ran her fingers through her curls, pulling out a broken twig from the dried blackberry bush. She splashed the cool liquid onto her face, feeling it run down the collar of her dress. Then she dabbed the cold water onto her scratches; some of which had become whelps on her fair skin. Next she scooted onto the bank and let her feet dangle into the coolness of the creek. From upstream came, "Look I'm a dog," laughed Sassy, down on all fours lapping the water with her tongue.

"You're so silly," Nadine giggled.

The two walked home slowly to allow their clothes to dry.

Coming within sight of the Taylor's, they breathed in the smell of cinnamon and cloves as the apples bubbled into a sweet thick reddish brown color.

Henry, sweat dripping off his nose, was busy chopping and carrying wood to feed the fire whose flames licked the bottom and sides of the copper kettle. Mrs. Taylor and Melinda sat about four feet away from the flame to escape the heat as they took turns stirring the hot liquid with a long wooden paddle.

*　　*　　*

The two women had talked away the morning as Melinda recounted her favorite story of how she came to be living along the banks of the Kanawha River. Mrs. Taylor never tired of hearing it. Even though it was a tragic tale.

"My daddy was a redheaded man," Melinda began. "That's the reason I've got this here color hair. Melinda put her hand on her short curly hair. He was the son of a landowner over the mountains there in Virginia.

Daddy came down with pneumonia, running a high temperature for days. My momma was one of his papa's young slaves. She took care of my daddy, fetchin' and carryin', cookin', washin', swabbin' him down with cold wet rags till his fever broke. Then she carried kettles of hot water, leanin' him over, so he could breathe the steam into his lungs in order to break up the phlegm and cough it up. Well, he up and fell in love with her. She was a right pretty thing; you know. Her name was Liza.

My daddy was too open about his affection to suit his papa. As you know, it wasn't unusual for a slave owner to have children by his slaves, but my daddy was a treatin' her like a white woman. The neighbors nor his papa weren't about to put up with that. So after many heated quarrels, my daddy took his share of the slaves, and his papa deeded him some land that he bought from one of George Washington's nephews. This tract of land stretched along the west bank of the Kanawha River about ten miles below Charleston.

It was a mighty hard trip over and through the mountains here to the western part of Virginia. Daddy hired a mule master, gathered up his belongings, including the slaves, and began their journey. One of those slaves was Liza, my momma.

Momma said she would never forget leavin home. Within a day or two, the split rail fences began to disappear, and the dog's barkin', growlin' and snappin' at their ankles and the feet and legs of the mules to protect their master's property got less and less. They traveled along what might be called rutted cart trails.

Every once in a while, they might ride past an outlyin' shanty where they could feel eyes peerin' from behind shuttered windows. A pack of mangy lookin' dogs might attack, but they too were left behind as the travelers entered into the dense forest of towerin' oaks, yellow poplar, maples, stands of hemlocks, and thickets of Rhododendron with their delicate pinkish purple blooms. There was a whole lot of poison ivy. The forest's trees, cuttin' off the sunlight, made the entire day seem like dusk. Finally, the cart trails disappeared, and the mules pulled the wagons through creek beds as those on foot followed, swattin' at gnats that they inhaled and swallowed and mosquitoes which buzzed in their ears and sucked their blood."

Without losing a word, Melinda exchanged places with Mrs. Taylor and began stirring the pot. Sometimes, in the act of remembering, Melinda's speech pattern took on that of her educated father's who had told the story many times.

"There was never a lack of food because the forest yielded up red and gray squirrels, deer and black bear, and the streams had plenty of fish: trout, catfish, and bass the length of a man's forearm. This gave variety to their supply of salt cured meat. Later in the trip, raspberries and blackberries were a'plenty.

There was always the knowin' of the copperhead and rattlesnakes. Because of the thickness of the green forest's canopy, they could move among the trees almost as easily as along the ground.

At about twilight when it became more troublesome to distinguish one form from another as the wagon train moved along a rocky ridge, Momma began walkin', havin' grown sick-like from bein' tossed about in the wagon. Out of the corner of her eye, she thought she saw somethin' move. Decidin' it was just shadow, she began to take another step when she saw the snake, with a diamond pattern on its back, arch its body. Its head stuck forward in order to move to the next rocky ledge. Then it slithered the rest of its body upward, and again the swayin' arched position and the slither to a higher outcropping. Momma was hypnotized by its gracefully smooth movement. It was like a slow dance—beautiful; it was.

Another slave, seein' Liza stop, stepped forward to see what she was starin' at. With this sudden move, the beauty turned to evil. The snake coiled, rattled its tail, projected its head forward and the forked fangs sent its poison into the slave's ankle. His scream and Liza's seemed to harmonize and echoed through the forest. The man fell to the ground writhin' in pain.

In a split second my daddy jerked the driver's thick whip from his hand, and with one mighty flick of the whip, the snake's head flew up into the air. Its body continued to jerk and quiver in the shadows.

Very calmly, as if in a dream, Liza ripped the man's pants leg apart and cut two marks across the two holes in the swollen flesh where the poison had entered. Leaning over, she put her mouth to the wound, and sucked the poison out and spit the blood on the ground. Finished, she made a poultice of herbs to help draw out the remainin' poison. As this was bein' done, somebody in the group, usin' a stick, picked up the head of the snake and buried it deep in the thick black dirt.

An extra day was spent at this campsite until the man's temperature broke. Time also was lost when they had to walk miles to find a place to cross the big waters, fordin' the stream with the cold water often hittin' them at their armpits or above. At night as they tried to sleep, they heard the lonesome like bayin of a not too distant red fox. When they awoke, they often looked up at a form shrouded in fog that looked like the back of a giant dinosaur. As the sun melted away that fog, the once dinosaur like form became the ridge along the top of the next mountain that had to be crossed.

As the group crested the next mountain and the next, often Momma said that some dare not look over into the distant valley. The mules footin' slipped, and loose rocks fell so far below that there was no sound when they landed. Always the mules moved forward under the whip of their master. Those who dared to look over the edge saw the blue green valley's stretching for miles, sometimes under the hazy fog which the sun had not yet reached.

The strangeness of this rugged western Virginia with its mountains at daybreak shrouded in fog and its misty valleys, when compared to their orderly plantation, made Momma think she had been sleep walkin' for weeks. Finally they came into the Kanawha Valley where my daddy lay claim to his land. The river bottom land along the Kanawha was rich and black. The slaves planted corn, tobacco and a vegetable garden, and built a house of yellow poplar. The bricks for its foundation were made right on the property. When they finished, the house outdid any in the valley.

Momma began givin' Daddy babies, and he freed her, livin' with her as his wife. Some of the neighbors got all fired up over that. When Momma and we kids were seen out, people often sneered at us and hurled insults. You bein' a white lady, I can't even say them out loud. They taunted Daddy as a "Nigger Lover." He got into some fights over that, comin' home all black and blue.

Then there was the night when they came ridin' up to our house, wearin' white sheets and carryin' a big cross. Can you believe they was hidin' behind the symbol of what our Lord gave his life on to cover their dirty deeds?"

Melinda's cheeks reddened as she talked, and she and Mrs. Taylor traded places to stir the apple butter.

"Daddy told Momma and us to stay in the house and not to come out. Then he took up his rifle that he had hangin' above the door and walked out on the front porch. The smell of whiskey and moonshine hung in the thick summer's night air. Nothin' of the men could be seen except their shoes, hands and the whites of their eyes with the veins in them all red from too much drinkin'. Mixed with the whisky smell was dried perspiration from the heat of the night, fear and anger.

"Some sat astride their horses, makin' them look even larger. The yellow flames of their torches flickerin' in the breeze made the men look as if they were pulsatin', recedin' and then gettin' big again. When the breeze stopped, the yellow torch lights, punchin' holes in the darkness, looked like cat eyes, starin' at you in the dark.

'The slurred voices of these men, whose common bond was hate, began screamin', 'Go back where you came from!'

'The likes of you ain't wanted around here!'

'Take them half-breed redheads with you.'

'We've come to give you a little of what you deserve.'

Then they fired up the cross which they had stuck in our front lawn. Flames shot upward burnin' the cross as they rushed toward the porch to get Daddy.

He fired his gun into the air. Then there was a crackin' sound. My daddy dropped the gun, his knees gave way and he crumpled to the porch floor.

Momma shot out the door, stooped down and cradled his head and shoulders in her lap, gazin' into the hole the size of a hen's egg above his eyes. She watched his wine colored blood seep out and drip down the steps, carryin' his life away. Momma began rockin' him back and forth as she would a child.

The only sound was a low moan which come from deep within her body. She just sat there rockin' for the longest time with the blood dryin' on her fingers, makin' them stick together. She could not look away from his sad bloody face which seemed to be askin', 'Why?'

Then you could hear the mob arguin' whether to torch the house or not, but some of the Klansmen had already begun to break up and retreat into the darkness."

My momma was stubborn and refused to give those who killed my daddy the satisfaction of leavin' the valley. She had to sell off parcels of land, which Daddy had deeded to her, to keep food on the table. But then, I'm still here to tell the story," Melinda said with a nonchalant shrug.

*   *   *

Mrs. Taylor, looking up from stirring the apple butter, saw a tear trickle down Melinda's cheek.

This story always made Mrs. Taylor feel sad and guilty that people just like her could hate so strong. She had grown to love and depend so much on Melinda. What made her feel worse was knowing that people listened to sermons on love, and as they exited the church door picked up their baggage of hate again to carry into the community. This hate continued to fester forty-five years after the war. Would it ever end? Light was supposed to follow darkness.

"You ain't had it easy either with your first husband's dyin' and leavin' this farm for you to wrestle with," said Melinda, breaking the silence as she took a rag out of her pocket to mop her damp forehead.

Mrs. Taylor gazed up toward the top of Goff Mountain which loomed above the farm, sheltering it from storms. "It's hard being a woman alone these days," she agreed. "But then Mr. Taylor found it hard after his wife's death. I don't know which would be the hardest, trying to run a farm with no husband or no wife."

"I guess that's why God put animals on the ark two by two," answered Melinda, shifting her ample weight in the cane bottom chair as she now stirred the bubbling liquid.

"It's been a sight easier since Mr. Taylor and I married. Even though Mr. Taylor spends a lot of his time on his farm down in Poca. Thank goodness he leaves Henry here to help. I don't know what I would do without you and

Henry." Mrs. Taylor patted Melinda's shoulder.

"Thank you, Ma'am," Melinda responded looking at the ground.

Trying to shift attention from herself, she asked, "Henry is as strong as a horse but a bit withdrawn. Where did Mr. Taylor get him?"

"Henry came off the poor farm. Hard to tell what he has been through, but he is a hard and willing worker," answered Mrs. Taylor as she stood and peered into the copper kettle with the verdict, "I think it's ready to be put in jars now."

"Look," said Melinda placing her hands on her hips, "There come Nadine and Sassy. They look a mess." Raising her voice, she yelled as the two girls came into the yard, "What have you two been up to? We sent you out clean and just look at you now."

"Just foolin' around," answered Sassy in her slow drawl.

"Nadine how did you rip the shoulder of your dress?" demanded Mrs. Taylor.

Before she could answer, Sassy stepped right up and looked Mrs. Taylor in the eyes and said, "We were playin tag, and a tree limb just reached out, grabbed the shoulder of her dress, and tore it."

Right at the end of Sassy's explanation, as if choreographed, Nadine stepped forward, pulled her hands from behind her back, and shot out two fistfuls of purple flowers. Offering one to Mrs. Taylor and one to Melinda, "We picked these for you," said Nadine with a broad smile.

Sassy flashed a toothy grin and agreed, "We fetched this iron-weed just for you."

"Uh ha," Melinda responded shaking her head and rolling her brown eyes as if to say, Yeh, I hear you.

"Thank you both. Now go wash up for dinner. We've just got to spoon this apple butter into jars, and we'll be finished." Mrs. Taylor shooed them away with a flick of her dishrag.

"Don't fall in the well while you're drawin water to wash up for supper neither," warned Melinda. "We're havin' tomatoes and dumplins."

"That's what we have every wash day, hog killin' day, and Cannin' day," Sassy fussed as she cranked up the water pail, containing the freshly churned butter.

Taking the butter out and unwrapping it, Sassy scraped her fingers across the underside of the butter where no one would notice and took a taste, and Nadine did the same, tasting the creamy smoothness. Then Sassy lowered the pail to bring up water to wash.

As she did, Nadine stood on her tip toes, leaned over the well, felt the coolness from it, breathed in the scent of water and watched her distorted features reflected in the rippling water as the bucket made its slow ascent upward.

*   *   *

Mrs. Taylor poured hot water heated on the wood stove into the metal wash tub. She then dipped her elbow into the tub to check the temperature. Satisfied, she coaxed Nadine into the water. The homemade lye soap made lots of bubbles in the soft water from the well. Nadine placed some bubbles on her hand, blew them into the air, and watched them float and disintegrate upon hitting the floor.

Mrs. Taylor, with Nadine's eyes closed tight, sudsed her hair and rinsed it by pouring a pan of water over her head. Then she began scrubbing her with a washcloth. "Stretch out those arms, so I can get your dirty elbows," she instructed. "What are those blisters on your arm? Looks like poison ivy to me." Meanwhile, Nadine sat and scratched. "That's what you get from running around in the weeds with Sassy."

As she continued the bathing, she talked of her trip to Charleston. "Tomorrow, Henry is going to drive me to Sattes Landing to catch the boat. I'm going to Sattes Landing because the Batemans have a livery stable where Big Red can stay." With that, she towel dried Nadine and then rubbed vinegar onto her poison ivy.

Nadine wrinkled her noise and exclaimed, "Ouch! Now I smell like a pickle."

"Indeed you do. Now what was I saying? Oh yes. I'll be gone most of the day, taking dinner on the boat. It's all part of the fare." She paused as she slipped on Nadine's gown and ran a comb through her tangled auburn hair. "Anyway, you and Mr. Taylor will have to take care of each other. I'll leave the leftover stewed tomatoes for you to warm up."

YUK, thought Nadine as she followed Mrs. Taylor, carrying the oil lamp with its yellow halo, up the stairs to bed.

After her bedroom door closed, Nadine reached in her dress with the torn shoulder and pulled out the small white pebble that Sassy had given her, unwrapped it, rolled it between her thumb and index finger, re-wrapped it in her handkerchief, and placed it in her top drawer. *I forgot to thank Sassy for this gift. The next time I see her I will,* she thought. Hearing a knock on her wall, she knocked back twice to tell Frances good-night. Then she looked at the picture of the two children and the angel over the raging stream and went to sleep.

Before sunup, Mrs. Taylor tiptoed into Nadine's room carrying a pan of oatmeal. Pulling the covers back, she said, "I fixed this for breakfast and Mr. Taylor did not eat it all, so I'll dab it on your poison ivy to sooth the itching. "My, look how it's spreading," she said shaking her head as she dipped a cloth into the sticky mixture. "Does it itch much?"

Nadine nodded her head.

"You just better spend the day inside with Frances."

"OK," Nadine said with a nod.

"Let it dry before you start moving about."

Nadine obediently stretched out like a scarecrow and drifted back to sleep.

She was awakened by the sound of a horse coming around the bend in the road. Thinking she had slept the day away and Mrs. Taylor was returning from Charleston, she jumped up and peeked through the lace curtains. Dust was the only visible evidence of the horse until it came over the rise, pulling a familiar looking covered wagon, swaying and bouncing with each bump in the road.

The driver also looked familiar. She was the old Gypsy woman with her brown front teeth worn almost into her gums. How could Nadine forget her? Sitting beside her was the beautiful Gypsy woman with the smooth olive skin.

A nagging thought came to Nadine, *Perhaps they are here to steal me.* This thought turned to panic as she wondered where Mr. Taylor was. Pulling her dress over her head, she ran down the steps and into the master bedroom. Peeking through the curtains again, she saw Mr. Taylor asleep in the oak swing on the front porch with his hands folded over his ample stomach.

The Gypsies passed and pulled the wagon to the side of the house, situating it behind Mr. Taylor. The old woman dismounted and tied the horse to the white picket fence that enclosed the yard. The young Gypsy followed her.

Mr. Taylor, awakened by the sudden silence of the usual chirping of birds, sat up, scratched his head, and straightened his shirt which had become twisted as he slept. Then he pulled his silver watch from his pocket to check how long he had slept.

Nadine started to tap on the window to gain his attention, but Mr. Taylor, hearing the women coming around the house, turned and saw them. Nadine heard the squeak of the gate.

Mr. Taylor greeted, "I've been meaning to grease those hinges with some lard."

As the two women walked under the row of golden maple trees, they filled in the gap of silence with idle conversation about how fair the weather was for October, except for the cold nights which caused arthritis bones to ache.

Mr. Taylor, having removed his boots and socks before napping, was trying to get them back on. Before he could, the women were standing in front of him with their full skirts swaying in the breeze.

"How can I help you, ladies?"

"Is the woman of the house about?"

"No, she took the boat to Charleston early this morning."

The old Gypsy seated herself in the rocking chair. "We just came to be neighborly. Thought we might buy some butter."

"Mrs. Taylor took the butter with her to sell," said Mr. Taylor, shifting a toothpick from one side of his mouth to the other with a flick of his tongue.

Nadine had a close-up view, and she could hear their conversation through the window. She noted the old woman's hooded black eyes dart about the property. The young one stood without a word. She had Mr. Taylor's attention as each time she breathed, her full breasts looked as if they were going to ooze out of her low cut dress.

The old Gypsy seeming to have quenched her curiosity shifted her black eyes back to Mr. Taylor as she pulled her shawl around her shoulders and leaned forward. With a quick movement, she pulled his hand palm up into her lap. She said, "I have a gift for looking into the future. My mother had the same gift. I'll tell your fortune for a nickel."

Mr. Taylor nodded, and the deal was made. She placed her dirty fingernail half the length of her finger onto his palm and went into deep concentration, almost a trance. Then her thin lips whispered in a unknown tongue as if

29

praying or chanting. Next, she began speaking in a slow steady drone.

Mr. Taylor, watching the long finger nail's repetitive movement on his palm and listening to the expressionless low voice, seemed to join in the Gypsy's trance, not noticing the young woman as she soundlessly stepped off the porch, heading toward the back of the wagon.

Nadine, to keep an eye on the young woman, ran to the side window which afforded a view of the out buildings and the side door. She dared not make a sound for fear the Gypsies would sneak in the side door to carry her off.

In response to the young Gypsy's quick hand sign, several men, women and children exited the back of the wagon. Without a word they went about their assigned tasks. One man came out of the smokehouse carrying a ham under each arm. Two women stepped out of the chicken coop one carrying brown chicken eggs in her skirt and another a sitting hen. The children had gone into the cool damp cellar house, returning with blue glass canning jars containing deep red beets, green beans, and golden corn. While still another woman was in the kitchen garden, gathering cabbage, turnips and a pumpkin. Another man loaded the back of the wagon with a basket of potatoes. The Gypsies whirled about the farm then suddenly disappeared into the back of the wagon.

The old woman noted when the young woman stepped back onto the porch. With that signal and having told Mr. Taylor's fortune, she turned her palm up for the nickel.

As the two women, with their business finished, stepped from the porch, the old woman tripped. Mr. Taylor jumped up to help in response to her fall and the moaning sounds she made.

As Mr. Taylor assisted and apologized over and over, the young one brushed up against him as her astute long fingers slid in and out of each of Mr. Taylor's pant's pockets, stealing whatever she could reach. He did not hear the click of the coins as she dropped them into her dress pocket.

The old Gypsy regained her composure and shook grass from her full skirt. She and the young one left swiftly with a wave and a flick of the whip to the horse's back. As the dust encompassed them, they disappeared.

Nadine, relieved that she had not become one of the Gypsies' children, with Frances found their source of pleasure in Mrs. Taylor's button box for the rest of the day. They dumped these beautiful treasures into several heaps on the floor. There were engraved gold and silver buttons, pearl buttons, and rhinestone buttons. The buttons were different sizes, colors and shapes. At first they entertained themselves sorting them by color, then size, and then shape. They picked out the ones they thought were the prettiest. They then made themselves bracelets and necklaces by stringing the prettiest ones onto the thread found in the drawer of the Singer treadle sewing machine in the master bedroom.

As shadows crept into the room, and the katydids began to make their loud shrill sounds, Frances and Nadine heard horse hooves, coming toward the house. Nadine's body stiffened, thinking that the Gypsies were returning. This time to take her away for sure! She went to the window, flattened her body against the wall, lifted the corner of the curtain and peeped out cautiously. She held her fingers across her lips to warn Frances to be quiet. Obediently, Frances sat frozen in the floor with her legs crossed. As before, the dust bellowed up, but this time as the horse cleared the rise, Nadine recognized it as Big Red.

She took a deep breath, whirled around and knelt down, grabbing handfuls of buttons, throwing them back into the box. Frances fell into the activity as Nadine said, "Hurry, we need to put all of this back before Mrs. Taylor finds them strung all over the floor."

Henry, taking Mrs. Taylor's gloved hand, helped her out of the wagon as Big Red swished his tail to ward off the ever present horseflies. Then Henry began unloading packages purchased in Charleston. Both he and Mrs. Taylor picked up armfuls and headed toward the house.

Seeing Mr. Taylor, Mrs. Taylor chatted as usual, asking questions that she answered herself. "Did you know the Gypsies are no longer camped along the creek? We just passed, and there is not a trace of them except the black pits where they burned their fires. Swan, that's a relief. That old woman approached me one day, offering to tell my fortune, talking about her ability coming from her grandmother. That old gray haired Gypsy was more than a half bubble off. I tell you that."

Mr. Taylor, leaning over in the swing holding his head in his hands thought, *that old woman is not a half bubble off. That sly gray fox sure outsmarted me.*

"Taking notice of Mr. Taylor's unresponsiveness, Mrs. Taylor cocked her head to one side and asked, "Mr. Taylor, are you ill?"

"I am down right sick to my stomach," he shook his head, never looking up. "Those dumb Gypsies, as you called them, have raided the farm."

"How could they raid the farm with you sitting right here on the porch?"

He just shook his head.

"What did they take?"

He shrugged his shoulders.

Henry stood with his arms full of packages and his mouth gaping open.

"Well don't sit there!" directed Mrs. Taylor. "Put your shoes on and let's see what is missing."

"Don't have any shoes."

"They took your shoes too?"

"Yep, sure did."

Nadine ran down the stairs and put the thread back into the Singer drawer before running out to greet Mrs. Taylor and Henry.

Flinging the screen door open she ran to Mrs. Taylor, grabbing her around the waist in a hug. "The Gypsies came. I thought they were here to steal me, but they took other stuff."

"What stuff?" Mrs. Taylor asked in an agitated voice.

"Two hams, a chicken, potatoes, vegetables, and canned goods.

The pretty one had her hands down in Mr. Taylor's pant's pockets."

"Do tell," Mrs. Taylor raised her eyebrows as she turned slowly around and looked at Mr. Taylor, waiting for an answer, but none came.

"I tell you, I can't even leave for a day." She dropped her packages on the porch and took off for the hen house. She came out madder than when she went in. "They've taken my best sitting hen," she stormed. Stopping at the porch long enough to ask, "Have you fed Frances or Nadine, yet?"

Mr. Taylor just shook his head. That seemed to be the last straw for Mrs. Taylor as she slammed the screen door so hard that it banged three times. She went in the kitchen talking to herself. "Just chalk everything up as gone. Sheriff Johnson will never find those Gypsies. Hard to tell where they are now."

Nadine sat scratching at the blisters which had raised up on her skin as she ate the tomato dumplings. Then she ate the special treat that Mrs. Taylor had brought from the bakery in Charleston a cinnamon roll all crusty, buttery, and sweet with sugar and cinnamon.

Mr. Taylor finally came into the kitchen, not saying a word. He poured some hot water into his cup, reached into the top cabinet, pulled out a bottle of amber liquid, stirred it into the water, added some sugar, picked up Frances' supper including the cinnamon roll, and said, "I'm going to bed as soon as I have my toddy."

There was no answer as Mrs. Taylor banged pots and pans, scrubbing them vehemently, stopping only to flip a strand of hair off her forehead.

*   *   *

Nadine stood in the pantry gazing at the jellies and preserves lined up neatly on the open shelves, exhibiting a rainbow of colors. Of the jellies, there were the bluish elderberry, purple grape, deep purple blackberry, red raspberry, and golden apple. Of the preserves, there were the pears which had been cut in half and placed in their natural juices thickened by adding sugar. Whole cloves and the pear halves floated in their sweet liquid as if suspended in animation, as did the wine colored damsons in their sweet liquid. The newest addition to the shelf was the dark red apple butter.

Mrs. Taylor took great pride in the fact that she did not add a drop of food coloring to achieve the apple butter's redness. "It comes naturally from slow cooking the Jonathan apples," she said, trying to remain humble. "All the canned fruits and vegetables come from this farm; you know," she added. They were her crown jewels earned by the hours spent growing and preserving.

Nadine walked to the drawer where the eating utensils were kept, pulling out a teaspoon. She returned to the pantry where she carefully ran the spoon around the edge of the beeswax, sealing in the red raspberry jelly's freshness. Then she lifted the edge of the wax and spooned the sweetness into her mouth. Carefully, she replaced the seal. The next day she remembered the sweetness of the jelly and returned to the pantry to reenact her clandestine activity of the night before. Gradually, she became addicted to the tastes of these wonderful delicacies, being careful to take only one spoonful from each jar as she methodically advanced across the shelves in her now nightly raids.

Meanwhile the household was astir in anticipation of Mrs. Taylor's sister, Ada Allen's, visit. Mrs. Taylor's maiden name was Allen, and Ada was her spinster sister. She, not having any immediate family, just popped in on relatives for visits of no shorter than a week.

Ada, being fastidious in her own habits and having the same expectations of others, set Mrs. Taylor and everybody around cleaning at least eight hours a day. This cleaning of course had to be absorbed into all of the other farm chores, so tomato and dumplings was frequently the item on the menu.

Henry ran here and there, chopping firewood, splitting it with a wedge and sledgehammer and placing the small pieces that accidentally split off into coal scuttles to be used for kindling. Having stacked several cords of wood near the kitchen door to be used in the stove, his next chore was to wash the outhouse down with lye. This allowed him some solitude, being out of Mrs. Taylor's range of vision. For anyone in her sight was stopped in their assigned task to fetch and carry whatever else came to her mind.

Melinda and Sassy were recruited for this "dire hour of need." Melinda had all the featherticks off the beds hanging on the clothesline, beating them with a broom handle to freshen them up when Mrs. Taylor said, "Don't forget to get that unsightly brass spittoon of Mr. Taylor's out of the master bedroom. Hide it, so he can't find it. Ada would be highly offended by its presence. That is such a filthy habit of his, and you'll have to clean the tobacco stains off the braided rug. Whatever am I going to do with that man?"

"Yes, Ma'am, I'll get right to it," Melinda answered as she continued the rhythmic beating of the bedclothes.

Nadine and Sassy had not escaped without their orders. They were to be certain that there were ample Sears & Roebuck catalogs and corncobs in the john for the "necessary," as soon as Henry finished cleaning it with lye.

"We need more red corncobs than white," Sassy said as she and Nadine dangled over the edge of the corn crib, retrieving the cobs with sparse kernels, then throwing the kernels they cleaned off to the clucking chickens. The chicken's darting yellow eyes watched to see where the next kernels fell.

"Why do we need more red cobs than white?"

"The white ones are for the last wipe," answered Sassy with her white tooth smile.

With this chore completed, they were to line all the pantry shelves with fresh newspaper. Nadine and Sassy carefully unloaded the shelves of their jewel colored contents, stopping every once in awhile to reward themselves with a spoonful of sweetness from a jar as they replaced it on the shelf. Finished with this, they tiptoed behind Melinda who now sat in the dining room, shining the only company crystal.

Sassy and Nadine both licked their lips, tasting the last remnants of sweetness and wiped their mouth with the backs of their hands to remove any tell-tale rings, just in case they encountered Mrs. Taylor.

As they stepped off the porch, they caught site of her scrubbing clothes on a scrub board in the washtub which sat under the downspout at the corner of the house to catch run off rain water. "There is nothing like the sweet smell of linens washed in rain water," she always said as she inhaled deeply while folding pillow cases and sheets.

Getting out of hearing distance, they took off running to escape the possibility of any more assignments. The rest of the crisp blue day was theirs as they walked along a wooded path covered with golden maple leaves which had fallen the night before. With the slant of the sun, the path looked like gold. "Do you think the streets of gold in heaven will be prettier than this?" Nadine asked.

"Heaven will be prettier than anything we've ever seen. There will be angels with wings like white down."

"I have a picture of a blonde angel in my bedroom. When I can't go to sleep, I just stare at her until I drift off."

"My angel will have curly hair and skin the color of mine," Sassy said thoughtfully.

"My angel will look like Angela, the pretty lady I met on the boat."

Sassy absentmindedly began singing a Negro Spiritual, "Every time I feel the Spirit to escape...I know I'll be crossing the Jordan River...Where there will be a train that runs to freedom."

"I've never heard that hymn in church," said Nadine.

"Before Mr. Lincoln set us free, Grandma Liza told me the slaves sang about escapin' on the underground railroad. If they sang plans like a hymn, the white masters didn't pay any attention. It was like a code among the colored folks. Jordan River stood for the Ohio, and train that runs to freedom meant Canada. Grandma Liza sang it as she went about doing her chores. That's how I heard it."

"Who was Mr. Lincoln?"

"Why, he was the sixteenth president of these United States of America who gave us colored our freedom from bein' slaves."

Nadine grew quiet as she studied on all that Sassy said.

"You'll learn all this stuff once you go to school, Girl."

Nadine thought about the underground railroad, deciding it must be dark like caves with railroad tracks going through them. But she had to be sure.

"The tracks ran underground?"

"No Girl," Sassy shook her head emphatically. "I'll give you an example. You see Willy had come from Virginia with Grandpa and Grandma Liza, but Grandpa sold him to the neighborin' landowner here, not knowin' what a mean man the landowner was.

Grandma Liza said her brother Willy was whipped by the overseer for takin' some sugar from Master's sugar cabinet. So he grabbed up some corn mash, lard, turnips, a knife and took off as soon as the sun dropped over the hill.

A boy ran to our house to tell Grandma Liza what happened. Grandma Liza ran back with him to comfort Willy's wife.

When Willy didn't report for field work, the overseer stormed into the cabin wantin' to know Willy's whereabouts. Both women denied knowin'. The overseer grabbed one of Willy's shirts and sicced the dogs on him after they got his scent.

Grandma Liza listened to the dog's barkin' and howlin' into the night as if they were chasin' a fox. It was not a fox they sought but her brother. Liza prayed Willy would get to the river quickly and walk along the shallow part, so the dog's would lose his scent.

Before daybreak, the overseer returned. His horse was lathered and its nostrils flared, snortin' out his hot breath, formin' a vapor which hung in the air. The dogs came trailin' behind with their red tongues hangin' out the side of their mouths as their drool dripped onto the ground. Praise the Lord, Willy was nowhere to be seen.

Under the cover of darkness and sleepin' in out buildin's and the woods by day, Willy probably traveled down along the Kanawha River, headin' for the big Ohio River where he could cross to freedom. Every once in a while he'd stop at a house of white abolitionists or freed coloreds, and they hid and fed him until he was able to travel. The people who gave food and shelter to the slaves were the underground railroad. It was the secret organization to help escaping slaves to move along."

"Where did they hide Willy?"

"Oh, maybe a hidden room or cellar with a trap door."

Nadine listened intently being projected into another place, time, and way of life.

"Maybe about Point Pleasant, some abolitionists smuggled him onto the ferry that crossed to Ohio. They probably packed him in a crate like to mail or somethin'. Then he'd cut his way out of the box once in Ohio and try to get to Canada."

These new words and ideas just boggled Nadine's imagination; Ohio, abolitionists, and Canada. "Well, how did he know where to go?"

"The abolitionists hung quilts on the line called Geese Pattern Quilts. The direction in which the geese were flying on the quilt pointed the way to freedom."

"Another code," gasped Nadine, as she covered her mouth just thinking of it all.

"Yep and then the people who hid Willy would give him handwritten maps on scraps of paper and more supplies until he made it to the next friendly place."

"What happened to Willy?"

"We never heard from him again."

"So, you don't know if he lived or died?"

"Nope!"

"I hope he got to Can-a-da," Nadine, said, trying to sound out the new word and feel it on her tongue.

"Well, one good thing, Willy left in the spring, so he had good weather, not like travelin' up north in the snow, so Grandma Liza said. But then he might have been shot before makin' it to Ohio," Sassy said with a shrug and a tinge of sadness. "But probably if he was caught, Willy would have been returned to his master, for his master ran a 'runaway slave ad,' carryin' a reward."

Sassy and Nadine ambled along, intent in Sassy's story, not going anywhere in particular, but ending up in the apple orchard which had been stripped for canning applesauce and applebutter.

Sassy and Nadine fell to their knees, hunting for at least two apples to eat. "I've worked up an appetite," Sassy said, throwing the rotten apples to the side.

"Might as well eat what we can. We are going to have tomato and dumplings for supper for sure," answered Nadine. Not finding any perfect apples, they selected the ones with the fewest bruises.

"The birds have been peckin' at all these apples." Sassy complained.

Apples in hand, they rolled over on their backs ignoring the stubble that pricked them, and looked up into the blue sky with floating white cumulus clouds. They quietly enjoyed their apple as the juice ran down their chins and the soft breeze brushed over their skin. Nadine broke the silence, "That cloud straight overhead looks like a lamb."

Sassy tilted her head to the side and, after much thought, agreed.

*   *   *

The next morning, Nadine awoke to the rustling of the wind through the dry oak leaves. Looking out her window she saw flocks of birds flying south. She remembered that today Aunt Ada would arrive, so she hesitantly went downstairs, anticipating more chores. The only thing that moved her along was the chill of her room.

Mrs. Taylor was not in the kitchen as she usually was, and the fire burned low. Nadine backed up to the fire to warm herself when she heard the solitary clucking of a chicken which seemed to come from under the house. She stepped out on the screened-in porch and saw Mrs. Taylor stalking a pullet. Quickly her arm shot out and grabbed the one which was hiding beneath the house. Holding it securely under her left arm, she grasped it by the head and with one flick of her wrist separated the chickens head from its body. Flapping its wings, it dropped to the ground where it proceeded to walk around headless with blood spurting out with each step. The rooster ruffling his red feathers shot his spurs out ready to attack Mrs. Taylor. Mrs. Taylor shook her fist at him, saying "I'll get you the next time."

Nadine shifted her eyes back to the headless chicken, which seemed to be moving toward her. With a shrill scream, she ran back inside.

Mrs. Taylor carrying the now lifeless chicken came into the kitchen grumbling, "I swear those chickens seem to have a sense that their execution is at hand because they can't be found anywhere."

After calming Nadine down and spooning oats with brown sugar into a bowl for her, Mrs. Taylor set to scalding then plucking and cleaning the chicken. Her fingers nimbly pulled out the pinfeathers, sometimes with the aid of a knife, and then proceeded to cut the chicken up for frying. She placed the heaped up feathers in a bag for stuffing pillows. Nothing was wasted on the farm if Mrs. Taylor had anything to do with it.

The preparation of the banquet was in process as Mrs. Taylor kneaded the bread dough, setting it on the shelf above the wood stove to rise. She peeled a bowl full of potatoes, putting them on to boil and later mashed with fresh milk and homemade butter.

Nadine made several trips to the cellar house for canned vegetables, carefully carrying one jar at a time. Mrs. Taylor added the white creamy icing to her almond cake; it's aroma permeating every corner of the house. Mrs. Taylor periodically went to the store of chopped wood to keep the hungry stove at just the right temperature. Checking her gold watch, she placed a big iron skillet on the stove and spooned in lots of lard from the coffee can on the back of the stove. The flour covered chicken went in next, being turned several times to assure even browning and crispness.

Aunt Ada arrived the same way Nadine had. Big Red pulled the wagon to the gate of the picket fence. Henry helped Ada down from the wagon and without a word carried her baggage into the house. She stood erect taking inventory of everything through her blue eyes. Unlike Mrs. Taylor, she was thin with a narrow nose and lips. Wisps of silver gray hair could be seen around the edge of her bonnet with a red rose. The rest of her hair was pulled back into a bun.

The Taylors, including Nadine, stood lined up on the porch as the receiving line. Mrs. Taylor broke rank and ran down the walk, swinging open the gate. The two women embraced.

Chatting as they walked, they stepped onto the porch where Mr. Taylor gave Ada a hug as Mrs. Taylor eyed a brown spot on his otherwise freshly laundered shirt. *He has sneaked out to the barn to chew his Mail Pouch again,* she thought.

"This must be Nadine," Ada said, extending her thin hand with blue veins showing through its skin. "My what a pretty girl you are, but then pretty is as pretty does; isn't that true?" With that, her narrow lips slid into a natural smile.

Since the Taylor's thought highly enough of Aunt Ada to turn themselves upside down for the past week, getting ready for her visit, she must be a nice lady Nadine concluded. So she took Ada's hand and led her into the guestroom to rest and freshen up after her trip. "I picked you some purple iron weed see," Nadine motioned to the dresser. "And here is your chamber pot, pitcher of water, and a bowl to wash in. I'll see you at supper." She then whirled on her heels and left Ada, so she could rest.

"Thank you dear," Nadine heard as she softly closed the door.

Following dinner, Ada and Mrs. Taylor cleared the dishes from the table and began washing them. Nadine loved to listen to grownups talk, so she seated herself at the end of the table. Mrs. Taylor with soapsuds dripping from her hands turned and said, "Why don't you keep Frances company while she eats her dinner this evening?" As she left Ada and Mrs. Taylor began to catch up on their gossip.

"How does it feel having a child under foot?"

"Nadine is a joy to have around, and she keeps Frances company sometimes."

"You are accumulating a lot of responsibility with Frances, Henry and Nadine. All three have their own set of problems. I don't understand how you do it or why. It has to be costly."

"Oh, I just give away what I can't keep, a little bit of money, to get what I can keep, love," Mrs. Taylor answered with a smile. "Although I am going to have to discipline Nadine. I just don't know how to discipline her. She's been here such a short while. I don't want to turn her against me."

"Discipline? What for?"

"She's ruining my jelly. She has been going into the pantry, breaking the wax seals and taking a spoonful out of each jar."

"Why on earth is she doing such a thing?"

"I guess she has a sweet tooth."

"If she keeps it up, she'll soon rot her sweet tooth out," said Ada. She stopped drying to think. "Just let me solve that problem," she added.

Hearing the oak swing squeaking, Nadine knew the women had adjourned to the porch. She tiptoed down the steps and into the dark hall, feeling the walls as she moved so not to bump into anything, alerting them she was downstairs. Walking into the kitchen, she saw the full moon filtering through the window, casting an eerie silver glow into the center of the room. The furniture in the shadows gave the appearance of darkened forms that with imagination could be anything, lurking in the dark. Nadine would have turned and run but for the desire of the sweet jelly.

Cautiously, she pulled the drawer open removing a spoon. She then carefully opened the pantry door and entered. In the dark, she counted down by touch to the third shelf and went to the fourth jar over, knowing this was the next seal to be broken. She dipped her spoon in.

As she tasted the sweetness on her tongue, something moved in the shadows, and then a shrouded white form leaped toward her. Nadine dropped the jelly jar which broke and splashed its crimson red contents onto her. Turning to escape, she was having trouble breathing, and she could not utter a sound as the white form moved toward her. As Nadine ran through the kitchen door, she looked over her shoulder. The white ghost-like form disappeared.

Once in the safety of her room, she stared at the picture of the angel guarding the two children as they crossed the raging stream. This calmed her when she was frightened. She smelled a familiar fragrance of talcum, but she could not recall where she had smelled it before. As she started to breath normally, the fragrance faded. She emphatically made a silent pledge never to bother the jelly in the pantry again.

*   *   *

The following evening Nadine went into the kitchen where Ada was peeling potatoes for supper, and Mrs. Taylor was mixing the biscuit dough. "Do you know how to peel potatoes, Nadine?"

"No."

"Well sit beside of me, and I'll show you. See, you want to peel close to the outer peel so not to lose the meat of the potato."

"Be careful not to cut yourself," Mrs. Taylor interjected.

"Hold the knife just so and see if you can peel the whole potato without breaking the peel. See, like this," Ada demonstrated.

Nadine watched Ada's long thin fingers cut as if doing a sculpture. She then took her turn, but try as she may, she could not peel without breaking the peeling into several pieces. She kept trying because it made her feel grown-up.

"Keep practicing," Ada instructed, "You'll get the hang of it."

"Why am I not to break the peeling?"

"If you do not break it, you can throw it over your left shoulder, and whatever initial the peeling forms when it lands is the first initial of the man's last name whom you will marry."

That is why Ada has perfected peeling, she keeps trying to find a man, Nadine thought. *It sure hasn't worked for her.* Nadine, even though it made her feel grown-up, soon grew tired of this tedious task and made an excuse to leave.

Once Nadine was out of hearing distance, Ada asked, "Have you been keeping up with Pig Woman's trial down in Winfield?"

Rolling out the biscuits, Mrs. Taylor wiped flour from her hands on the corner of her apron and fumbled through a stack of newspapers, returning with one. "Right here in the *Putnam Democrat* is an article. You know Nadine's brother, Carl, was taken by his Uncle John Miller who owns the paper. So, Mr. Miller has been sending us free copies, since Nadine came here to live. Mrs. Taylor began reading the article which quoted the judge when sentencing the Pig Woman.

Matilda Meeks, you have been indicted, tried by a jury of your county, and convicted of murder in the first degree. Murder with malice aforethought—of willful, deliberate, premeditated murder. Of the correctness of this verdict there is not only no reasonable doubt, but not even a shadow of a doubt.

The atrocity of your crime is almost without a parallel. The deed of which you have been convicted is one of the foulest that blackens the annals of time. You were a poor girl, in the humblest walks of life. An honest, sober, industrious young man, with no fortune but his own strong arm and manly resolve, led you to the altar. You there gave him your hand, and he supposed your heart. He vowed to love, protect, and cherish you, and forsaking all others cleave alone unto you, and he pledged this vow to the most high. He made you the partner of his bosom and mother of his child, and provided you with reasonable comforts. He purchased a handsome little farm.

Yet whilst your poor husband is standing before the fire, all unconscious of impending evil, he sees the uplifted axe, and has but time to say, 'Oh! don't kill me!!' and blow after blow falls on his head, mashing it, as it were, to a jelly. Next the head is almost severed from the body with a butcher's knife.

He is then taken by the head and heels and buried in the dung and filth of the pigpen, and hogs are turned in to trample upon his already mangled remains. In a few days your husband is missing. Alarm is felt by the neighbors. All turn out to make the search, and in the pigpen, buried in the dung, trodden over by the hogs, there is found where the hogs have rooted up the mangled remains of a man who had lived amongst their community and commanded their respect and esteem.

You are a woman, and woman is Heaven's best, divinest gift to man, and made a little lower than the angels. But, like the angels who kept not their first estate, she sometimes becomes fallen, and when she falls, great is the fall.

It may be mercy to you to have your days prolonged as preparation to meet the judge of all the earth; but still your fate is hard, very hard indeed. You are to be excluded from society and housed with its outcasts, without regard to race, color or precious condition, and doomed to hard labor and coarse diet all the days of your life.

When you leave this place you will have gazed, perhaps for the last time, upon your little girl whom you leave in the world without a mother's oversight, and with no father save the Father in heaven. O Woman! prepare to meet thy God. Give up all hope or expectation of worldly pleasure.

The sentence of the law is that you be taken to jail, and the sheriff of this county convey you from thence to the public jail or penitentiary house of the State, and that you be therein confined during your natural life. And may you there learn to unlearn what you have learned amiss!

Judge

Putting down the paper to resume her bread making, Mrs. Taylor shook her head in disgust. "What's this world coming to when a woman kills her own husband? It's our role as wives to nurture our children and through our actions remove our husband's natural inclination to coarseness. Women are becoming as coarse as men!"

"Well, you can't believe everything you read in the paper."

Ada pressed her thin lips together before continuing, "I sat beside the Pig Woman's closest neighbor on the boat. She boarded in Winfield. She said Matilda killed her husband in self-defense. The neighbor said Matilda's husband had broken her nose so many times that it looked like a pig's snout.

"I thought she was called the Pig Woman because she buried her dead husband in the pigpen, not that she looked like a pig."

"Well, I don't know about that, but this is the story Matilda told her neighbor."

Me and my young daughter Iola were a fixin' supper. She was settin' the table, and I noticed she picked out a cracked plate to put at her pop's place. I asked her why she did that, and she said he was so mean he deserved a cracked plate. I guess it was the meanest thing she could think to do without him slappin' her down.

He came in from the field in one of his moods. So I knew I'd better hurry and get his food on the table, or I would suffer the consequences. He had punched me in the face so often that I turned my head when passin' his shavin' mirror which hung by the fireplace, not wantin' to see my disfigurement starin' back at me. My arm is crooked at the elbow where he bent it backwards till it broke.

We just sat down to eat when he took a bite of fried taters and threw his fork straight at my head screamin', "You good for nothin' ugly bitch, you can't do anythin' right. These taters are so salty I can't eat them. I slave in the field tryin' to make a livin', and this is the slop I come home to." He was out of his chair, movin' in my direction with his large fist wadded up and his unkept greasy hair fallin' across his forehead. I could smell his stinkin' breath. The sick numbin' knot came to my stomach, knowin' what came next. I saw the familiar anger flashin' in his green eyes like he was demon possessed.

When Iola saw that he was aimin' to beat me, she jumped up and threw her plate at him. It missed and rolled across the floor, splatterin' food all over. He went to take his next step toward me and lost his footin', slippin' on a potato.

At that moment he turned on her. With quick strides, he was beside the mantle, grabbin' his straight razor in one hand and Iola with the other, placin' the razor to her throat.

My fingers danglin' beside of my chair touched the axe that I had split kindlin' with and had leaned against the wall. I grasped it. Seein' the terror in Iola's eyes, I struck him, and he turned toward me with his face twitchin' in rage. I hit him again and again. I couldn't stop. It was as if somethin' had taken possession of me, as if it were'nt me.

Mrs. Taylor stopped her bread making and stood in silence as Ada related the neighbor's version of Matilda's self-defense explanation. If it were true, what a terrible miscarriage of justice had been done. The Pig Woman was no longer an abstract monster, but a person with a name, Matilda, who had a daughter Iola. "Where is the daughter now?"

"She's living with Matilda's aging father. So I'm told, and well, the sheriff has a kinder heart than the judge. As of yet, Matilda is still at the Putnam County Jail. During the day she has the run of the town, so Iola gets to see her mother."

"That poor woman. I guess it's true that you have to walk in an Indian's moccasins. . . What some people go through."

Supper that night was more somber than usual as Mrs. Taylor thought about the Pig Woman. This made her count her blessings of having Mr. Taylor, a kind gentleman, Frances, Henry, and Nadine.

*   *   *

It had been a gray wet day, and Nadine went to sleep that night to the sound of rain gently walking across the tin roof. Awakening, she heard not a sound. When she breathed, vapor hung in the air. She ventured from under her warm covers to look out the window, seeing a world of black and white. Everything was snow covered except the trunks of the trees which were black silhouetted against the white. The low bushes and farm equipment seemed to lose their identity, looking like banks and drifts of snow. The tree branches coated in ice appeared to be elongated diamond fingers, reaching skyward. The only disturbance to the smooth layer of snow was biscuit crumbs that Mrs. Taylor had thrown out for the birds and her footprints which led to and from the well house.

Nadine wrapped a cover around her shoulders and ran down the steps because it was Christmas morning. Entering the master bedroom, she saw the spruce tree that Henry and Mr. Taylor carried in yesterday. Now, it held small, white, wax candles clipped near the tips of its branches. In the darkened room, the tiny flickering flames looked like twinkling stars in the sky all clustered together, and the heat of the candles spread the woodsy scent of pine throughout the room.

Under the tree were five colorfully wrapped gifts with Nadine's name. Mr. Taylor, looking like Santa himself, sat by the blazing fire that he kept poking and adding coal. Mrs. Taylor had positioned herself beside the tree. Behind her was a bucket of water just in case the tree caught on fire. She motioned toward the tree as if she were going to introduce it, and said, "Santa left you some gifts."

Mr. Taylor turned his rocker toward Nadine to watch as she, without hesitation, ripped away the wrapping. Inside the first box was a blue wool sweater that she knew Mrs. Taylor had knitted, knowing blue was Nadine's favorite color. Another box held blue wool mittens from Ada. She held the sweater briefly to her cheek and hurriedly tried on the mittens.

There was also a picture book of *Grimms Fairy Tales*. Her eyes widened as she flipped through the pages and smiled at the pictures. There was a new feed sack dress for Miss Betsy, and a box which said, "To: Nadine, From: Carl." Inside was the most beautiful doll that she had ever seen. It was a china doll with a cloth body except for its head, hands and feet. Her features were delicately painted. She wore an aqua antique satin dress that buttoned with tiny buttons at the neck, and there was a tiny pearl necklace.

"That's from your brother down in Winfield. Handle it very carefully because it will break. I'll keep it in the top of the closet, as soon as you finish looking at it, so it will stay pretty."

Nadine reluctantly gave Mrs. Taylor the doll. Then she let the blanket drop as she pulled on the sweater which itched but felt warm. Mrs. Taylor pulled the sleeves down to Nadine's wrists saying, "It looks like Santa knew exactly your size."

Mr. Taylor interrupted, "Look over here, hanging on the back of the chair. I believe Santa left something else." Nadine recognized one of Mr. Taylor's freshly washed socks hooked over the chair arm, stretching almost to the floor. It was filled with an orange, a peppermint stick and nuts.

"Wait!" Nadine cried. "Now it's my turn." She turned and ran upstairs, coming down with her gifts for Mr. and Mrs. Taylor, Mail Pouch tobacco and a small sack of hard candy from the general store. "I saved for these out of the penny you pay me for every two chicken eggs I find outside of the hen house," Nadine said proudly. "I had enough for a bag each for Frances and Henry."

Mr. Taylor showed his gratitude by dipping into the Mail Pouch and pulling out a pinch of tobacco which he tucked into his jaw.

Mrs. Taylor knelt down to be on Nadine's level, and said, "Do you know the very best gift you could give Mr. Taylor and me?" Nadine shook her head.

"You could call us Mom and Pop."

"But I had a Mom and a Pop."

"Ok, how about Mom Taylor and Pop Taylor?"

Nadine nodded her head in agreement.(Later, however, Mom and Pop Taylor would be shortened to Mom and Pop.)

"It is a deal then. Now, go give Henry and Frances their gifts. You and Frances can show each other what you got while I get dinner on the table."

"Can Henry eat with us today since it's Christmas?"

"Henry is shy and usually likes to eat alone, but you can ask him."

Nadine visited Henry first, so he could get ready for dinner, in case he wanted to. Putting on her boots, coat and new mittens, she walked carefully down the snow and ice covered steps of the screened in porch. As soon as she was on the walk leading to Henry's one room frame house, she saw smoke curling out of his chimney and dissipating in the wind. She pulled her coat close to her neck to guard against the frigid chill. The snow seemed to insulate the world from sound. The chickens weren't clucking and the frozen creek was mute.

Nadine tapped on the door. She could hear movement inside, but no answer. She had just raised her fist to knock again when the door swung open. Framed in the doorway stood Henry, wearing a brown cardigan sweater over his bib overalls and red shirt. "Well look, if it ain't Nadine. Is something wrong at the Taylors?" He cleared his throat after the question.

"No, Henry. It's Christmas. I brought you a gift." Nadine held out his bag of hard candy.

Henry shyly took the candy. "Well, I ain't used to getting gifts, and here I get two, this here sweater from the Taylors and now candy from you."

Nadine thought she saw the glisten of a tear in his eye as he waved her into his house. The fire roared, and in front of it, a black dog lazily stood and stretched, having been awakened from sleep. "This here is Dutch Christopher Ebenezer. I just call him Dutch."

Dutch wagged his tail at the introduction, and Nadine heard his toenails clicking on the pine floor as he came to her.

"He's saying, 'Hello,' to me with his tail," Nadine giggled as she sat down in the floor to pet Dutch. "He's so shiny."

Dutch began wiggling all over and jumping around with all of the attention. "Have you had Dutch long? I've never seen him."

"Well, Well," Henry stuttered, putting his hands in his pants pockets. "You see it's, ah, like this. Mr. Bird down the road there was having trouble with Dutch and was going to shoot him, so I said I'd take him. I ain't wanting this dog killed; you understand."

Nadine shook her head and asked, "Trouble?"

"Well, you see Dutch here has got a taste for chicken eggs and goes in the hen house and steals eggs to eat. So you see, I've been keeping Dutch in until I can break him." Henry paused and then added, "Could this be our little secret cause Mrs. Taylor wouldn't abide me having no dog inside my house. She thinks all animals should be kept outdoors."

Nadine, smoothing Dutch's coat, agreed with a nod.

"Dutch here is a real good dog cept for that one bad thing. He's good to have because he's a snake killing dog. I've seen him hunt snakes and pick em up in his mouth, shaking them till they're plumb dead."

"That sounds good to me, " Nadine agreed.

"Come now you two and sit by the fire to keep warm." Henry pulled the chair back for Nadine to sit in as Dutch put his paws in her lap for more petting. "I think you got a friend there, Nadine. Now just sit for awhile, and I'll fix you some hot tea sweetened with honey."

Nadine looked around the sparsely furnished room which was immaculate. The only thing hanging on any of the walls was a picture of an older boy who favored Henry, but who was much smaller, skinny in fact. The picture hung by a nail above the bed.

Henry handed Nadine the sweetened tea, stirred the fire and sat down, holding out his hands to warm.

Nadine noticed his nails were dirty from farming. They were quiet for a few minutes. Then Nadine asked, "Is that your picture over the bed?"

"Nope that's my brother, Ned. He died at fifteen when we were a livin' on the poor farm."

"How?"

"Oh, I don't know. I guess hard work, and he weren't very strong. Always had asthma. Smart though. He taught himself to read, unlike me."

"What is as-ma?"

"It's where you can't hardly get your breath. Many a night he'd have to sit straight up in bed or in a chair next to an open window to get any sleep. I'd rub Vicks Salve on his chest and cover it with a hot cloth. That seemed to give him some relief."

"Didn't you have a mom and pop?"

Henry ran his hand down over his face, "Well, you see Mom died early on, and our pop just got to drinking. Then he just walked out one day and forgot to come back. Ned and me were sent to the poor farm."

"What's a poor farm?"

"Where people go who ain't got enough to take care of themselves. I never want to go back there, no sir."

"Is it a bad place?"

"They feed you and give you a place to stay, so it wasn't all bad." He shook his head from side to side adding, "They made us work like dogs for every bite we ate, from early till late. On hot days we'd sweat, so we'd take our shirts off. Then we'd burn so bad that the sheets would stick to us at night. You'd think a long time before turning over. It hurt to move."

"Did they make Ned work even though he had as-ma?"

"Yep, sure did. The fall had been real dry. The fields turned to dust and the woods were on fire all around. Between the smoke and dust, he wheezed and wheezed, and then suddenly the wheezing stopped. His lungs give out."

"That's a sad story, Henry." Nadine reached over and patted his hand.

"Well, it has a happy ending cause Mr. Taylor came and brung me here and gave me a house. This is my first house ever. The Taylors, them sure are good folks."

"By the way, besides my bringing your gift, Mrs. Taylor said you could come to dinner."

"Oh, I'll just be happy here."

"Please, Henry, for me?" Nadine's voice raised to a little whine.

Henry scratched his head, "I don't feel comfortable around people; you see."

"Please, please."

"Oh, ok, just for you, Nadine."

*   *   *

The Taylors had just sat down to Christmas dinner, and Mr. Taylor was carving into the juicy white meat of the turkey when there was a wrap at the kitchen door. Nadine looked up at Mrs. Taylor, who smiled and said, "You may answer the door but don't stand there with it open, letting in the cold air. Just tell Henry to come on in." Nadine followed Mrs. Taylor's directions. Opening the door, there stood Henry holding his cap which he fidgeted with, turning it around and around. He quickly came in and quietly found his seat at the table.

After prayer, thanking God for the birth of Christ, the only sound was the clicking of eating utensils and Henry's chewing with his mouth open.

Mr. Taylor broke the silence, "You know, Henry, we have tobacco rights in the bottom land along the creek, so I think as soon as the weather breaks we'll start clearing. We have to plow the rocks out and then burn it off.

Henry never looked up from his plate as he grunted in agreement. After finishing his turkey and dressing, green beans, and mashed potatoes he proceeded to lick his plate clean.

Nadine shot a look out of the corner of her eyes to see Mrs. Taylor's reaction, knowing Grandmomma Dunlap would have been horrified.

All Mrs. Taylor said was, "I see you enjoyed your food, Henry."

"Yes um" he nodded, making the unruly hair which stuck up out of his cowlick bob up and down.

Following Christmas, work pretty much involved survival through the cold gray winter days and of course planning for spring planting. In the evenings, the family gathered around the fire where Mr. Taylor read from the *Grimms Fairy Tales*, with Nadine sitting on his lap. From time to time he paused to spit an arched stream of amber tobacco juice onto the hot coals, causing a sizzling sound and sparks to fly. Nadine particularly admired how he could make a perfect arch. She tried to imitate, but spit dribbled down her chin. So she gave up trying. When it was bedtime, Mr. Taylor bearded her with his long white whiskers which scratched.

"Don't do that," she retorted.

"Goodnight Sweet Pea," he'd say in his jolly voice.

With wrinkled brow, Nadine looked at Mrs. Taylor who, never missing a stitch, responded, "One of these days when you catch him sleeping, just cut that beard off." This caused Nadine to giggle.

Mrs. Taylor's favorite reading was the *Farmer's Almanac* and seed catalogs. Planting by the cycle of the moon was important, so said the almanac. If cucumbers were not planted by the right cycle, there would be lots of blooms but few cucumbers. Of course the potatoes had to be planted on St. Patrick's Day which was also Nadine's birthday. *I guess that's how we'll celebrate my birthday*, she thought, *plant potatoes*. When not reading, Mrs. Taylor's hands were busy doing needle work and mending.

After there was no more snow in which to make snow angels, the yard began to come alive with Sweet Williams; Forsythia budded at the side of the house; the dogwood and red bud began showing color on Goff Mountain; and blue birds nested on the fence post in the front yard.

Mother Nature also spurred Mrs. Taylor beyond her usual hustle as spring house cleaning topped her list of priorities. It became even more rigorous than usual when word was received that Pastor James and his wife were going to stay with the Taylors when he came to preach at the Pleasant Hills Missionary Baptist Church where Mrs. Taylor attended. Just as when Aunt Ada came, Henry, Melinda, and Mrs. Taylor launched into their chores, handing out some to Nadine and Sassy when they could be found.

The kitchen windows stayed steamed up from the constant cooking and baking in preparation for the company and the picnic lunch which came between the three sermons in the morning and the two in the afternoon. Following supper for the preacher's family the night before the services, Melinda, as she plunged her hands into the sudsy dishwater, fussed to herself, "I swan, that preacher and his wife done eat like hogs. There is hardly any table scraps. Just this little bit of gravy for the cat."

Nadine dried dishes as Mrs. Taylor entertained in the parlor. "All I got was a chicken neck." she complained.

"No wonder Mr. Taylor is a Freewill Baptist and won't have anything to do with these goins on," continued Melinda. "Here it is plantin' time and in comes company as if we don't have enough to do around here. Miz Taylor done had us clean everything in sight except the wooden clothespins."

*　　*　　*

Nadine and Mrs. Taylor were seated on the front row of the white frame church. Mrs. Taylor pulled her shawl around her to ward off the chill. Nadine, not daring to move, stared at the simple wooden cross, hanging behind the podium. Services started by singing *Amazing Grace*. Nadine was always glad for the singing part where she could stand rather than sit on the hard bench. Her dress collar was starched so stiff she had a hard time swallowing which prevented her from singing her very best.

Then Preacher James began his sermon in a sing-song tone about the devil, death, and hell. Nadine watched his Adams apple bob up and down, and the blue veins in his temples pop out when he talked about the devil and death. At one point she thought, in his excitement, that his false teeth were going to shoot right out of his mouth and land in Mom Taylor's lap. Then her attention shifted to Mr. Bird, their neighbor, who, when he dozed off to sleep, awoke with a startled jerk every time Preacher James hit the pulpit with his fist, or somebody in the back shouted, "Amen, Brother."

The sermon continued, Mom Taylor shed her shawl, and the cardboard fan, with pictures of Jesus and lambs on the back, began to vibrate as the congregation fanned vigorously to ward off the heat suggested by the sermon. Toward the end of his sermon, Preacher James was describing hell so vividly that Nadine envisioned the bright orange flames lapping at the hem of her long skirt and imagined the smell of burning flesh. Finally, everybody joined in singing the altar call, "Shall we gather at the river, the beautiful, beautiful river." Nadine hoped to remember all of Preacher James' sermons and gestures, so she could use them when she and Frances played church.

That night, and many nights to follow, Nadine drifted in and out of sleep remembering the images of death described by the preacher. Upon awakening, she felt her fingernails cutting into her palms, and her body was rigid. Only when her eyes caught a glimpse of the blonde angel in the picture and her nostrils breathed in the sweet familiar smell of talcum did she drift back to sleep. Sometimes her disturbed sleep brought screams which awakened her and brought Mom Taylor to her bedside. "Scoot over Nadine," she would say softly, as Nadine returned to sleep in the safety of her arms.

*   *   *

The rooster had just crowed as Nadine gulped down her rolled oats that Mom Taylor left on the stove for her. She listened to the clean clothes on the line snap in the brisk wind and smelled the wild green onions. Mom Taylor took great pride in how early she could wash and hang the clothes out to dry. In the kitchen garden, even strokes of a hoe were heard as it turned the soil, exposing its richness made by the rotting roots of past plantings and regular doses of horse manure.

"Nadine, get dressed. You can help me plant the peas," Mom Taylor called. "Don't forget your bonnet. You freckle so badly!"

Nadine bounded two steps at a time up the stairs to get dressed. *Planting must be fun*, she thought, being that Mom Taylor has done nothing but pore over the *Farmer's Almanac* and seed catalogs since Christmas. Mom Taylor was excited about the sunny days which allowed her to start gardening. She even walked more briskly now that planting time arrived.

Mom Taylor wasn't the only one who was enthusiastic about the arrival of spring. Henry and Pop Taylor were up and off early to curry, feed and harness the horses who were friskier than usual as they were hooked up to the plow. Coming home in the evenings, Pop Taylor and Henry bragged about the number of acres plowed and went into great detail on what to plant, where, when and how much. "More rows of field corn need to be planted this year. Last winter there was hardly enough to feed the livestock," said Pop Taylor.

Nadine tied her bonnet under her chin as Mom Taylor directed, "Walk between the rows, Nadine. See, like this, not on top of the rows. The soil has to be loose for the seeds to take root and plant one seed at a time. We can't afford to waste. Plant each seed, let me see your arm." Nadine held it out. "Plant them the distance from your wrist to your elbow apart. When you finish a row, go back and cover the seeds with dirt. See, like this." Mom Taylor again demonstrated. "Don't pack the dirt down, you hear?"

Nadine did as directed, but her pocket full of seeds diminished slowly. The even strokes of Mom Taylor's hoe became fainter and fainter as Nadine's energy began to ebb. Her shoulders and arms ached, and her tongue stuck to the roof of her mouth. It became quite apparent to her what strange creatures adults were to get so, "up in the air" about planting seeds and getting blisters on their hands from hoeing. *This is not fun at all*, she thought. This thought was intensified as she sighted Sassy heading toward the creek, fishing pole in hand. So she began dropping two seeds in each hole, then three and at the end of the row, she dumped the remaining seeds into one hole. Dropping the hoe, after covering the seeds with dirt, she took off after Sassy.

Mom Taylor's voice came from a distance. "Nadine, where are you off to? Have you planted all those seeds? Look at me when I talk. Do you hear?"

Nadine faced Mom Taylor and turned her pockets inside out. "All empty," she yelled and took off again.

Having joined Sassy on the creek bank under the sycamore tree with green buds forming on it, Nadine sat content.

Sassy rigged up a fishing pole for her out of a piece of string and a thick stout stick. Both girls watched the fat pink worms hooked at the end of their fishing lines wiggle in the water, inviting a catfish to just take a bite. Then, for supper, they could have fried catfish dipped in that special corn meal batter that only Melinda knew the secret recipe for, fried potatoes, and maybe leaf lettuce wilted with hot bacon grease and bathed in vinegar with a pinch of sugar with some green onions mixed in.

"I thought I saw you plantin', Girl. How did you get finished so quick?"

"I got tired of planting, so I dumped the seeds I still had left in one hole."

"Your sins will find you out when them plants come up in one clump. You goin' to be in big trouble then." Sassy shook her index finger in Nadine's face as she spoke.

Besides death, now Nadine had a guilty conscience to deal with and the fear of being caught in her evil deed. She squeezed her eyes closed as she squeezed that thought out of her mind. Anything could happen between now and then. *Right now I'm having fun fishing*, she decided as she watched a big ole catfish swim by on the other side of the bank. She tried to tempt him by extending her pole out as far as she could from where she sat, but he swam on down the stream like nothing was going on. "I sure do like fishing."

"Yep, the second most fun thing to do is to catch lightnin bugs. Ain't long till we can do that," Sassy said as she dangled her feet in the cold creek.

Sassy certainly can think of more fun things to do than these adults, thought Nadine.

*   *   *

One morning, Nadine heard Henry out at the barn, harnessing Big Red and hitching the wagon to him. Big Red snorted and pawed the ground. "You might as well calm down. Ain't no use fussin' cause you and me are goin' to take a ride," Henry said.

"Where you and Big Red going?" asked Nadine as she ran to the barn to check out the commotion.

"Mrs. Taylor done ordered some baby chicks from Charleston, I'm goin' to the boat landin' to pickem up."

That afternoon, Nadine heard the chirps of the chicks, announcing Henry's return before Big Red came into sight. Mom Taylor heard them too and was at the hen house waiting as Henry guided Red into the chicken yard where the chickens flapped their auburn wings, squawking at the intrusion of their yard. The ole rooster strutted around with his yellow eyes darting about as if to say, "You better tread lightly on my territory."

"May I hold one?" Nadine asked, jumping up and down. Mom Taylor tenderly placed the downy soft yellow chick into Nadine's small out stretched hands. Nadine held the ball of fluff in one hand as she stroked it softly with her index finger. "I think she likes me."

"Thanks for picking up the chicks," Mom Taylor said turning toward Henry.

"Yessum," was his only response as he finished unloading the crates of chicks.

On Easter morning as Nadine came downstairs, she heard "chirp chirp," coming from the master bedroom. Pop Taylor sat in his rocker, stroking the ball of yellow fluff. "Look here what the Easter Bunny done left for you, Sweet Pea," Pop said as he motioned her into the room. Mom Taylor stood beside him smiling.

Nadine covered her mouth with her small hand, but the wrinkles around her eyes were evidence of a wide smile. "I've never had anything alive for my very own," she said, reaching for the chirping chick. She felt its little heart going pity pat.

"Got to give it a name." said Pop.

Nadine thought for a minute and said, "Biddy, cause it is so small. I love you, Biddy."

"You'll have to feed Biddy and give it water. It's not like Miss Betsy who you can set in the corner until you get ready to play. This chick has to be tended to daily."

Nadine nodded her head in understanding.

*   *   *

After planting time, Aunt Ada boarded the boat in St. Albans, coming for another visit. This time she did not come alone, but brought her niece Elizabeth, named after Mom Taylor. Elizabeth was a year older than Nadine, so Nadine was thrilled that Elizabeth had come for the summer. She and Elizabeth became soul buddies. In fact, Nadine called her Buddy.

Buddy had the same soft blue eyes as Mom Taylor, Ada and Frances. She also had dimples when she smiled. Nadine so wished for blue eyes because it was her favorite color—the color of the sky—and because she would feel more like a real part of the family. She also loved those dimples, so when no one was looking, she sucked her cheeks in, thinking if she kept sucking she too would have dimples.

When it rained, they played inside with Frances, but on fair days, they explored and roamed the countryside with Sassy. Sassy knew where the best swimming and fishing holes were and even where there was a secret cave.

As the days drew to a close, the sky often turned pink and orange streaked with wisps of purple clouds. These vivid colors in the western sky evolved into the deep dark purple of twilight. Somewhere between twilight and night when the earth grew suddenly quiet and the humidity clung close, one light flashed then in response a second and a third. The earth became alive with tiny yellow-green flashing lights of lightning bugs and the giggles and yelps of delight as Sassy, Buddy and Nadine snatched the lightning bugs out of the air. Then they carefully placed the bugs delicate bodies into glass canning jars and quickly replaced the lids which were punched full of holes, so the bugs could breathe but not escape.

On one of these evenings as the three gracefully soared higher and higher with out stretched arms, their forms were silhouetted against the darkening sky with the lights flashing on and off in their three containers. The earth seemed to shimmer. Mom Taylor sat in the oak porch swing, enjoying the sight of three dream-like images dart here and there like fairies in *Grimms Fairy Tales*.

"We'll give these to Frances, and she can watch them in her room," Nadine said. She made her next leap forward for another catch, and her foot twisted as she landed. She was sent catapulting to the ground. A sharp scream cut through the darkness.

Mom Taylor jumped up as two containers with flashing lights converged over Nadine who writhed in pain as blood pulsated from her hand. The lightning bugs dispersed from her shattered jar, flittering silently into the night. Mom quickly took her apron off and tore it in half. One part she wrapped tightly at the pressure point on Nadine's arm to stop the bleeding. The other part she wrapped around and around Nadine's thumb which was almost severed from her hand.

"Is she goin' to live?" Sassy asked in a high pitched voice.

"Yes, but find me a thick strong stick, Sassy, quick."

In minutes, Sassy returned with the stick. Buddy stood frozen with tears washing down her face as she watched Nadine in pain. She finally stepped forward to sweep a strand of hair out of Nadine's eyes.

Nadine let out uncontrollable sobs as Mom Taylor twisted a piece of the cloth around the stick and then twisted the stick to exert more pressure to stop the bleeding. "Elizabeth, go on up to Frances' room. She probably heard Nadine and wonders what happened. Keep her calm. Sassy, run on home now. Nadine needs to be quiet, so the bleeding will stop."

"Yas Miz Taylor," Sassy answered as she reluctantly turned to go home. She opened the gate and then turned again to watch Mrs. Taylor carry Nadine to the porch swing where she continued applying pressure, holding the thumb in place with her blood soaked apron, and swinging back and forth, cradling Nadine in her lap.

"Do you want me to ask Grandma to come?"

"No, Nadine will be alright." Mom Taylor felt Nadine's sobs slowly subsiding.

As Sassy walked down the road, she heard Mrs. Taylor's singing drift through the night air, "There were ninety and nine. . ."

Sleep did not come quickly as Nadine felt what seemed like her heart beating in her thumb, but that familiar smell of talcum which came in times of stress brought peace. Sleep encompassed her.

The next day Mom Taylor tended the wound, and Nadine complained of the pain. "Stop, you are squeezing too tight!"

"I know it hurts, but you must keep it wrapped tightly, so your thumb will grow back and not get infected. You'll have to be a brave little girl, and you'll probably have it wrapped most of the summer." Nadine let out a whine at that thought. "Remember Nadine, without God putting some pain in our lives, we would end up being shallow people."

Nadine did not have the slightest idea what Mom meant, but she wore the bandage all summer.

Mom dressed it daily and applied rosin from a white pine tree. The rosin was boiled until thin enough to spread. This formed a seal on the cut.

Her thumb mended, but the tendons were severed. For the rest of her life, Nadine would not be able to move her injured thumb.

*　　*　　*

"I found two more dead chicks when I went out to the hen house," Mom Taylor announced as she joined Ada who was sitting on the front porch stringing green beans. For a few minutes the only sound was the snapping of beans.

"Liz, you just got a batch of infected chicks. They'll probably all die," Ada said, shaking her head.

A few days later when Buddy and Nadine went to visit Biddy, she lay limp in the corner of her cage. Nadine picked her up, but there was not a sound, not even the pity pat of Biddy's heart.

"Is she dead?" Buddy gasped.

"She is," nodded Nadine as tears silently seeped down both of her cheeks.

"You took good care of her." Buddy said stroking the top of Nadine's head. Nadine sat there for what seemed a long time. The only movement was her wiping tears with the back of her hands.

"Are we going to bury the poor thing, Nadine?"

"Yes," she whispered, but it has to be a real Christian burial."

"What do you mean?"

Nadine cleared her throat. "First, we need a coffin."

"I think a kitchen match box would be the right size," Buddy suggested.

That afternoon, Buddy, Frances and Nadine sat in Frances' room, lining the match box with scraps of antique satin left from making the living room drapes. Frances smiled as she fitted the cloth neatly into the box. She loved working with her hands and being with the girls. After the proper casket was prepared, Nadine reverently placed Biddy in her resting place. She then carried it to her bedroom, hiding it under her bed, so it would not be discovered by Mom. *Henry said that Mom didn't like animals in the house and especially dead ones,* Nadine recalled.

After Mom and Pop had gone to bed, Nadine placed the coffin in her window sill. "What are we going to do now?" Buddy asked.

"We have to have a wake for Biddy."

"What's that?"

"We must sit up all night with the body."

"Why?"

"I don't really know," confessed Nadine. "I just remember that when

Grandmomma Dunlap died a group of friends sat up all night with her body. And we're the only friends Biddy has."

The full moon positioned itself right behind the coffin. The coffin was a dark form in contrast with the moon's white light that waned only when a cloud briefly passed over it. The two girls sat staring at the dark form. At first, there came the, "Who, who, who," of the hoot owl, and then Dutch began howling mournfully at the moon.

Buddy moved closer to Nadine who sat wide eyed in bed, leaning against the headboard.

As the night went on, the, "Who, who, who," stopped, but Dutch's howls did not. The girls rubbed their eyes to ward off sleep.

"Look!" Nadine pointed, did you see that coffin move?"

"No."

"Watch."

Another cloud passed over, making the room dark then light once more. Just at that moment, Buddy let out a scream, "It's moving; it's moving; oh, Nadine the coffin is moving."

Footsteps were heard coming up the stairs, taking two at a time. The bedroom door flung open. There stood Mom Taylor silhouetted in the doorway, gasping for breath. "What is the matter? What is moving?"

Buddy pointed at the corpse. "What is it?" Mom asked, moving quickly to pick up the coffin. Seeing it's contents, she called for Pop; who came in rubbing his eyes. "Take this out of here," she directed. Then she turned toward the girls. "That chick is diseased, and you can't be bringing it into the house."

"Where is Pop going with Biddy?"

"Outside. Now you two settle down and get some sleep."

"Will Biddy go to heaven? I sure don't want her to burn in the flames of hell."

"Yes, Nadine, Biddy will go to heaven, now go to sleep." Mom pulled their covers up and tucked them in, so they could hardly move. She quietly closed the door and tiptoed downstairs.

"I hope a big ole chicken hawk doesn't swoop down out of the sky and have Biddy for breakfast."

"Now, why did you have to go and say that?" Nadine turned over and fluffed her pillow. "If you hadn't screamed, Biddy would still be here."

"You said you saw it move too," replied Buddy.

Finally sleep came.

Catching Pop before he went out into the field, Nadine asked about Biddy's whereabouts. "Biddy is right out there by the screen porch door," Pop motioned as he pulled his billed cap down around his ears.

Buddy and Nadine buried Biddy, said a prayer and sang "Jesus Loves Me." They pounded a small, white, wooden cross that they had made into the ground. On the cross was written, Biddy. Then they placed a fist full of white daisies on the grave and somberly left.

*   *   *

Summer was drawing to a close. The leaves that had been yellow-green and tender in the spring, turned dark green and drooped toward the ground, seeking water in this dry spell. The cicadas, which Buddy called school bugs because they became more vocal right before school, began their screeching.

Pop Taylor recruited several field hands to help gather in the crops. It was Mom's job to be in charge of preparing the lunch for these hungry men. She, Ada and Melinda stayed busy in the kitchen, frying chicken, peeling and mashing pounds of potatoes, slicing the Big Boy tomatoes which had turned bright red in the hot summer's sun, and crisp green cucumbers. There were stacks of corn on the cob, and cornbread. Besides the gallons of ice tea, there were glasses of grape wine that Mom had made from the grapes which dangled like deep purple amethyst from the arbor in the backyard.

After the tables were ready, Mom went to the front door where a conch shell served as a doorstop. She picked it up, placed it to her lips and blew. Out came a loud bugle like sound.

Hearing this sound, the men dropped whatever they were doing, to hurry to the well house where Melinda ladled a dipper of cold water over each man's head and hands. They then anxiously found a place at the table. They were tired, sweaty, hungry, and Mom's cooking was renowned in these parts.

The three women served as forks, knives, plates and glasses clanked, and loud chewing and talking proceeded. Nadine, Sassy, and Buddy were sent to the screened-in porch to eat, so not to be exposed to "men's talk." The women would eat after everyone had finished. Meanwhile, they ladled out more and more food, wiping beads of perspiration from their foreheads with the corner of their aprons.

As the three girls ate, Sassy hummed. "What's that you're humming?" asked Nadine.

"I feel like a motherless child," she answered. "My grandma she sang it all the time, that and 'Nobody Knows the Troubles I've Seen.'"

"I don't have a real mom, you know. She died."

"Mrs. Taylor is your mom now," interjected Buddy, picking at a kernel of corn with her fork.

"I know," answered Nadine, and a smile spread across her face. "I always wanted a home, a mom and a pop. Now I have all three."

Melinda stepped to the kitchen door. "You youngin's finish up now. You need to clear off the table where the men folk done eat while we come out here where it's cool." With this she waddled back into the kitchen.

"If we hadn't talked so much, we could've been down by the creek. Now we have to work," Sassy grumbled as she stood with her hand on her hip.

This wine left in the glasses sure is a pretty color, thought Nadine, as she held a glass up to the sunlight. She then tipped a half empty glass to her lips and licked it with her tongue. Then making smacking sounds with her lips, she whispered, "That sure is good, something like grape jelly."

Buddy and Sassy were easily persuaded to sample that sweet purple liquid. Having a few swigs, their chore did not seem so hard. In fact, by the time the table was cleared, left over food divided into separate containers for Dutch and then the pigs, and all of the wineglasses emptied of their liquid, the girls were feeling giddy. They were laughing, tripping over themselves and rolling on the floor.

As Buddy scraped the last dish clean, she tripped over her own feet, and the plate went crashing to the floor, breaking into several pieces. All three girls were down on their hands and knees, trying to pick up the evidence before discovery, but to no avail.

Mom heard the crash and was standing over them asking, "What is going on in here?" "We just accidentally broke a dish," Nadine answered, holding up a piece. With this, Sassy and Buddy could no longer stifle their laughter.

"What are those purple rings around your mouths?"

In sync, they shook their heads and shrugged their shoulders, indicating they had not the slightest idea.

"Nadine, come here. Now open your mouth and blow. Nadine," Mom said in a disbelieving tone, "you've been into the wine."

The girls froze in their positions and looked at each other. What could they say? "Just a drop or two," Sassy took the initiative to speak.

"You're drunk!"

Buddy's hand flew to her mouth to suppress a hiccup. By that time, Ada and Melinda were standing in the kitchen shaking their heads in disbelief.

Melinda, saying over and over, "What am I goin' to do with you, Sassy?"

"Take them out on the porch to get fresh air while I brew some strong coffee."

Ada and Melinda marched the girls onto the porch where Ada began lecturing them on the evils of alcohol with her fingers wagging in their faces.

In the background, Melinda was saying, "Yessum," in agreement to Ada's words.

The screen door slammed as Mom carried three cups of black coffee out, "Drink," she commanded.

Nadine's stomach began to feel queasy. She made a dash for the porch door, followed by Sassy and Buddy. Nadine didn't think she had ever been so sick. The three heaved and heaved. After that, they were sent to bed for the remainder of the day. None of them felt able to argue at the punishment.

As they were ushered into separate rooms, they decided never to drink wine again, NEVER!

*   *   *

Ada sat swinging on the front porch, enjoying the last few evenings before she had to take Buddy back to St. Albans for school. The coolness and the oak leaves tipped with red reminded her that fall was not far away. Mom sat in a rocking chair, sewing buttons on Pop Taylor's shirts. "I swan, I don't know how he manages to lose so many buttons."

Other than such sporadic remarks, the only sound was the creaking of the swing. Then Ada, with raised eyebrows, asked, "Did you read the reprint about Assessor Stark's murder in the *Putnam Democrat*?"

Liz, concentrating on threading a needle in the twilight, shook her head. "Summer is too busy for me to do much reading. I save the papers to read on the long winter evenings."

"Well, it was a gruesome murder. It had everybody in Winfield bolting their doors and pulling down their shades at night."

"Do say," Mom answered with interest.

Ada leaned over so she could speak softly. She didn't want the girls to hear. Nadine was nervous enough about death already. "Assessor Stark lived alone, you know. His house was situated on a hill right about where the road that runs along the river intersects with the road going toward Hurricane."

"I know about where that is. Mr. Taylor's Poca farm is above that and across the river."

"Well, anyway, Assessor Stark's sister lived nearby. She came every morning, it seems, and fixed his breakfast. This one morning as she stepped onto the porch, she noticed broken glass where the front window was out. She knocked several times, but Stark never answered."

Ada stopped her monologue. She arched her eyebrows again, making her eyes round like an owl's. "I can see it in my mind's eye almost as if I were there. The sister walked across the porch to the broken window and peered in. There lying in his own blood, was her brother. Not knowing if he were dead or alive, she crawled through the window, being careful not to cut herself on jagged pieces of glass." Ada stopped as if she indeed visualized what transpired.

"Well, was he dead or alive?"

"He was dead!" Ada said wringing her hands. "Dead as a door nail. His sister seeing that the house had been ransacked, surmised the motive was robbery. Since, as an assessor, he kept a sum of money in the house from the head taxes he had been collecting. Plus, he had money of his own. She also realized the window that she crawled through was evidently how the murderers entered. In fact, they could have still been lurking about. With this thought, she hightailed it out and down to her house for help, screaming all the way."

"Did they catch the murderers?"

"I'm coming to that. Upon investigation, it was determined that Stark had been sitting and reading by the light of the fireplace because a half burned book was found lying at the edge of the fireplace. The murderer(s) crept up to the window and shot Stark in the back of his head. The force pitched him forward. His spectacles were half on and half off. He never saw his killer. The sheriff began asking questions. There was gossip about Stark's having a falling out with a neighbor over the cost of a basket. There was some animosity between John Shelts and Stark. Shelts, it seems, was a half a bubble off, if you know what I mean?" Ada stopped to see if Liz comprehended.

"He was none too bright?"

"That's right. The sheriff, harassed by the people of Winfield and those about who were living in 'mortal fear,' took Shelts in. And, not being too smart, and with the sheriff interrogating him, Shelts confessed."

"So, that was that!"

"No there is more." Liz's rocking almost stopped and the swing creaked no more. "Seems a private investigator by the name of Howard Smith from Charleston got interested in the case. He also heard gossip. This time it was about a handyman who worked for Stark. His name was Bright. Seems he and Stark argued about wages. Bright left in a huff, telling Stark that he, Bright, would see him again but that Stark wouldn't see him again."

Ada swallowed then continued, "Smith had two bloodhounds which led him to a houseboat down about Leon where a Mr. Hawkins lived. Searching the boat turned up Bright's shoes with mud on them and a good sum of money that he or Hawkins could not explain."

"Oh my," interjected Liz. "Now we have three suspects. Who did it?"

"Detective Smith said the mud on Bright's shoes matched the soil around Stark's property. Meanwhile, Shelts recanted his confession, and somebody gave him an alibi for the evening of the murder."

"You're not going to get anybody else involved in this story are you, Ada?"

Ada holding up her hand said, "Hold on Liz. The sheriff questioned Hawkins and Bright."

"And?"

"Seems Bright moved in with Hawkins after he and Stark fell out. Bright, stewing over the fight, kept telling Hawkins about all the money Stark kept in his house, and how they could get rich fast. So after dark on the night of the murder, they dismounted their horses after reaching Stark's property and crawled on their bellies till they reached Stark's house, sneaked onto the porch, and watched Stark for a few minutes as he sat reading. Then they shot him in the back of his head. They fired twice, so they said. Sure enough the sheriff went back to the house and found a second bullet lodged in the mantle."

Mom tilted her head to one side, "Why didn't a dog bark or anything?"

"Stark's dog didn't consider Bright to be a stranger. As Stark's handyman, Bright had lived on the farm for a time.

The moral to this is not to let questionable characters move onto your property." were Ada's final words, shaking her fingers in Liz's face."

"What happened to Hawkins and Bright?"

"As we speak, they are cooling their heels in the Moundsville Penitentiary."

*   *   *

Pop Taylor couldn't help but notice that Nadine was moping around after Buddy left, so at breakfast he said, "Sweet Pea, I'm going to ride over to the general store. You want to ride along?"

"Can I ride on Prince too?"

"Sure thing."

Nadine looked at Mom who nodded her head, adding, "You can pick up some school supplies. School begins next week you remember."

Nadine let out an excited giggle as Pop headed to the barn to curry, feed and saddle Prince, his prized Tennessee Walker.

She rode astride holding onto the saddle horn while Pop held her around the waist with one arm while guiding the reins with his other hand. The trip was enjoyable except for Pop's white beard which scratched the back of her neck. Every once in a while Pop let Prince nibble grass along the road or stop for a drink from the creek. Prince snorted loudly after each swallow of water.

Approaching the general store, Nadine saw two men slouched down in their chairs on the store's porch, spitting tobacco onto the dusty road. As Pop and Nadine stepped onto the porch, they proceeded to tip their hats, "Howdy Mr. Taylor and Nadine."

"You men solving all the worlds problems?" joked Pop.

"We're givin' um a lot of thought, sure enough," they replied with a smile which showed the brown tobacco stains on their teeth.

Having been in the bright sunlight, Nadine's eyes had to adjust to the dark interior of the store. The proprietor stepped from behind the counter, shaking Pop's hand like he was priming a pump by its handle. "How can I help you, Mr. Taylor," he asked squinting through his gold rimmed spectacles.

"Well Tim, I have a list here," Pop said pulling out a brown paper bag with some writing on it.

"That certainly is a pretty little girl you have there. This must be Nadine," Tim said with a wink in her direction. With that he reached in the candy jar and handed her two chocolate drops.

"What do you say, Nadine? Cat got your tongue?"

"Thank you."

"You are welcome young lady." Taking Pop's list, Tim began moving quickly about the store filling the order. Pop was right on his heels, chewing on a licorice stick. The store owner only stopped once to get a lady's mail, for he was also the postman.

Nadine stood there taking in all the sights. She had never seen so many things under one roof: candy, toys, clothes, groceries, medicine, seed, fabric, hardware, dishes, pots and pans, and chicken feed. The general store carried about anything anybody would want. "Sweet Pea, we better get a bite to eat before starting back. "Let's see Tim; we'll have a slug of longhorn cheese. Oh, and that there bologna and some saltine crackers. By the way, put two pounds of peppermint candy and these chocolate drops Nadine likes with the rest of my order." Tim began attending to Mr. Taylor's request and with some bologna, cheese and crackers in hand, Pop sat on the porch steps to gossip with whomever came by.

Meanwhile, Nadine nibbled on her lunch as she continued to take inventory of the store. She spied a small celluloid doll and asked Tim, "May I see that doll, please?" Nadine stood on her toes and pointed.

"Sure enough, young lady."

The doll had a pretty painted face with bright blue eyes and wore a flowered bonnet to match her dress. "I sure would like to have this doll," she said out loud while thinking, *she would be company for Miss Betsy while Sassy and I are playing.*

"Ready to go? Prince is loaded," Pop motioned to Nadine.

"Nadine says she fancies this doll." Tim held it up.

"If she wants it, she can have it. Stick it in the bag and total it with the rest of the order."

Each school day, Pop took Nadine to school, riding Prince. She wanted to get there early because she liked helping get water from the spring. Other students, mostly the boys, gathered wood for the pot belly stove which served to warm the one room frame school house. Grades one through eight met in the same classroom.

Mr. Scott, the teacher, spoke with a nasal quality which the older boys imitated behind his back. This always made Nadine laugh which encouraged them even more. They would hold their noses with their fingers and recite

Evangeline, the narrative poem that all eight graders had to memorize.

Nadine's favorite subjects were geography and history. She liked history because Pop always made it come alive when he talked about fighting as a young boy in the Civil War. One reason she liked geography was because the book was large enough to hide behind while Mr. Scott was busy teaching a lesson to the upper grades.

Once Nadine was sneaking and eating an apple behind her book. She always got hungry around two. She was savoring the sweet apple juice, wiping it from her chin with her handkerchief when she must have crunched too loudly. "Nadine, are you eating in class?" questioned Mr. Scott in a somber voice.

The class suddenly became quiet as all eyes turned toward Nadine, waiting for her answer. Lowering the geography book until her eyes made contact with his serious no nonsense glare, she smiled as big as she could and replied, "Yes sir, would you like a bite? It is mighty good and juicy." She held the half-eaten apple up for him to view.

This honest reply caught Mr. Scott off guard, and he tried to restrain his lips from turning upward into a smile by clearing his throat and covering his mouth with his hand. "Young lady, throw that apple in the trash and go stand in the coat closet."

Nadine was very familiar with the interior of the coat closet. By the time she was in grade three, she had spent quite a bit of time there. She really didn't mind. There were advantages, especially when it was getting close to Mr. Scott's dismissing class for the day. She could grab her coat and be out the door to retrieve the asafetida bag that she hid under a rock to the side of the school each morning after Pop rode off. Mom made her wear it on a ribbon around her neck, saying it would make her healthy by keeping germs away.

At first she put up a fuss, telling Mom that she was the only one in class who wore an asafetida bag. There was no persuading her. Nadine decided on passive resistance. She wore it until getting to the school yard, but not one minute longer.

Nadine liked school because she had fun being with other children. In fact the weekends, at times, seemed long. One Saturday in early fall, Henry drove Mom to catch a boat to Charleston to sell eggs and buy winter supplies, leaving Pop in charge with her now standard warning, "Don't let the Gypsies carry away the farm this time."

Pop just waved his hand as if to say, "Go on get out of here, everything will be okay." As Red's hoof beats faded into the distance, Pop laid down in the swing for a nap.

For awhile Nadine played with Dutch. They had become good friends. As Henry predicted, Dutch made an excellent farm dog. He accompanied Nadine each evening when she went to get the cows. Mom would walk onto the porch at milking time and call, "Sook Jersey, Sook, Sook…" The cows began ambling toward the barn. Nadine hurried them along as Dutch ran barking, helping herd them homeward.

Thirsty from play, Nadine opened the front gate and saw Pop, snoring in the swing. Instead of stepping onto the front porch, she detoured to the screened-in porch door. She tiptoed into the master bedroom where the Singer sewing machine sat. Quietly she opened its drawer, pulling out the scissors. Just as quietly, she stepped onto the porch.

With Pop's snores assuring her that he was in deep sleep, she cautiously bent over him and began to snip away at his long white beard, thinking, *he won't beard me ever again.*

As a pesky fly began to buzz about, Pop's hand instinctively swiped it away with a wave almost hitting the scissors. With this close call, Nadine backed away from her task. Returning the scissors to their place, she made herself scarce.

Not long after, Red with his cargo pulled up in front. Nadine forgetting herself ran to greet them. Pop hearing the crackle of paper bags jumped up and rubbed his eyes. With one look at him, Mom began laughing. "What on earth happened to your beard?" she asked.

Pop looked down with dismay, recognizing that half of his beard was missing. "Look what that Nadine has done! Look what she has done to me!" He shook his head, going to check himself out in the mirror to see how much damage was done.

"Nadine, you've brightened my day," Mom said as she and Henry unloaded the wagon. Henry looked over at Nadine with a wink.

Nadine waited for Pop's reaction. At supper he came to the table with his thick whiskers trimmed into a neat goatee.

"My how handsome you look," said Mom, trying to ward off as much negative reaction as possible. "I do believe I see a resemblance to General Lee."

Nadine taking this as a cue, slipped onto his lap, saying, "You do indeed look more handsome than ever." She planted a big kiss on his cheek, and he to her surprise bearded her with his goatee. With that she jumped down, thinking, *I wish I had cut it all off and the next time I will.* Pop got the last laugh.

*   *   *

May had arrived, and it was hot in the classroom. Nadine watched for a droplet of sweat which dangled at the tip of Mr. Scott's nose to drop onto his grade book. This helped keep her mind off the heat and the odor of sweat drenched clothes of her classmates. Flies and wasps darted in and out of the open windows at will. Every once in a while Mr. Scott smacked at a bothersome fly with the fly swatter that he kept on top of his desk. The loud slap made the students liven up, rousing some from their form of escape—sleep.

Nadine's stomach drew into a knot, alerting her that the lunch hour approached. She restlessly shifted in her hard desk seat, thinking of the butter and grape jam on biscuits that awaited her in her lunch basket. She moistened her dry lips with her tongue as she glanced toward the dipper in the bucket of now warm water, but water nonetheless.

Mr. Scott slowly pulled his silver watch from his trouser pocket and announced that lunch time had arrived. Students, however, did not dare to budge from their seats until their row was dismissed. None wanted to be kept in during lunch for not following "the rules."

After finishing her long awaited jam sandwich washed down by a dipper of warm water, Nadine joined the girls jumping rope: "Jimmy and Sally sitting in the tree K-I-S-S-I-N-G," went the chant as the rope turned, and the dry dust floated upward, settling on the girls' socks and hems of their dresses.

While taking a turn at holding the rope, Nadine caught sight of Mr. Hodges, the mailman, riding his mule. Without hesitation, she handed the rope off and ran into the classroom. Grabbing a piece of paper and a pencil, she wrote a brief note. Exiting the school, she caught sight of the top of Mr. Hodges wide brimmed hat as he rode over the hill. Clutching her note, she walked quickly.

Clearing the school yard, her walk broke into a run followed by, "Mr. Hodges, Mr. Hodges, please wait up." Mr. Hodges being hard of hearing just kept bobbing up and down on the mule. "Mr. Hodges," Nadine yelled louder followed by a shrill whistle. Her whistle caught the mailman's attention, and he turned to look in Nadine's direction. Pulling his sweat stained hat off, he mopped his forehead and bald head with his red bandana handkerchief. "What are you doing off the school yard, Nadine?"

"Please take this very important note to Mom or Pop Taylor."

"Ok, but you best get back to the school yard young lady, or you'll have Mr. Scott after us both."

Nadine obediently turned back toward the school. Her mission was completed.

*   *   *

"Remember some of the letters of the alphabet give off more than one sound. For example, the g can be hard as in goat or soft as in giant, having a j sound...," Mr. Scott droned on in his nasal twang. Then there was a sharp rap on the door. Mr. Scott excused himself and with a few quick strides swung open the door; on the other side was Pop Taylor.

"I understand you have a sick little girl, and I've come to take her home."

"Well, if Nadine is sick, she didn't let me know," Mr. Scott answered with raised eyebrows.

Mr. Hodges delivered a note to my wife, saying Nadine is sick, come and get her immediately. Pop punctuated this by crossing his arms across his chest and continued, "So Mrs. Taylor came out in the field where I was haying, sent me, and here I am."

Mr. Scott with raised eyebrows turned toward Nadine, "Are you sick Child?"

"I sure am. My tummy is just in knots, sir."

"Why didn't you tell me you were sick?"

Nadine shrugged and looked at the floor. A moment later, when Nadine grabbed her lunch basket, she heard feet shuffling and stifled giggles. As she looked up, she caught sight of her classmates' expressions of disbelief. This did not deter her from taking Pop's hand and escaping the hot, smelly, boring room.

Nadine tried to hide her delight as she rode behind Pop Taylor astride a lathered Prince.

"How you feel Pussy Cat, any better out in this fresh air?"

"I think I'll make it." Nadine was glad she did not have to look Pop in the eyes because she had an inkling that he knew her trick. She just held on and swayed to and fro with Prince's slow gait.

Nadine's happiness was short lived, however. As Pop lifted her from Prince, she caught sight of Mom Taylor standing at the front door with a bottle of castor oil.

"What on earth is ailing you, Child?"

"My tummy is cramping awful," Nadine answered, leaning over as if in pain, so as not to make eye contact.

"All she needs is to be put to bed and to drink a nice hot toddy," volunteered Pop Taylor.

"No! She'll have the bed rest, all right, and a good dose of castor oil," insisted Mrs. Taylor. She stood aside, so Nadine could enter the house. Nadine found herself ushered upstairs, which was hotter than the classroom, dressed for bed, tucked in under blankets and had spooned into her mouth the awful tasting castor oil which indeed made her stomach cramp.

"Just lie here a little while until the oil clears your stomach, and you'll feel better," directed Mom, patting Nadine on the head and securing the blanket under Nadine's chin.

"That fried chicken, apples and biscuits sure smell good cooking," Nadine said. "Maybe I can have some when I feel better."

"Oh no, not with your upset stomach. I'll fix some squab broth out of nice tender pigeon."

The thought of eating a baby pigeon, the heat, and the oil was just too much for Nadine. Waves of nausea swept over her. Everything, including the grape jam and biscuits came up. Nadine began to wonder if escaping school and the ride on Prince was worth this torture. Besides, she was still starving for some of the fried chicken and apples, but to no avail. It was pigeon soup or nothing. After cleaning her up, Mom sent Nadine back to bed.

Nadine heard dishes' clanking as Mom cleared the supper dishes from the table. Then she heard Pop shuffling down the hall and into her room, holding a glass with some amber colored liquid she often saw him drink before bed. "Here sip some of this hot toddy; it'll make you feel better and let you sleep."

Sure enough as the warmth of the sweet liquid spread through her body, Nadine fell asleep as the afternoon light faded, and the cool evening air began to stir through the room. Drifting in and out of sleep, Nadine felt Mom and Pop's presence and heard their voices. "Just let her rest until around noon, and I'll take her to school on Prince."

"Well, she does seem to be resting but look how flushed her cheeks are," answered Mom Taylor, leaning over to tuck in the covers. "I'll send for Dr. Davis to come and look at her to be sure she is fit to return to school. You go on about your work!" Pop knew there was no use arguing with Liz, so the matter was settled.

Dr. Davis did not arrive at the house until late the next evening. After her examination, Nadine watched by lamp light as Dr. Davis with his index finger flicked powdered caramel into a small piece of paper and folded it as if making a cigarette while giving Mom directions. Mom jabbed her hands into the pockets of her dress and cocked her head to one side. "Liz, Nadine is to take six doses in twenty-four hours. Mix a teaspoon of this, 1/2 teaspoon of cinnamon with ginger, add to boiling water, steep for a few minutes, then strain and serve. Tomorrow wrap her in a blanket, let her sit up to gain her strength back, and feed her baked potatoes."

Mom repeated the directions to Dr. Davis' satisfaction then noting how tired he looked, said, "You look like you've had a hard day yourself. Henry caught some catfish, so I've fried them up with potatoes, fixed wilted lettuce salad and baked an apple pie for desert. Why don't you join us?"

"You're right, Liz. It's been a long day. The Lovejoy girl up the road had a difficult delivery. The baby came early and is just a tiny thing. I'm going to stop back before I go home, so I'll take you up on your offer of supper. Nadine was left thinking of the menu Mom had just rattled off, and the baked potato she was going to get.

The next day, sitting wrapped like a mummy in a room whose temperature had to be over 100 degrees, sipping her hot tea prescription, Nadine thought of Sassy's words, "Your sins will find you out, Girl."

Two days after Dr. Davis' visit, Mom tiptoed into Nadine's room where she sat wrapped up in the rocking chair. "I think you can go to school tomorrow Nadine," Mom said softly. "There are only a few days left before school is out for the summer." Leaning over to brush a red curl from Nadine's forehead, she continued "Mr. Taylor rode over and picked up your books, so you won't be behind. We'll do some lessons now. After lighting the oil lamp and opening the window to let the air and light in, she patted her lap, and Nadine went over and sat with her arms around Mom's neck.

Nadine had decided that school might not be so bad after all, especially with only a few more days left. When she returned to school, maybe Mom would let her have something to eat besides squab and baked potatoes. She began reading Dot and Dan aloud. Later Pop came in to check her arithmetic.

* * *

Early the next day, Pop returned from taking Nadine to school and found Mom still sitting at the kitchen table. "Are you not feeling well?"

"I've just been thinking," she answered biting her lip and then crossing her hands in her lap.

"That's not good." Pop joked.

"Sit down."

"Oh my, this is serious." Pop said as he pulled up his cane bottom chair.

"How did Nadine do with her arithmetic last night?"

Pop took off his hat and ran his fingers through his hair. "Not too good," he answered slowly.

"She didn't do well in reading either. Well, not as well as I know she can." Again she bit her lip and then continued, "Nadine is not getting the education she should have here."

A frown came across Pop's face, "What are you suggesting?"

Mom pulled a folded letter from her pocket and unfolded it but did not read from it. She just got to the point, "My sister Effie writes that the John Hansford house is for sale in St. Albans."

"And," Pop coaxed.

"And, I think we should sell my farm here and yours at Poca and buy the house."

"Do what? Give up farming?"

"There is land with the Hansford house and a slave cabin. We can fix it up for Henry." Mom rushed on. "There are houses we can rent out, and it is beautifully situated with a large yard sloping to the river."

"Um," Pop growled. "That house almost burned down once, and it's old—been standing since the 1840s or 50s. Besides, I don't abide living in town, especially St. Albans. The town has been flooded and in 1906 there were two fires that almost wiped it out."

"But this is 1917 and everything is new. Why there is telephone service, city water, a trolley car, and they say the mayor is talking about paving some streets. Besides, on Smoky Road, we would still be out." Mom sat folding and unfolding the hem of her apron.

The room was quiet except for the ticking of the mantle clock. Feeling uncomfortable with the silence, she spoke again. "Very good families live there about, descendants of the Washington's and President Grant's brother lives just up Brown's Creek."

"Talking about Grant to a Confederate soldier is not good strategy Mrs. Taylor, by gum. As for descendants of George Washington, Melinda and Sassy, if the truth were known, are probably that." With these words, he stood to exit.

Mom meant to have the last word. "Mr. Taylor, you and I aren't getting any younger, and two farms are too much for us to run. Besides, we've lost sight of the point of the conversation. Nadine is not getting the proper education here."

"I'll think on it."

"Effie said we could get the property cheap, and the Thomas' have really fixed it up," yelled Mom above the slam of the screen door as she watched Pop head for the barn, shaking his head.

Summer was a blur, all revolving around the move to St. Albans. Since the Goff Mountain farm belonged to Mom, she could sell if she wished, and she did. Pop held onto his Poca farm until sometime later. "But he finally saw the light," as Mom said.

Part II
Move to St. Albans, WV

It was a gray rainy day when Nadine first came to the John Hansford house where she would live with the Taylor's. She stood at the bottom of the concrete steps and looked up. It was a large square house with a porch running across the front, and in the center was a large door with a glass panel above. The house looked foreboding silhouetted against the thick dark clouds, and the wet leaves which had not been raked from last fall gave off an acid smell. Gazing up at the house, Nadine, out of the corner of her eye, could see the railroad track to the right.

Carrying Ms. Betsy in one arm, she slowly ascended the steps and entered into a hallway as large as a room. Here she stood at the bottom of another wide stairway, leading upstairs where she and Frances would sleep. She noted the shiny stair railing and banister, which ended with a large wooden ball at the foot of the steps. She smiled to herself, thinking *what a great slide that banister was going to make*. To her right, was Pop and Mom Taylor's bedroom. She continued exploring and noted the stuffed furniture wrapped with white cloth, losing its identity and looking instead like white dinosaurs, crouching along the walls. She walked down a step into the dining-room, then into the kitchen and out onto the back porch. Henry's house was just beyond.

She heard Mom's excited voice, giving orders on where everything was to be placed. Finding Nadine, she took her hand and led her upstairs. "Here is your bedroom. Doesn't it have a beautiful view of Coal River? As soon as we are all settled in, I'm going to have a porch built on this upper level. On hot nights you can sleep there and listen to the sounds of the river." Mom placed her hands on each temple, exclaiming, "We are all going to be so happy here. I just know it!" Nadine nodded her head wanting to share in Mom's joy over her new home. "Ok," continued Mom, "You can begin putting your things away."

First Nadine placed Ms. Betsy on the bed, arranging her dress just so. Then she stepped over to straighten the picture of the blonde angel, watching over the children as they walked across the bridge over the turbulent water. As she did, she smelled the familiar aroma of sweat talcum powder which always gave her comfort.

Whistling as she dug into the boxes, her fingertips touched a wad of tissue paper. As she unfolded it, she saw the smooth white pebble that Sassy gave her the day they met. That seemed like years ago. As she had done upon receiving it, she felt its smoothness. Her throat contracted and her eyes stung as she thought of saying goodbye to Sassy. Nadine tried to think of a special gift for Sassy. She cut a lock of her own hair and gave it to Sassy with a note saying, "Remember, redheads are special."

Sassy nodding her redhead up and down in agreement, turned and ran down the road and was swallowed up by the dust. What wonderful times they had together. Sassy's pragmatism and zest for life had been absorbed into Nadine's personality. Nadine would miss Sassy.

She would always live in Nadine's thoughts, and she would think of her often. It comforted Nadine, knowing that she would see Buddy most everyday because Buddy lived across the river from the Hansford house.

"Nadine, time for lunch," came Mom's voice from the foot of the stairs. Nadine carefully re-wrapped the white pebble and pushed it to the back of the drawer. As she whizzed down the banister, being stopped abruptly by the wooden ball, she noticed a large irregular brown spot on the hardwood hall floor right inside the front door. She thought maybe it was wet from the rain, but when she leaned over, it was dry to the touch.

"Watch your head, Sweet Pea," boomed Pop's voice as he leaned over in order to clear the glass panel above the front door with the new grandfather clock that Mom bought for the hall. "I wouldn't want to break either this clock or the glass panel over the door, or I'll get the wrath of Mrs. Taylor."

"What's this big brown spot?" Nadine pointed.

"That, Sweet Pea, is a blood stain that can't be scrubbed away."

"Yuk, a blood stain from what?"

"Well nobody really knows," answered Pop as he and Henry put the clock down. "Some say a wounded Civil War soldier laid here following the Battle of Scary. Others say it's John Hansford's blood. He was hit by a train while walking across the railroad trestle over there." Nadine could see the black railroad bridge strung across Coal River where Pop pointed. "He supposedly managed to make it back to his house, collapsed, and died right here."

Nadine's hand shot to her mouth and her eyes widened at the thought of either version. "Which do you think it was?"

"Probably the Civil War version. Fort Thompkins was here in St. Albans. Following the Battle of Scary, right down the road here, we brought the wounded back to St. Albans. I think this house and St. Mark's Episcopal Church both served as hospitals."

"We? Did you fight in that battle Pop?"

"Sure did, Sweet Pea."

Mom stepped into the hall, wiping her hands on her apron. "Mr. Taylor, you two come on for lunch. We've got lots of work to do and don't be filling Nadine's head full of explanations for that stain. You'll scare her. She's nervous enough about death."

*   *   *

It was the time of evening when the primroses begin to unfold, and the moths gather about. Pop had just finished hanging the oak swing on the porch, and he and Nadine were trying it out. Nadine initiated the conversation, "Pop, tell me about your being a soldier in the Battle of Scary."

"Well, what do you want to know?"

"Why was it called the Battle of Scary?"

"That's an easy one. It was fought at Scary Creek about two- and-a-half miles below St. Albans which then was called Coalsmouth. You see Scary Creek runs into the Kanawha River above the junction of Teays Valley Road and Winfield Road.

On July 17, 1861 when the battle was fought, four days before the first Battle of Bull Run, this here part of the country was Virginia."

"Coalsmouth, Virginia," said Nadine, "That sounds like a different time and place."

"Indeed it was," agreed Pop. "Indeed it was." A distant look came into his eyes. "Right here in Coalsmouth, the Confederates set up Camp Tompkins under the command of Captain George S. Patton who drilled us 800 or more soldiers endlessly. You see, Nadine, the Confederates knew an invasion by the Yankees was imminent in the Kanawha Valley."

"Why here?"

"Well, it wasn't to free the slaves as your school books might tell you because there were only about 2,000 of them in all of Kanawha Valley. Most of us soldiers were small farmers, not owning any slaves. But the valley grew a lot of grain and had large salt deposits for preserving meat. Most importantly the Kanawha emptied into the Ohio, and the fastest way to Richmond, the Confederate capital, was through the valley."

Pop spit tobacco into the yard and continued, "Word came that the Union Army under Brigadier General Cox had started their invasion, crossing from Gallipolis, Ohio into Pt. Pleasant, Virginia and was moving along the Kanawha River. They were being harassed by our scouts all the way. Information was received that they were better equipped and trained than we were. Us country boys had brought our hunting rifles with us. Besides this, they outnumbered us. You see, it was hard to recruit here in these parts because of all the northern sympathizers. We had an advantage though. We had hunted and farmed these hills and knew them like the back of our hand." With that, Pop swatted at a pesky mosquito.

"Patton got a report that there was a large shipment of coffee and sugar landed about nine miles down the road at Winfield. He knew that meant the Yanks were coming, so some of our soldiers started digging in at Scary."

"Did people live there?"

"Not many, there was the Simms house, a log building and a crude bridge, mostly cornfields and trees."

"How about the battle?"

"There had been firing back and forth, starting on the fourteenth. Two Union scouts were fired on and killed. Tension was running high; we realized this wern't no game."

Pop was quiet for a few minutes, and Nadine patiently waited for him to gather his thoughts. He cleared his throat. "The battle began around 9:00 a.m. on July 17th when Yanks opened fire on Confederates, and our boys fired back. It was then that Captain Thompson rode out to get Captains Patton and Jenkins. So Patton's 450 boys were at Scary by 10:00 a.m. Bullets zapped all around, puffs of white smoke hung in the air, and tops of trees were ripped off by the cannon balls.

The Union, under Colonel Norton, had around 1,500 soldiers. About 1:00 p.m. the battle really erupted. It was like a debate back and forth with the Yanks trying to dislodge us from the log church, which they did."

"Were you scared, Pop?"

"Scared spitless, I was just a boy less than sixteen. I actually went behind a tree and vomited. The night before sleep wouldn't come, so I said lots of prayers and wrote my fiancee."

"Mom?"

"No, what became my first wife. In the letter, I asked that if I survived, would she marry me?"

"Go on," said Nadine who could not imagine Pop married to anybody but Mom.

"One time, I looked up, and the hills seemed like they were cloaked in blue with the Yanks all over, and the cornfields came alive with them. It was a sweltering hot day, the sun glancing off the metal of the guns, and the sweat dripping off my eyebrows blinded me. My hands shook, so it was hard to load my shotgun.

You see that gun had a kick. My shoulder was bruised, and the muscles in my firing arm began to quiver. I seen some Yanks killed, not much older than I was. One got his hip shot off. But then I saw one of ours get his head nearly ripped off. Yep, I dropped to my knees to shoot to keep them from knocking together. I could hear my heart beating in my ears. I thanked God for that sound.

By a little after 2:00, the Ohio infantry had pretty much silenced us, and turned their attention to the Simm's house. Splinters and body limbs flew all over. It wasn't long till the Union controlled both buildings and moved toward the bridge which we still held."

"Oh my gosh, those ole Yanks were winning."

Pop shook his head, "It's not over yet, Sweet Pea. The Union boys are low on ammunition, and there didn't seem to be any on the way. Out of desperation they made a bayonet attack. There ain't nothing as horrifying as hand to hand combat!"

Pop suddenly stopped. His mind's eye turned inward. He could no longer speak of what he saw or felt. His mind spiraled through time. He was on the bridge, hearing curses, clanks of bayonets, screams of the wounded and moans of the dying. He felt the impact of the butt of his gun split his enemy's skull. He then felt his bayonet, which he had grabbed from a dead yank, sink into flesh, and the warm grape colored blood spurt forward into his face as he placed his foot on the fallen soldier's stomach to dislodge the bayonet. It had pinned his opponent to the ground.

He turned his eyes from his victim's face, twisting in agony as life began to leave his body, and his final plea came, "God help me." The young man quit struggling and went limp. The feeling of his blade penetrating into the enemy's stomach like into the meat of a watermelon would always haunt him. His knees almost gave way. As he turned he saw a Yank shoot a young coatless Confederate who had fallen behind. His knees straightened as he moved on.

Nadine did not see the tear escape the corner of Pop's eye because he quickly wiped it away with the back of his hand.

Only Pop knew what happened the day after the battle, when the soldiers from Camp Thompkins returned to Scary to dig the mass graves. He checked the pockets of his victim on the bridge for identification. He looked into the young soldier's brown eyes, staring skyward, and saw flies swarming about his blood that had made small rivulets on the dusty earth. Pop unfolded a letter he found in the soldier's pocket addressed to the soldier's fiancee in Athens, Ohio, proposing marriage. It almost matched the one he, himself, carried into battle, but the answer to this soldier's letter had been sealed. Pop leaned over and closed his now kindred spirit's eyes, carried him to the straw lined pit, and placed him along side of the others. He then stood and watched the vultures circling above.

Nadine looked up at Pop. "Go on!" she said with a nudge.

With Nadine's prodding, his thoughts turned from the young soldier back to the battle scene. "We managed to hold the bridge, kill and wound some Yanks and take some prisoners. But, as I looked around, Confederates were beginning to flee other parts of the battle field. Patton rode his horse onto the field, trying to rally his men, and wham, he was wounded and fell from his horse."

"You haven't mentioned Captain Jenkins."

"It was him that helped turn the battle for sure. Well, him and the Coal Mountain boys who came riding over the hill on mules and whatever else could move. They were such a motley looking crew that our soldiers mistook them for the enemy, even killed one."

Pop's voice became a little less serious. "Then Jenkins, with blood streaming down his face and neck, got the cannons back in condition by firing anything metal—chains, horseshoes, scrap iron-anything to tear up a human body. By 5:00 p.m. the Yanks were out of ammunition. They retreated from the field. The funniest thing, we did too. The battlefield was empty. Then one of our officers realized it and retook the field, giving us the victory."

Pop leaned back laughing and slapping his knees. "That wasn't the only funny thing in that battle. We were raw recruits in our first battle, so there were some less than heroic deeds happening that day. But we'll talk about that another time," he said, bringing his hands together with a clap that punctuated the story.

*   *   *

Being dismissed by Pop, Nadine went inside and was starting up the stairs when, through the partially closed door to Mom and Pop's room, she saw Mom unwinding the bun she wore her hair in. Nadine stepped in, "Let me brush and fix your hair."

"Ok, young lady," Mom answered as her shining, dark, silver streaked hair tumbled down her back.

Nadine began combing, feeling the silky strands between her fingers. As she platted Mom's hair into one long braid and rolled it into a bun, she thought again of Pop's fighting in the Battle of Scary. "How do you like that?" asked Nadine.

"It makes me look too stern, don't you think?"

Nadine unbraided and brushed Mrs. Taylor's hair until it was smooth again, and piled it into a soft bun on the back of her head.

"Enough," said Mom, "We got a lot of work accomplished today, and I need to pick some things up tomorrow in St. Albans. You can go with me." With this adventure to look forward to, Nadine obediently went to bed.

Before going to sleep, Nadine knocked on her bedroom wall, and a knock soon came back followed by a giggle. Nadine knew Frances was fine, so she dropped off to sleep only to be awakened by Dutch's howling at the moon. Then she slept again.

The next morning as she gulped down her rolled oats, Mom alerted her that Henry and Red had pulled up in their new spring wagon and were all set. As they bumped along, Mom pointed out some of her rental houses on the property, giving the names of the families that rented them. "This here is where your father's brother Lucian lives with his wife Emma and daughter Esther.

"How old is Esther?"

"Oh, probably ten years older than you, I'd say."

Crossing the bridge into St. Albans, Mom pointed out Teays Hill Cemetery perched high above the town. "That's where I go to decorate graves on Decoration Day."

After making the rounds of the stores and stopping at Charlie Woo's Laundry to pick up dry cleaning, Mom asked if there was any place Nadine would like to go before heading home. "How far is the St. Mark's Episcopal Church?"

"Not far, why do you ask?"

"Pop said it was used as a hospital during the war."

"Henry, take us to the church," Mom directed.

On the way, they passed by a two story red brick house with black ornate iron trim and fence. Sitting on the porch rocking was a heavy set elderly man dressed in black. He waved and tipped his hat as they passed.

"Who's that?"

"That is James Teass."

"Does he have children?"

"No, he never married. It's said he was engaged, but his fiancée broke it off. That soured him on females. Supposedly he won his money in a lottery. He keeps to himself. Except he runs a saloon on main street, but young ladies don't need to know or be about saloons."

The red brick church came into view, and Henry pulled up in front. "There is a cannonball lodged in the church wall. Left from the war, I guess it was," said Mom with a shrug. "Mr. Taylor can tell you about that. I do know the Yankees also used it as a livery stable and did a lot of damage."

Henry turned to get his next directions. "Let's stop at my sister's bakery before heading home," Mom said, mopping her brow with her lace handkerchief as the sun positioned itself directly overhead.

As they rode along, Nadine asked Henry why Dutch was barking last night. Henry shrugged his shoulders, "Suppose, bein' in a new place, there are sounds about he never heard before."

"Well, we live closer to people now, Henry. He can't bark all night, keeping people up." Mom interjected.

"Yessum," Henry replied, pulling up to a building on West Main with a sign saying, "Wickline's Bakery." Effie Allen had married a Wickline who had died a few years ago.

The bell on the door rang as they entered the shop that gave off the aroma of yeast, flour, fruits, sugar and mingled spices. In response to the bell, a plump lady, with dark hair swept up in a loose bun, turned in their direction. "I swan, I've been wondering when you'd drop by," she said coming swiftly from behind the counter with outstretched arms to embrace Liz. "And here is Nadine just growing prettier and taller everyday." She gently pinched Nadine on the cheek. Nadine responded by a quick curtsy as she eyed the cookies, pies, sweet rolls and cakes behind the glass shelves.

"You just go behind there and help yourself to a cookie while Liz and I chat awhile." Nadine was quick to oblige.

"Don't you love the house, Liz?"

"Well it needs some fixing."

"You got the rest of your life to do that. It's just so good to have you close by, Liz. How is Frances taking the move?"

"I keep her busy hemming curtains, so I don't have to buy new ones."

"Well, I know she's happy then. She loves to do handwork and feel helpful."

"She's real good at it too!" added Liz.

Heading toward home, Nadine munched on her second oatmeal and raisin cookie and listened to Mom. "Nobody is happier about the success of Effie's bakery than I am. However, I just can't believe women have gotten so lazy that they won't do their own baking." Pausing a minute she said, "Henry, as soon as we get home, please put that block of ice in the icebox. It won't do any good setting in this wagon."

"Yessum, Mrs. Taylor," Henry answered rolling his eyes, as if to say, "Don't she give me credit for any sense?" Nadine flashed a smile.

*   *   *

When they reached home, Mr. Taylor was swinging on the porch. Nadine ran up and plopped down beside him.

"What do you think of St. Albans, Nadine?"

"I like the bakery. Here you want a bite of my cookie?"

"No, I don't want to get my sweet tooth a going."

Nadine finished the cookie, licked the crumbs from her lips and shook them from her hands and skirt. "I saw Mr. Teass who owns a saloon, but Mom said I didn't need to worry about that."

"Did you see that big gold pocket watch he wears?"

Nadine shook her head, "But, I did see the church that was a hospital in the Civil War and has a cannonball stuck in its wall. That reminds me, would you tell me some more about the battle? You promised?"

Not wanting to experience the flashback of the part of the battle that he had yesterday, Mr. Taylor wanted to tell of the "comedy of errors," which occurred at Scary. He wet his lips and began. "As I said there was a lot of valor shown in that battle. It lasted about five hours. There is no way of knowing how many died as a result of that five hour encounter because some of the wounded crawled into hollow trees, barns, any hiding place so as not to be discovered. I do know we buried fourteen Union soldiers. One dead Confederate was taken up to Lower Falls for his mother to bury." Pop pressed his lips together a minute and then said, "Remember in the Civil War, more died of wounds after battle than on the field.

Now about the humor of the battle. Mind you some of this is hearsay. On July 17 at 9:00 a.m., John Thompson and his Border Rangers positioned themselves on high ground. Astride their horses, they watched the Yankees moving through the cornfield. When the Yanks opened fire, Thompson's false teeth shot right out of his mouth, and his hat flew straight up into the air. No wonder he went a running back to Camp Thompkins to fetch Patton and Jenkins."

"Picture this distinguished man ready to battle with his gums and bald head a shining." laughed Nadine.

"One time I was down on my stomach firing as fast as I could, looking mostly through the legs of horses when I saw this skinny feller dancing about and waving his hat in the air as he ran across the battlefield. Turns out he is a Yankee officer's cook, and he had sighted some geese that he was chasing after to cook. I'll give it to him, he did catch them. Amazingly, he didn't get shot in the rear." Pop smiled as he pictured this scene in his mind. "But the funniest thing was at the end of the battle."

"What happened?"

"The Yanks, even though they supposedly were better trained than we, became totally disorganized. Having run out of ammunition and having lost the bridge, they retreated in every direction." Pop threw up his hands, "Lo and behold, if we didn't retreat too, leaving the field deserted, as I said yesterday. Catching on, we returned.

Well, anyway, there was this zany French Yankee who was told we were in retreat. Meanwhile, those Coal Mountain boys, that I said came a riding in on mules, had brought some good ole moonshine. With our nerves raw from the battle and to celebrate our victory, there was a lot of drinking followed by burning of out buildings." Pop shook his head in disbelief. "It was already night, and this here French Yankee Col. DeVillers, seeing the celebration, thought we were the Union army celebrating victory. He and his men came a riding in congratulating us, saying, 'You sent Johnny

Reb a running today, boys.' In no time flat, those Yanks found themselves prisoners, shipped out to Libby Prison at Richmond."

"Did you fight in any other battles?"

"Yep, Gauley Mountain and Winchester, following Patton. He was wounded two more times. The last time was fatal. He was astride his horse at Winchester."

"What happened to Jenkins?"

"He became Brigadier General, fought at Gettysburg, and died at Battle of Cloyd's Mountain."

"War sounds awful with all those people dying." Nadine patted Pop's knee.

"It sure is, Sweet Pea. It sure is."

*   *   *

Nadine and Buddy soaked their dusty feet in the cool green river water, watching for another big iridescent catfish or carp to pop up out of the water and plop back, creating ripples that made perfect symmetrical circles. "We should have our fishing poles. I bet we could catch one of those big ole fish. Pop says there are carp and muskie four feet long just a swimming at the bottom of the river."

Buddy scratched a mosquito bite before commenting, "Right below Lower Falls, Mr. Jarrett caught a mud catfish and brought it to town alive. It filled the bathtub Mr. Loftis had sitting in front of his store. Why, I've seen turtles caught out of here that filled a wash tub."

"I hope one doesn't bite our toes off. The fish can just see these twenty pink little things a dangling in the water," said Nadine. With that thought they both jerked their feet out.

Nadine swatted at a flying insect. "What is that thing?"

"That is a snake doctor. You know what that means; don't you?" Buddy said in a low creepy voice.

"That there is a sick snake around here?" asked Nadine.

Buddy scooted up and whispered, "I don't know if they are sick or not, but they are about."

"I swear Buddy you know how to take the joy out of the most fun experience." Nadine stood up to leave.

"Sit down, Nadine. I was just teasing."

They quietly watched fallen leaves being carried by the current and felt the soft breeze on their skin. Nadine leaned back on her elbows. Looking up through the lacy leaves of the sycamore and weeping willow trees into the soft blue sky, she watched a robin silently wing through the trees. Afraid to anger Nadine again, Buddy decided to talk about a more pleasant subject. "What do you want to be when you grow up?"

"A wife and mother," came Nadine's quick response. "I want to have a husband that won't leave me like my dad left me to go play in a band somewhere." Nadine started to speak again but stopped.

"What were you going to say Nadine?"

"Nothing."

"Friends share secrets," Buddy nudged Nadine on the arm.

Nadine with eyebrows knitted turned and looked Buddy in the eyes.

Buddy made a sign of an "X" across her heart, "Cross my heart, hope to die if I tell."

"You know I have a brother, Carl, four years older than I am."

Buddy nodded in agreement.

"Well," continued Nadine, "I worry, since I've never seen him, what if I met him, fell in love and married him?"

"Oh my gosh, Nadine, you can't marry your own brother. That's against the law and immoral."

"But I wouldn't know he was my brother."

Buddy saw a cloud of worry come over Nadine's face. She folded her hands in her lap. "We just have to put on our thinking caps." There was a pause. "I know. Now that you live in St. Albans, you're closer to Winfield. You just tell Aunt Lizzie you want to meet your brother."

"But she might think I don't love her and Pop and give me away again."

"No such thing Nadine. How could you think that?"

A smile came over Nadine's face at such a simple answer.

"Ok, now what do you want to be when you grow up?" asked Nadine.

Buddy, placed her finger on her temple and wrinkled her brow in deep thought. "I want to be a singer and travel up and down the Kanawha, Ohio and Mississippi on a showboat. That reminds me, have you seen the posters advertising that the showboats coming?"

"I've seen them, but Mom says I can't go," she answered digging her toes in the soft mud at the river's edge and squishing it between them.

"Why on earth not?" Buddy placed her hands on her hips.

"She says there will only be riff-raff there—gamblers and such."

"There will be a band. For all we know your dad might be in that band."

Nadine's face flushed. "Oh, Buddy that might be true. I just have to go, but I don't have the fifteen cents for the ticket."

Buddy scratched her head and thought, "We'll get some apples off our tree and sell them."

"Who to?"

"We'll just go down Main Street. It won't take long to sell fifteen cents worth of apples. Any extra we'll use for candy on the boat."

Nadine and Buddy stood on the corner of Main Street peddling the apples that they had gathered, washed and spit polished until they shone in the bright sunlight. "I think the best place to sell these apples would have been in front of Wickline's Bakery. Then customers would relate apples to apple pie, and how they could save money by baking their own," suggested Buddy.

Nadine shook her head emphatically, "No way! Effie Wickline would tell Mom for sure that I was selling apples, and I'd be in real trouble. Look, here comes Mr. Teass."

"Wow," whispered Buddy, "Look at that heavy gold watch chain he has. I'm surprised, he's able to keep his britches up, toting that and his gold watch in his pocket." She shook her head and continued, "He's rich, but don't bother trying to sell him anything. They say he's as tight as the bark on the tree."

Buddy had no more finished her sentence than Nadine walked up to him, holding a shiny red apple up in his face. "How about buying some fresh apples, Mr. Teass? They're good and juicy for baking, frying or eating."

Mr. Teass reached out and took the apple to scrutinize. "How much, young lady?"

"Two pennies a piece, Sir," answered Nadine, flashing a broad smile."

"Do tell," Teass turned the apple over for further examination. "How about three for two pennies?"

"Yes sir, it's a deal," answered Nadine. He stuffed two apples into his pockets, paid, bit into one and sauntered on toward his saloon.

Nadine flipped a penny into the air, caught it and did a quick shuffle of her feet. "Look there. We've made our first sale."

"Yep, but the old tightwad got a bargain," replied Buddy. "We don't have to sell cheap today. Look at all these people who have come into town to go to the showboat."

As Nadine looked down the street to see, she saw men riding horseback, wagons full of ragged children and buggies carrying women and men all dressed up.

"Why, is this little Nadine?" came a robust woman's voice as she stooped over to be on Nadine's eye level. "You don't recognize me?"

Nadine shook her head. Even though, there was something familiar about the friendly woman's face. She just couldn't place her.

"I'm Nanna Rimmer, honey. Well, I wet nursed you when your poor mom died, but then you wouldn't remember."

Nadine had no idea what "wet nurse" meant but decided it must be an act of kindness by the look of this woman.

Nanna, seeing no recognition in the child's eyes, pursued. "Do you remember your Aunt Vonzine?"

Nadine's eyes widened at this name, "And Grandma Dunlap? Yes, I remember. Where is Aunt Vonzine? Is she here in St. Albans?" Nadine rushed on.

"No honey, I'm afraid not." Nanna hesitated and weighed her words, patting Nadine on the head. "Your Aunt Vonzine took her husband to the TB sanitarium at Terra Alta, you know. She stayed there to be with him and contracted TB herself. May she rest in peace," Nanna pointed up toward Teay's Hill Cemetery. "Poor thing was put to rest up there."

Nadine swallowed hard and felt the sting of tears at hearing that yet another connection to her past had been severed.

Nanna pulled Nadine to herself, "Now, now child. I didn't mean to bring you sadness. You perk up there and sell me some of these good looking apples." After counting out the money, Nanna cupped her hand around her ear. "Listen, the showboat is approaching. Hear the concert on the steam calliope beginning? The Majestic has arrived! You two come along with me. I'll see that Billy Bryant, the greatest river showman of all times, lets you two carry the banner in front of the band that'll march down Main Street soon. Billy and I go way back."

After Billy Bryant unrolled the banner, with "Majestic" written in bright red shiny letters and instructed Buddy and Nadine how it should be carried,

Nadine anxiously examined the band members' faces as they gathered their instruments for the parade. They were all decked out in colorful blue and red uniforms with gold trim and buttons, but there was no redhead. Nadine's father was not a member of this band.

Her disappointment evaporated as the band struck up a tune and began marching down Main Street. Nadine and Buddy, with the banner stretched between them, were in front of the band but behind the two white horses that led the parade. After about a block of marching, Nadine began to wonder if the free ticket promised to Buddy and her for carrying the banner was enough. Nadine walked in front of the trombone player who kept bumping her in the back of her head with his long slide as she jumped over and around the horses' poop left as evidence that indeed the white horses had been there. Nadine on second thought decided it was worth the pain. Indeed, she felt like a celebrity. Looking over she saw people lining the sidewalk to watch and barefooted children running along side of the parade, whipping up dust, giving everything a dreamlike appearance.

*   *   *

"Ok, Nadine as soon as you hear the calliope begin to play start walking, and I'll meet you halfway." Nadine nodded her head in agreement. "Now, you've told Aunt Liz you're spending the night with me, right?" Buddy asked, raising her eyebrows as she unfolded the plan for the evening.

"Right", answered Nadine as chills of excitement and anticipation flooded her.

"The calliope starts playing an hour before the show begins, so we'll have plenty of time to get good seats and a bag of peanuts and candy."

At the first sound of the calliope playing *Beautiful Ohio*, Nadine was out the front door. As she and Buddy walked and ran along the river, they saw row boats full of families, moving down Coal River to its mouth, feeding into the Kanawha. All were headed toward the Majestic.

Nadine began to feel down right giddy, breathing in the thick humid air and listening to the river water lap against the shore. In their haste she almost stepped on a turtle whose head instantly recoiled into its shell. The sound of the crickets reverberated from both sides of the river, and friendly excited voices greeted each other as their boats glided in the same direction.

Rounding a bend in the river, Nadine looked up and saw the blood red sun sinking in the west, forming a red, orange, and yellow path down the middle of the river. At the end of the path, was the great Majestic with its name glowing in tiny white electric lights mirrored in the river like a diamond necklace. Nadine had never seen anything as beautiful, and she instinctively squeezed Buddy's hand.

The sound of the calliope ceased. It was replaced by the band standing on the bow playing, Dixie.

When crossing the plank, leading from the shore to the Majestic, Nadine felt a presence. The face of Angela who befriended her on her boat ride to the Taylor's house six or seven years ago flashed across her mind. *She did look like the angel in the picture in my bedroom*, Nadine thought. Just as quickly the shutter on her mind's camera snapped closed, and Angela's image was gone.

"Come on, come on," came Buddy's voice as she handed the tickets to the ticket taker.

Seated, Nadine looked about the interior of the boat in awe as she popped salty shelled peanuts into her mouth. Even as a child, she could appreciate the beautiful ornately carved red mahogany and the heavy stage curtain with a scene of New Orleans painted on it.

"Look Nadine, there is Mayor White, sitting with his wife up there in the box seat. See?" Buddy pointed.

Suddenly the door leading into the center isle swung open, and in marched the band. Nadine examined each face as it filed past to make sure she had not missed her father earlier in the day. No, he was not here, for she knew she would recognize him. There would be a sixth sense.

Just as the band seated itself in the orchestra pit, the lights dimmed and the footlights on the stage flipped on making the sign with the title of the play visible. Where Is My Wandering Boy Tonight? was written in large shiny black letters.

Thunderous applause erupted in the room as the beautiful brunette, with the black beauty mark penciled on her cheekbone, stepped onto the stage. Likewise, when the villain wearing a black mustache curled up on the ends and a black hat entered, there were boos and cat calls. Then a hush settled over the audience as the first act unfolded. Nadine and Buddy, as did the others, sat mesmerized.

As the scenery changed, the curtain closed, and a juggler dressed in a white costume began his act, first with three red balls then four, five, and six. Up and down, over his shoulder, and behind his back the balls flashed in the air. "I'm going to practice until I can do that," Nadine whispered.

"What are you going to juggle?"

"Apples," Nadine answered with a shrug.

"I'm going to be just like the heroine," Buddy sighed.

"I can paint a beauty mark on my cheek just like her; you know?"

Nadine thought, *It will take more than a beauty mark*, but refrained from speaking.

During the intermission, Buddy and Nadine rehashed the play, daring not to leave their seats when Buddy felt a sting on the back of her neck then another and another. She whirled around and looked at those seated behind her, but they were absorbed in conversation and laughter.

Then Nadine became the victim. As she whirled around, a peanut shell which lay on the collar of her dress slipped down her back, so every time she leaned against her seat, the ragged edges of the peanut shell stuck into her flesh. She felt her face flush with fury. In response, she began tearing pieces of paper from her program, chewing them and then rolling them up into hard spitballs. "What are you going to do with those?"

"You'll see, but first I have to go somewhere to get this peanut shell out of my dress." Nadine pointed to the tortured area.

With concern in her voice, Buddy warned, "Don't get us thrown off the boat. We have to see the second act, or I'll just die!"

Fishing the peanut shell from her dress, Nadine stationed herself in the doorway leading to the middle isle. Squinting her eyes, she carefully scanned the audience row by row. Suddenly from the gallery she saw a hand shoot up and release its missile—peanut shell—toward an elderly gentleman with a shining bald head. As the shell hit its target, three boys leaned back, covering their smiling faces with their hands.

Nadine stepped forward, taking careful aim, and ping, ping, ping the spitballs hit the offender hard right behind his left ear. Quickly she stepped behind the doorframe to hide. Waiting a few minutes, she stepped forward again. Ping, ping, ping, ping her shots took down her prey with two hits on each of the other two boy's heads and necks.

With the feeling of triumph unfolding within her, a smile spread across her face as she bought a box of jelly beans for Buddy and a bag of candy corn for herself. Then her smile faded as she thought of the possible repercussions. Very quietly and without expression, she walked down the aisle to her seat, keeping as low a profile as possible. Neither she nor Buddy were pelted again.

*   *   *

The spell of the evening continued to cast its magic as Nadine and Buddy set out walking toward Buddy's. Their way was lit by those who had brought lanterns to guide them home. Slowly the light became less and less as people took different paths to their destinations. Finally, the last lantern light drifted off, and Buddy and Nadine found themselves in pitch darkness. The atmosphere became ominous as the sounds of unseen nocturnal creatures, moving about, became louder. "I hope we don't step on a snake," Buddy said. "You know after a hot day like today, they come out in the coolness of night to get a drink, especially along the river."

"Stop talking about snakes, Buddy. You know I hate them."

Buddy ceased talking. The only sound other than those of the creatures of the night was the river's rhythmic lapping against the bank.

Nadine was wiping away the remnant of a cobweb she had walked into when there was a zigzag flash of lightning in the sky and the deep roar of thunder echoed. The streaks continued, and the thunder came closer. The trees joined in nature's show, gently waving their extended limbs. As the wind increased, the rustle of the trees became louder and louder as they whipped and thrashed about above Nadine and Buddy's heads. A single drop of rain made a loud splash. Then the sky seemed to open, pouring its contents upon the earth. "Run, Buddy, run."

"I can't see which way to go."

"Here take my hand," Nadine grabbed Buddy's wet hand, and they stumbled hand in hand over gnarled tree roots, slipping and falling onto the muddy ground.

"Do you get the feeling we're walking in circles," asked Buddy. "Since we've left the river, we have nothing to follow." The jagged bolts of lightning stabbed the earth repeatedly with claps of thunder roaring across the sky.

Nadine caught the aroma of talcum that always brought comfort and peace to her. Her mind began to clear. "Just look for a light in a window. Once we find a house, we'll know about where we are."

"You're right, Nadine. I know every house in this town," Buddy boasted.

With a plan, they continued to walk, straining their eyes to see a light. "Over there, over there," Buddy pointed, wiping rain from her eyes and pulling strands of wet hair out of her face.

"Where, I can't see anything."

"That's the Russell house. It's okay. We're close to the railroad bridge. Once we get there, we'll take a left and walk along the river again. In no time, we'll be at my house."

*   *   *

The next morning Nadine headed home, breathing in the clean smell that follows a thunder storm, trying to think of an explanation to give Mom as to why her dress, shoes and socks were matted with mud. Walking down Smokey Road toward her house, she looked up and saw Mom sitting in the swing. Nadine slowed down to think of an excuse.

"Stop your dawdling along, Nadine, and get up on this porch, right now!" came Mom's stern voice as she stood up, and walked toward the stairs.

"She knows," Nadine whispered to herself in panic.

As soon as Nadine hit the top step, she felt Mom's heavy hand take a firm hold of her shoulder. "Young lady, I understand you were hawking apples on Main Street that you stole off my sister's tree like a common beggar. Is this true?"

Nadine looked at her muddy shoes and nodded.

"And after I said you could not go to the showboat where there would be all kinds of ungodly people, you went anyway. Did you or did you not disobey me?"

The affirmation almost stuck in Nadine's throat, but she managed to whisper, "Yes."

"Yes, what?"

"Yes, Ma'am, I disobeyed you."

"Look me in the eyes when you speak, Nadine. Then you and Buddy proceeded to walk home in the dark alone and got caught in that awful storm? It is a wonder one of those ruffians from the boat didn't follow you and kidnap the two of you, or you could have slipped in the mud and fallen in the river and drowned or been struck with lightning." Mom shook her head and wrung her hands as she enumerated all of the horrible things that could have transpired.

With all of the effort Nadine could muster, she made eye contact with Mom, seeing concern and thinking this woman knows and sees everything. She's all knowing. "Yes, Ma'am, but how did you know?"

"I have my ways and remember," Mom shook her finger, "this is a small town. Well at least you are not lying," said Mom quickly moving on. "Look at that mud all over your clothes. What if your Uncle Lucian saw you pass his house looking like that? He'd think I was not a fit mother."

With this, she bent Nadine over her knee smacking her on her behind. With each strike, Mom cried, "This hurts me worse than it hurts you, Nadine."

Nadine thought, *If it hurts you so badly, why don't you stop*, but she dare not speak.

Nadine was saved by Ada who came running through the yard and up the steps screaming, "Murder, murder."

Mom immediately ceased the application of learning being applied to Nadine's rear, thinking that Ada made reference to her, spanking Nadine.

"What are you talking about, Ada?" Mom quickly dabbed away a tear that escaped down her cheek, so Ada could not see.

"There has been a murder right here in our town!" Ada answered, folding and unfolding her arms.

"Who? What on earth?"

Nadine didn't want anybody murdered, but she thought the message arrived just in time. Mom released her hold, and Nadine quietly sat down on the top step to eavesdrop. Mom, in all of the excitement, didn't notice that "little ears" were listening.

Ada caught her breath and fanned her flushed face. "These three young good for nothings boarded the streetcar at Stop Nineteen this morning."

"You mean it happened on the streetcar?"

"I do."

Tears pooled in Mom's eyes again as the thought pushed itself into her mind of Nadine and Buddy out in the dark, wandering around with murderers about. "Oh my dear!"

"Anyway, these three, wearing khaki pants, got on. Two remained in the front while the other sauntered toward the back. Mrs. White, who told me, was on the streetcar, heading for the dentist office. You should see her with her jaw all swollen out like this." Ada motioned with her hand.

"Ada get on with the story and forget Mrs. White's tooth."

"Well, Mrs. White was who told me."

"Never mind, just get on," Mom flipped her handkerchief to make the point.

"The two up front shot their guns right through the top of the car, "Bam, bam just like that," Ada held both hands as if shooting upward. "They screamed at the passengers if they knew what was good for them to get their hands up."

"Oh, my dear Lord!"

"You haven't heard anything yet. The conductor, Mr. Harvey, tried to get away and the punk in the back shot him in the side. Mrs. White said blood spurted all over the streetcar."

Mom clasped her hand over her mouth and gave out a low moan.

"With the car stopped, one of the robbers, up front, pistol whipped the motorman. While this was going on, a passenger scrambled out a window. The third robber's gun jammed when he tried to shoot the escaping passenger." Ada again imitated the gunman.

Nadine thought if Ada had on a costume that this drama was almost as good as the one on the showboat. To think this was for real and here in St. Albans. Goosebumps ran up her arms just thinking about it. She guessed Mom was right. Buddy and she shouldn't be going off in the dark alone.

"Then the robbers demanded the passengers' jewelry and money. They even took Mrs. White's wedding band."

"Better that than her life," interjected Mom.

"Indeed, after witnessing Mr. Harvey being shot and the motorman whacked in the head with the butt of a gun, I don't think anybody resisted."

"You certainly can't take material things with you," was Mom's observation. "Where are those good for nothing murderers now?"

"They're hunting them," Ada swatted at a bumblebee and shifted her body to get out of its path. "All they know is they headed toward the Kanawha River. Probably had a boat to escape. Hard to tell where they are now."

"Here we sit alone with three murderers on the loose, and Mr. Taylor and Henry are down at Poca, working on the farm. I hope he soon finalizes the sale of that place."

"Well, I best be on my way," Ada moved toward the steps.

"Not before you have some cold ice tea." Mom motioned toward the side of the house, "I got the mint for it out of my herb garden."

Mrs. Taylor saw a movement on the step and turned her attention to Nadine. "You have been there since Ada came?"

Nadine did not deny the question, just rolled her eyes to one side.

"Young lady. I want you to stay inside today."

"Ah, no, do I have to?"

"Yes! Now, you go upstairs and help Frances with the mending." Feeling guilty over the earlier discipline, Mom added, "There is some ice from the ice house in the ice box. Chip off some and fix Frances and you some ice tea."

That did seem to make the mending a bit more palatable, as she hurried to obey.

Later as she and Frances sang hymns and sewed, they heard Ada leaving. Mom's last words were, "Keep me posted on the manhunt. I have to stay close to the house with Nadine and Frances."

"I'll do just that," Ada answered as she walked down Smokey Road, glancing from side to side.

*   *   *

Remnants of corn hung on Nadine's chin from the sweet Silver Queen corn that Mom had prepared for supper. "Don't forget to wipe your mouth when you eat. Here, might as well finish up the rest." Mom motioned toward the bright red tomatoes still warm from the sun and the golden brown fried potatoes. "I've already fixed Frances' supper."

Nadine licked the butter from her top lip and rubbed across her chin to remove the corn. "Where do you think those three murderers are now, Mom?"

"Could be in Pt. Pleasant or Charleston by now. Don't worry about it," Mom began clearing the table. Then she sat down with her second cup of coffee.

Nadine twisted a strand of her hair. "I wish Pop and Henry were here."

"We'll be fine," Mom put her cup down, "Nadine why did you disobey me and go to the showboat?"

Nadine traced around a flower on the oil cloth tablecloth with her index finger and bit her lower lip. "Buddy said there was a band. I know my dad plays in a band. I thought I might find him." She covertly glanced up to see if she had made Mom angry or hurt her feelings.

Mom looked down into her coffee cup. "Are you not happy here with us?"

"Oh, no, I love it here, and I love you and Pop. This is my home," she quickly added. "I just wonder about my relatives. Nanna Rimmer told me that Aunt Vonzine died."

"I didn't know that." Mom Taylor had a special place in her heart for the woman who had trusted her with Nadine.

While on the subject and remembering her and Buddy's conversation, Nadine said slowly, "I also wonder about my brother, Carl. I have the dolls he sends at Christmas, but I've never seen him, my own brother." Again she glanced up to see Mom's expression.

"Well, it certainly won't do any harm to travel to Winfield to meet Carl and your Uncle John and Aunt Noni." Her brow wrinkled in deep thought. "I knew there would come a time when you became curious about your family." Concern showed in her eyes. "Well, enough of this. It will soon be time for bed."

Nadine heard the locks on the front and back doors click and saw Mom checking the latches on the window screens. Something seldom done because everyone felt safe in St. Albans.

Heat lightning could be seen in the distance as dusk folded into night. The wind whispered through the trees and their leaves white underside reached upward for a drink as a slow drizzle began. Nadine was glad to be home this evening.

She had dozed off and was awakened by the whinny of a horse. Her body became taut as she strained to hear, but it was now quiet except for the soft rain on the roof. She raised herself up on her elbow, listening. She thought she heard men's voices out toward the barn. Dutch began barking. Now she heard footsteps coming around the house. Dutch's barking increased. Nadine could hear him jerking at his leash. "Hush," came a man's warning to the dog who now whimpered softly.

The latch on the front door clicked. Then there came another click. Nadine's throat tightened as she debated on running downstairs to Mom's room or just staying put. Someone began pounding on the door. Nadine felt her heart beating against her rib cage.

There was a shout, "Let me in. A man could catch his death of cold standing out here in the rain."

Mom's voice could be heard as she unlocked the door. "That's a good way to get yourself shot, sneaking around in the night like this, scaring a soul to death."

"I wouldn't call a man coming to his own home exactly sneaking."

It's Pop, thought Nadine easing herself back onto her pillow as the tension began to drain away. Thank goodness.

"What are you doing, coming home this time of night?" continued Mom.

"I heard about the murder on the streetcar. I thought, with three killers loose here abouts, that I best be getting home." Pop removed his hat and shook the rain off.

Mom left a small gaslight burning in Nadine's room that night. Trying to go back to sleep, Nadine looked at the picture of the angel guarding the boy and girl over the raging stream. She hadn't thought of Angela for a long time, but being on the boat last night brought back memories of her boat trip to the Taylors.

"I'll be praying for you," were Angela's last words to Nadine.

Lying there, Nadine tried to picture Angela's face in her mind. She could see her blond hair, soft delicate facial features and sky blue eyes. She glanced back at the angel. They do look alike. Something clicked. The scent of the talcum powder that brought Nadine comfort, that was the fragrance Angela wore that day when she had befriended the little girl going to live with people whom she had never met and to a place she had never seen. A smile crept over Nadine's face. Could Angela be an angel? A personal angel that God sent to guard me? Wow, wait until I tell Buddy. Nadine snuggled under her cover and went to sleep, feeling very special.

Nadine awoke early and walked out onto the second floor porch Mom had had built. She looked out over Coal River. A silvery white mist rose above it. The earth again had a fresh smell and the air had been cooled by the night's rain. She watched squirrels scamper from one tree to another and listened to the multiple birds singing. Clutching her nightgown around her, she walked down the wide hall and downstairs.

She heard Pop talking to Mom, "Russell just rode by a few minutes ago to tell me those three murderers had been caught."

"Thank goodness. We can breathe a lot easier now. Surely they weren't from around here?"

"Nope, but they were soldiers stationed across the Kanawha River at Nitro."

"War is evil, not only on the battlefields but in the communities where soldiers are stationed. Along with the good young men, it brings riff-raff too." Mom ran her fingers around the rim of her coffee cup. "These young men are so far from home."

"Yep, I hope, as President Wilson promises, that this is the 'War that ends all wars.'" Pop looked off in the distance, thinking of the battles he experienced with the sights and sounds of young men maimed and dying on the field. He remembered the aching knot in his stomach before battle, his prayers to escape death, and smelling the stench of death all around.

Mom gave Pop a penetrating look which broke into his memories, "I was thinking that the young man who confessed to the murder was nineteen years old and only seventeen when he joined up to be taught to kill," Pop said not wanting to share his thoughts for he feared they would reveal weakness.

"That was older than you were. Still you didn't kill a streetcar conductor with six mouths to feed."

"True enough," said Pop as he grasped the edge of the table. "No one deserves to die before his time."

"Did Russell say any more about the confession?"

"Yep, it was premeditated for sure, and it was for money; it appears." Pop took another gulp of coffee. "They came over on the ferry, hid their uniforms in the bushes along the river bank, and changed into coveralls. After the robbing and shooting, they changed back into their uniforms, took a boat back to Sattes and walked to their camp at Nitro."

"What did they do with their coveralls?"

"Threw them in the river, seems."

"Did they all stick to the same story?"

"Nope," Russell said. "At first the young man who injured no one, confessed. While the other two denied the whole thing. Later the other two came around."

When Nadine appeared at the kitchen door, the discussion ceased.

*　　*　　*

On the next Saturday night, Buddy slept over at Nadine's. It was one of those humid nights when not a twig moved, and the heat became a blanket pressing in on you. "We'll open the porch door, and you two can sleep out here in the upstairs hall. Maybe you'll catch a breeze," Mom said as she began to spread out the bedding and left the gas lamp burning. With a bowl of popcorn, the two girls talked into the night, sharing the latest events in their lives. "Mom was mad as an old wet hen about me running off and going to the showboat. She flipped me over her knee and gave me a spanking."

"Did you cry?"

"Nope, with all these petticoats she makes me wear, I hardly felt it," Nadine shook her head. "I did ask if I could visit my brother Carl."

"Was she angry?"

"I don't think so. She is making me a brand new blue dress to wear. We're going this week before school begins."

Buddy munched on her popcorn thoughtfully. "About how old is Carl?"

"I guess fourteen. I just can't wait to meet him."

Finally quieting down, they watched the shadows on the ceiling made by the lamp and drifted off to sleep. After midnight, Nadine woke with a start. The lamp light was going off and on. Lying quietly, she heard shuffling like someone walking across the floor, but there was no one there. Other than Buddy she was alone in the hallway. Nadine nudged Buddy.

"What is it? What's wrong with you, waking me up?"

"Listen."

Everything was silent, "I heard someone walking, but there was no one in the room, and the light was turning off and on."

"It's probably your own personal angel. Now go to sleep." Buddy turned over and pulled the sheet over her head.

Nadine lay down, and there was not another sound. The light continued to burn brightly.

* * *

"Carl, Carl come on now. Your sister is here to visit." Nadine stood in her Uncle John and Aunt Noni's yard looking at the white house with a cupola and large front and back porches. Nadine had never seen a house with a cupola before. It made it look like a small castle, she decided. From the back yard she looked across the street and up at the red brick gothic style Putnam County Courthouse that loomed over the town atop a hill. In the large back yard of the house, were lacy weeping willow trees, offering shade and making soft rustling sounds when the wind blew. "I swan, I think that boy is hard of hearing," said Aunt Noni.

With the second call, Carl came around the corner of the house. He did not appear to be happy. All his friends were down at the river swimming, and Aunt Noni had awakened him to announce that a dumb girl, his

CARL MILLER

sister, was coming to visit. At fourteen, Carl was shy around girls. To make things worse, Aunt Noni dressed him in a starched white shirt, bow tie and knickers. He knew he looked like a sissy. He stayed in the house until he was sure all his friends had drifted down to the river.

Nadine watched, with her heart beating fast, as he approached. She could not control herself any longer and ran to meet him. When they were face to face and he looked down at her, she felt as if she were gazing up into a mirror. He had hair the color of varnished copper that glistened when the sun shined through it just like hers. His eyes were the same green with golden specks, and there were freckles matching hers dusted across his nose. Before Nadine could embrace him, Carl shot his hand out to shake her's. When their skin touched in the handshake, she couldn't resist throwing her arms about him. She felt his body mold to hers but then quickly stiffen.

"Ah, Nadine," Carl said feeling awkward, "Would you like to ride my goat, Nanny? She can pull you in her goat cart?" He shifted his feet, waiting for an answer. Nadine clapped her hands with delight.

"Now you entertain your sister," Aunt Noni directed. Mrs. Taylor and I are going into the parlor for a cup of coffee."

"Wait right here while I hitch her up." He was glad to escape into the weathered wooden shed. He did not like shows of emotion. It made him feel uncomfortable, especially with a girl. Even though she was his sister and did seem nice enough.

Nadine began looking for four leaf clovers, while waiting for Carl's return. She was very good at finding them—much better than Buddy anyway. Indeed she spied one and leaned over and plucked it up.

She then heard the tinkle of a bell and looked up to see Nanny, pulling a small homemade wooden cart. The metal bell hung from a string tied securely around her neck. She was soft gray with white markings around her face and nose.

Carl tossed Nadine a carrot. "Feed this to her, and she'll be your friend forever. But watch your fingers around her mouth. She'll think they are more carrots and just keep chewing."

Quick as a wink, the carrot disappeared into Nanny's mouth. Nadine could see Nanny's teeth and pink gums as she devoured the gift. She carefully touched Nanny's soft, wet nose and gently petted her head.

"Okay, jump in, Nadine," Carl lifted the reins and they were off, making circles in the yard as Carl proudly showed off his expertise in handling Nanny. They went bump, bump, bump.

"Carl," Noni called from the porch. "Don't go too fast. You'll dump your sister out."

Nadine repeated the word "Sister" to herself. That was her. She was somebody's sister and that somebody was right here beside her. She couldn't believe that this very moment, in this very place she was bobbing up and down in a goat cart with her very own brother. No one could deny their relationship if they saw them seated together.

"Carl," came another directive, "take the cart out into the road. It will be smoother. Besides you're making wheel tracks in the grass. Remember don't go fast."

Carl pulled to the left, and they were riding on the wide road which ran in front of his home and the courthouse. To the left of the courthouse was a small one-story red brick house with a brick chimney on each side. It, as the courthouse, sat on a knoll above the road.

"That's an interesting house," Nadine pointed.

"It's haunted, some say," Carl answered matter-of-factly.

That sent a chill up Nadine's spine, "Why do they think that?"

"Some say they've seen a headless horseman riding through the yard."

"Have you seen it with your very own eyes?" Nadine questioned with her own eyes showing their whites.

"No," Carl shrugged. "Uncle John says it's probably just a vapor. Right behind that house and to the side there is a grave of a Confederate soldier." Carl motioned toward the direction.

"Sure enough," Nadine remembered the story of the Battle of Scary that Pop had related. "My pop says wounded soldiers from the Battle of Scary tried to run and hide. Maybe that's what happened to that soldier. Do you think he was shot in that battle?"

"Could be. It's a grave with no name." Again Carl pointed, this time to a tall oak tree, "Aunt Noni said one day, when she was a girl, school was dismissed to see a colored man hanged right on that very tree."

"What for?"

Carl's face flushed, "For a reason boys and girls just don't talk about," he stammered.

"Oh," Nadine nodded wisely but had not the slightest idea what the colored man's crime was.

"We better go back home. It's getting close to lunch."

Lunch sounded good to Nadine, "Will Uncle John come to lunch?"

"They are printing the paper today, so I doubt it. It's the best weekly paper about," he said with pride as he guided Nanny right into the back yard.

Aunt Noni saw the two children and called, "Hurry, get your hands washed. Lunch is ready."

As Carl returned the goat to the shed, Nadine washed. From the bathroom, she could hear Mom and Aunt Noni's conversation. "I thought, since John is Phil's brother, it would be better for you to write, asking about my adoption of Nadine and yours of Carl."

"The news is not good on that matter. Phil says he will never allow his children to be adopted."

"But he never sees them. Do you think some day he'll come along and take them from us?" Mom's voice raised with concern at the thought of losing Nadine.

"Phil is a good man. He is doing what he believes is best for the children. He knows they are in stable homes. He even says he'll never interrupt with their upbringing but can't bear to adopt them out."

Mom breathed a sigh of relief. "He has never remarried?"

"No, Phil was so broken hearted when Hazel died." Noni cleared her throat, "He is a good man, as I said, and very intelligent. He just can't seem to find his direction. John and I worry about him." Noni's voice cracked with emotion.

"What's for lunch?" Carl bounded into the kitchen, stopping the conversation.

"I fried the catfish you and John caught yesterday and cooked fresh vegetables. As soon as you and Nadine finish, you need to take a plate over to your Uncle John. He won't have time to come home. He will want to meet Nadine."

Carl was glad that Aunt Noni mentioned he helped catch the fish. It made him feel grown-up. He sort of liked being the older brother.

"Mind your manners, Nadine," Mom whispered.

Aunt Noni, who was erect, thin, large boned and wore her hair loosely piled on top of her head, turned her attention to Nadine, "That certainly is a beautiful blue dress you are wearing."

"Yes, I mean thank you. Mom made it to wear today."

Carl, not interested in women's talk, cleaned his plate in no time and picked up Uncle John's lunch. "Are you ready?"

Nadine licked the milk from her upper lip and excused herself. She and Carl bounded out the door together.

Winfield was a small town, and Carl seemed to know everyone as they greeted each other by name. Entering the newspaper office, Nadine spied a plumpish man wearing a long printers apron over his pants and shirt. His shirt sleeves were rolled up, and he was scrutinizing print that a plain looking woman with salt and pepper hair had just set up to go to press.

As soon as the bell on the front door jingled, he looked up, clapped his hands, reached down, lifted Nadine up to his eye level and in a jovial voice said, "This here is Nadine. Look at those pretty long red curls and that beautiful blue dress." A big smile spread across his face as he hugged her tight. "I'm your Uncle John."

"Nice to meet you, Sir."

"My, my, Phil would be so proud of you. You and Carl both have his red hair. Yes, you do. You ever been in a newspaper office, Nadine?"

"No, sir."

"Well, Carl here and I will show you around." He nodded toward Carl. "Carl is my right hand man in this newspaper office."

"I help with Mom and Pop's garden and take and go get the cows from the pasture."

"Yes sir, sounds like you and your brother are both helpers."

Nadine just had a natural fondness for Uncle John. She wondered if her dad was like him and decided he was. As Carl and Nadine left the office, Uncle John gave them a nickel for candy at Burke's General Store down the street.

Carl's bedroom was upstairs in the cupola, so it was octagon shaped. It had windows that afforded a view from several vantage points of Winfield. "Aunt Noni, that is an unusual name," said Nadine as she and Carl sat in his bedroom floor examining his arrowhead collection that he had found when people plowed their fields for gardens or dug up an area for building.

"Her real name is Nora, but just about everybody here calls her Noni."

"She and Uncle John are nice. I like them."

"Yes, I'm happy here." Carl volunteered.

"Mom and Pop are good to me too," responded Nadine. "They took me to raise when no one else would."

A look of compassion washed over Carl's face. He quickly went to another topic. "Over here are some Civil War bullets and a belt buckle I found." Carl stood and walked to his closet and pulled out a paper bag.

"Wonder if this belt buckle belonged to the soldier buried up there in the hollow behind the haunted house?" Nadine rolled it over in her hand.

"Could be."

"You two come on down now. Mrs. Taylor and Nadine have a good ride back to St. Albans before it gets dark."

Carl startled Nadine by quickly kissing her on the cheek and pressing into her hand one of his prized arrowheads. She in turn pulled the four leaf clover out of her pocket and pressed it into his hand. Without a word they went downstairs to say their formal farewells in front of Mom and Aunt Noni.

*   *   *

Mom spoke as she opened the oven to check the browning biscuits, releasing their delicious aroma into the kitchen. "Nadine, as soon as you take the cows to pasture, hurry on to school. This is your first day at Fairview. You don't want to be late. First impressions are lasting, you know."

Nadine pulled on her new shoes, not answering. She was excited about meeting new children but not about the daily routine of school itself. She loved the unstructured days of summer.

Closing the gate to the pasture where the cows grazed, she set out toward Fairview Elementary on West Main Street. As she passed her Uncle Lucian's house, she heard, "Nadine, Nadine." It was Esther, her cousin whom she had not spent time with because she was several years older. "Momma says you are to have this picture of your mom and dad, Hazel and Phil. She came across it when she was cleaning out some drawers." Esther handed Nadine the picture over the picket fence and started back into the house, calling over her shoulder, "I can't talk now. I have to get to school, and you better too."

Nadine thanked Esther, stuck the picture carefully into her new school dress pocket, and hurried on. When she neared Coal River Road, the brown two-story house came into view. It had two rooms up and two outdoor johns. Nadine quickened her pace, entering her classroom just as Mr. McCormick, her teacher, was closing the door. "You must be Nadine Miller?" he asked in a friendly tone.

"Yes, sir."

"Just stand beside the blackboard with the others until I seat you alphabetically." He gestured toward the board.

Nadine felt all eyes upon her as she entered. Looking around, she did not see a familiar face. Contrary to her nature, shyness washed over her, and she desperately missed her old school. The only familiar thing here was the musty smell of the room from being closed all summer and the smell of chalk. Seated in front of her was Charles Miller with his brownish hair neatly parted and combed to one side. He wore freshly washed and pressed knickers and a brown shirt. She wondered with the name Miller if he could be her cousin.

Mr. McCormick, looking over his spectacles, began a lesson on hygiene. "Cleanliness is next to Godliness, boys and girls, so every morning I'll inspect your ears and nails to see if they are clean. More over, I'll check to see if each one of you has a clean handkerchief. Promptness is also a virtue. When the bell rings you are to be seated. Also we have a new student, and you are to exhibit your best manners toward her." Nadine felt blood rush to her face as again all heads turned in her direction. She forced a smile but avoided eye contact.

As he continued, Nadine looked around the room. Hanging smack dab in the center above the blackboard was a picture of Lincoln and one of Washington. She decided Lincoln looked approachable but not Washington. Last February they learned that Lincoln grew a beard because a young girl suggested it in a letter. An adult listening to a child certainly raised Lincoln in Nadine's eyes. Mr. Scott said Washington did not smile because he had wooden teeth. Nadine thought that was just an excuse. If she needed an answer to a math problem, Lincoln looked like he might help her out, not George. Her attention was jolted back from a morning of day dreaming when Mr. McCormick announced lunch, and there was a scramble to line up in front of the door.

She went to the edge of the school yard and sat alone, eating her lunch. She watched girls jumping rope and boys playing marbles. After finishing her apple, she pulled the picture of her mother and father from her pocket. Beyond this faded picture, she knew little of her parents. They were two strangers staring back at her. Her throat contracted and her eyes burned. She did know her father refused to let Mom Taylor adopt her. Why, then, had he abandoned her and Carl? Was it fear of raising them alone, grief, anger at God for taking their mother, irresponsibility?

Her thoughts were interrupted by the sound of her name, "Nadine?" She looked up to see a girl about two years younger than herself with blond hair and a big smile. "My name is Lillian Miller. My daddy told me that I would have a new cousin at school today, and you were a pretty little thing with red curls. He said you are Phil's daughter."

Nadine quickly pocketed her parent's picture. She was glad to have someone to talk to, and to think, it was a new found cousin.

Lillian continued, "My brother Charles is in your class."

"Yes he sits in front of me. So he is my cousin too?" When the noon bell rang, Nadine did not feel as alone, returning to Mr. McCormick's class. After all, she had two cousins in this school.

*   *   *

Having Cousin Charles seated in front of Nadine proved to be an advantage. Coming from a one room country school, she was deficient in some of the basics. Charles, a sweet, bright boy, volunteered to tutor her. Nadine and Charles came to school ten minutes early each morning to check her homework. Charles never let a problem stump him. If he came to one he couldn't figure, he would sit and twist a lock of his hair between his index finger and thumb until the answer came. When she needed an answer during the day, she could just look over his shoulder. Which she often did.

As soon as the three o'clock bell sounded, Nadine was out the door to walk home with Lillian and Buddy. She and Buddy did not have the same lunch period. Which floor a child's class was on, determined lunch time since there were grades one through eight at Fairview. So she, Lillian and Buddy caught up with their daily gossip as they walked home. "What are you going to be for the school Halloween Party Buddy?"

"I can't decide, maybe an angel."

"That's a hoot. You as an angel," Nadine rolled her eyes in disbelief. They all three laughed.

"I'm going to be Little Bo Peep," volunteered Lillian. "I'll wear a bonnet and a long skirt with lots of petticoats."

"What are you going to do about sheep?"

"Well, I hadn't thought about that."

The three became pensive. "I know," said Nadine. "Since your dad owns the meat market, you can carry a lamb chop."

"Yuk, she can't carry a raw lamb chop to school."

"Cook it then."

"Now, you are being silly. What are you going to dress as?"

Nadine raised both eyebrows in thought. "I'm going to be the devil. I'll wear Pop's long red underwear and carry a pitch fork."

"I think that will be very fitting for you."

"Me too." added Lillian with a broad smile.

"Remember, there is no school the day after Halloween."

Lillian nodded in agreement with Buddy.

"I'm in favor of that, but why not?"

Buddy flung both hands up into the air as if everybody should know the answer to that question. "On Halloween night, all kinds of evil things happen here. Trees are cut down and put across roads; windows are soaped; bags of horse and cow poop are put on people's porches or on their walkway and set on fire."

"Pewie," she and Lillian both held their noses.

"But, the favorite thing is to turn the outdoor john's over or, even worse, carry them away."

"Yeh, children never go out on the night before Halloween." Lillian shook her head emphatically.

Buddy continued. "Of course the favorite targets for those hellion's are the two john's behind Fairview. We can't have school without toilets.

"Hallelujah!" Nadine responded, "If that gets us out of school, I wouldn't call them hellions. I'd call them angels of the night."

*   *   *

The day after Halloween, Nadine leisurely ate her cream of wheat, turning it with her spoon looking for the big lump she knew would be there. "What do you have planned for your day off?" asked Mom as she cleared the table.

Before Nadine could answer, she heard Pop knocking the mud off his shoes before entering the kitchen. There was another man's voice, but it wasn't Henry. The door opened, and a stranger entered, carrying his hat in hand. He waited for Pop to introduce him. Pop cleared his throat as he closed the door against the cold damp November air. "Mrs. Taylor, this here is my first wife's cousin's son, LeRoy.

"Nice to make your acquaintance, Ma'am." He shot out his hand and gave a quick bow as a smile spread across his face.

"Likewise."

"This here is our little Nadine." Pop motioned toward her.

LeRoy tipped his head in acknowledgement," I see you are out of school today?" His eyes which seemed too small for his face peered into hers.

"Some hellions tore down the john's at school"

"Nadine, what language!"

Nadine blushed but continued to size up LeRoy. To her, he seemed tall, thin, large boned, and he had brown hair slicked back with the imprint of the comb's teeth evident. She would call him pretty boy handsome.

"Mrs. Taylor here will whip you up some ham, eggs and biscuits."

"I'd appreciate that very much. It's been awhile since I ate a country breakfast, being in the war and all."

"Sunny side up?" Mom asked, cracking the eggs on the side of the black iron skillet.

"Yes Ma'am, that's the way my mom always fried them, so I'm partial to my eggs that way." He sat down at the table in anticipation as Mom poured him coffee. As he watched Mom move about the kitchen, he ran the tip of his fork beneath his finger nails.

Pop cleared his throat again. "LeRoy is going to spend a few days with us until he gets on his feet."

"I sure appreciate this," he said, brushing crumbs from the table. "It's hard getting back into things after returning from the war."

"I do understand that. I fought in the Civil War, you know. I'll tell you about that sometime." Pop stroked his beard.

"I certainly look forward to that, Sir."

"While you're eating, I need to change shoes before going out to the barn." As Pop left, Mom was right on his heels.

"This sure is a delicious breakfast, Mrs. Taylor." LeRoy said with his mouth full just as Mom disappeared through the door.

"Thanks," she called over her shoulder.

With Mom and Pop gone, the only sound in the kitchen was LeRoy's chewing. "How about you warming my coffee, Nadine." He asked, holding her in his gaze.

Nadine obliged, "Do you have any boys or girls?"

"Nope, never been married."

Again the room was silent, making Nadine uncomfortable. "I need to be excused." She carried her plate to the sink and started upstairs. Passing Mom and Pop's bedroom, she heard loud whispers.

"How well do you know this LeRoy, Mr. Taylor?"

"I told you he is my cousin by marriage."

"But do you know him? I mean how much time have you spent with him?"

Pop scratched his head, "I'd met him a couple of times when he was a young boy, why?"

Concern showed in Mom's voice, "You just can't be too careful whom you invite under your roof, that's all."

"For heavens sake, he is my cousin. Even if he weren't, he is a soldier who defended our country and now needs food and shelter."

"Mr. Stark, down in Winfield, invited a stranger in, and now Stark is dead."

"Yes, Mrs. Taylor, and there was a woman in Putnam County who murdered her husband, cut him up and buried him in a pig pen, but that doesn't make you a suspect."

"Well, how about those three soldiers who murdered the conductor?" With that spoken, Mom opened, then slammed the bedroom door behind her and marched down the hall, not noticing Nadine seated on the steps.

*   *   *

The Spanish flu that struck the nation in 1918, killing 675,000 Americans, ten times the nation's loss of soldiers in World War I, made its way into St. Albans. Black wreaths, indicating death had paid a visit to a house, dotted more and more front doors. Mr. McCormick became positively insistent that each child bring a handkerchief daily to be used when coughing and sneezing.

The flu was the main topic of conversation. Walking home from school, Lillian pulled her coat collar closer to her face for protection against the icy mist which fell that December afternoon. The three girls huddled closer than usual, and the cold made them walk faster. "Everyday when my dad comes home from his meat market, he whispers to Mom how many graves were dug that day at Teay's Hill. You know he can see the cemetery from his market's front window."

Buddy joined in, "You know little Katie Cox died. She was only two years old—the sweetest little girl with sandy colored hair. Her dad worked for the railroad."

Nadine shoved her hands deeper into her coat pockets for warmth and added, "As if her dying wasn't enough, when her mom and dad, who were from Richmond, took Katie back to bury her where the Cox's family lived, they never returned here after Katie's funeral. Come to find out, they died from the flu on the way back."

Lillian wiped away a tear with her coat sleeve. Momma went to Mrs. Hick's funeral yesterday. She said it was so sad. Mrs. Hick's little girl kept crying, "I want my momma, I want my momma."

"I guess the Spanish Flu is a horrible death. My Mom Taylor says it's like drowning in your own lung's fluid." The three girls agreed that was not how they wanted to go, and they prayed it did not visit their homes.

The cases continued to multiply. Finally, schools, churches and all public places were closed, and the sick were quarantined. If a family had members with the flu, healthy neighbors brought cooked food and left it on the porch, afraid to enter.

At the Taylor's home, there was no sign Christmas was approaching. Both Mr. and Mrs. Taylor contracted the flu and were bed ridden. The smell of Vicks Salve permeated the entire house.

Dr. Wilson prescribed rubbing Vicks on the chest and placed a hot washcloth over it to keep the lungs open.

Mrs. Taylor said LeRoy was a Godsend, for it was he that took care of their needs. He could be seen running about carrying bed-pans, keeping the humidifier full of water with liberal amounts of Vicks added. He also turned out to be a fair cook, supplementing the food brought by neighbors.

Throughout the night, Nadine was awakened by racking coughs coming from the master bedroom. In the mornings when she awoke, the house was quiet except for the periodic coughs, and LeRoy's quick footsteps, carrying needed medication, water or food to Mom and Pop. Looking out at the gray river reflecting the slate gray sky certainly didn't cheer Nadine.

The somber mood even affected Frances. Nadine sat combing Frances' long salt and pepper colored hair, and Frances began singing:

"I stole the gold from your hair and put the silver
    that is there.
When I was a baby upon your knee, you sacrificed
    everything for me.
I stole the gold from your hair and put the silver
    that is there.
When I was a baby upon your knee, you sacrificed
    everything for me.
I stole the gold from your hair and put the
    silver that is there.
I don't know any way I could ever repay you for
    my cradle days."

"Frances, why are you singing such a mournful song?"

"It's true. Mr. Taylor and Liz have always been good to me. They're downstairs sick."

"Well, it's not because of you, Frances. Now cheer up. You hear?"

After going to bed that night, she heard LeRoy open the front door and heard Dr. Wilson's tired voice, "What's going on here?"

"Mrs. Taylor is burning to the touch, Dr. Wilson. I don't know what to do?"

"Let me check her." Dr. Wilson felt her forehead. "She is hot. Get me a washcloth and some cool water. We'll swab her down until her temperature breaks."

Nadine slipped out of bed. The floor was cold on her bare feet. Holding onto the stair railing, she tiptoed downstairs and sat on the bottom step. She could hear Mom's raspy breathing.

LeRoy came and went, carrying bowls of cool water as Dr. Wilson rubbed her body down with the dampened cloth. Her head was propped up on two feather pillows to help her breathe.

"Dear God," Nadine prayed, "please let Mom live. Don't let her die, please God." Nadine continued watching Dr. Wilson's no nonsense demeanor as he worked into the night. Finally she dozed off.

The floorboards creaking under Dr. Wilson's weight woke Nadine. She saw the sun was up and heard the rooster's crowing.

Dr. Wilson was slipping his arms into his heavy black wool overcoat while giving LeRoy directions, "I think the worst has passed. Keep the humidifier with Vicks going. Be sure they both drink lots of liquids. If their throats are sore, let them gargle saltwater—one teaspoon of salt to a glass. Call me if you have any more problems. I've got other patients to tend to now. Lord, it seems there is somebody sick in most every house. It's keeping Dr. Phillips, Dr. Shirkey, and me all running.

"Yes sir," LeRoy nodded, "I'll do exactly as you say."

Dr. Wilson turned before going out the door. "Keep Nadine and Frances away from the sick room."

LeRoy nodded again, exhibiting a broad smile.

*　　*　　*

Christmas day arrived, but there was not the familiar smell of turkey and dressing and pumpkin pies browning in the oven. There was no sound of Mom's clanking pots and pans together, or the kitchen door opening and closing as Henry and Pop fetched and carried needed supplies for the Christmas feast. There was no smell of pine emanating from the Christmas tree with brightly colored gifts underneath.

There's nothing, Nadine thought as she rolled over in bed, not ready to face the day. As she breathed, vapor hung in the air, and she pinched the end of her nose to warm it. The smell of talcum came to her and accompanied the thought. *Shame on you. Mom and Pop Taylor are alive. Is that not Christmas enough?* She thought of the little Hicks girl with no Mama, and shame washed over her.

She got out of bed. Looking out the window, she saw Henry feeding Dutch. Even Henry seemed sullen lately, she thought. But not Dutch who jumped all around with his tail wagging back and forth, greeting his master and his food.

After breakfast, Frances and Nadine kept each other company, stringing buttons from Mom's button jar to make necklaces and bracelets.

Well into the afternoon, there was a knock on the front door.

Nadine slid down the banister and flung it open. There sat a wicker basket with newspaper covering its contents. Picking it up, Nadine found it to be heavy. She carried it to the dining room table and excitedly checked out the contents. There were thick slices of turkey breast, dressing, cranberry sauce, mashed potatoes and a whole pumpkin pie.

Nadine ran to the door and looked down Smokey Road. Lillian and Charles' father was the solitary figure walking toward West Main. He turned and gave Nadine a wave and walked briskly in the cold Christmas evening. Returning to the dining room, Nadine began setting the food out, so there would be a Christmas dinner after all. To the side of the basket wrapped separately, was a kewpie doll for Nadine and an orange and a peppermint stick.

LeRoy fixed the plates for Mom and Pop, and Nadine prepared a plate for Frances and one for Henry. Since Pop was sick, Nadine did what he faithfully did each meal, took Frances' meal upstairs to her. She also decided to give the peppermint stick to Frances and the orange to Henry, so they each received a Christmas present.

As she started upstairs, she heard Mom say, "God does provide," in response to the Christmas dinner, and Pop responded, "Amen, that is the truth."

Getting Frances settled, Nadine pulled on her coat and headed for Henry's little house which originally had been slave quarters. Beneath it was the cellar house. She watched her footing on the icy walk and breathed the fresh cold air into her lungs, a relief from breathing Vicks vapors.

With just one knock, the door flung open. Henry was silhouetted against the glow of the fire in the fireplace—the only light in the room. Nadine could tell that Henry was agitated, but he seemed to calm down, seeing her. "I brought your Christmas dinner and a gift. She held out the orange.

"My, my, an orange. I don't know how long its been since I ate one. Thank you kindly. Come on in. Here, sit down while I eat and keep me company."

He pulled up a rocking chair. As Nadine sat down, she felt the warm wood against the backs of her legs where the rocker had been setting up close to the roaring fire.

Dutch got up, stretched and ambled over to Nadine with his tail wagging.

At first, he nuzzled his chin onto Nadine's lap to have his head stroked. Then he began sniffing at her pocket. Nadine giggled and said, "Now you've found your present," as she pulled out a ham bone that Mom kept to make soup. But, it would be awhile before Mom would be making any soup, so Dutch might as well enjoy it. That was Nadine's reasoning anyway. Dutch greedily took the bone over to the fireplace and began gnawing.

Nadine unbuttoned her coat and watched the flames make dancing patterns on the ceiling and walls. She felt cozy in Henry's place.

"Mr. and Mrs. Taylor doin' better?" Henry's voice broke the silence.

"Mom's been sicker than Pop, but LeRoy has taken real good care of them. Mom says, 'He's a Godsend.'"

These words were no more out of her mouth than she sensed agitation come over Henry again. "Humph," was his reply.

"Is there something bothering you, Henry?"

"Lots."

"What is it?"

"It's that LeRoy fellow. That's what."

"Has he said something bad to you?"

"Don't have to," Henry grunted, "It's his uppity attitude. That's what it is." Henry's eyebrows bunched together as he brought his fist down on the table, splattering coffee onto the plate.

Nadine jumped back in surprise. Henry was always compliant. She looked at his ruddy complexion and his callused hands. She noted the deep furrows in his forehead. He probably looked much older than he was. His movements and slow drawl exposed his simpleness of mind.

Henry looked startled by his sudden show of rage. "I'm sorry," was his simple reply, but the anger lingered in his eyes. He closed them and shoved his plate away.

"It's just LeRoy's way. He's quiet like." Nadine spoke softly, trying to smooth the anger away.

"He ain't quiet around Mr. and Mrs. Taylor. Always up in their faces with that big smile of his, saying 'Yessum'. He repeats that hard luck story about the war, over and over." Henry now sat looking down, but his knuckles were white from gripping the edge of the table.

Nadine leaned forward. She loved Henry and did not want to leave him in such a state of mind. "What has set you off so against LeRoy, not just his attitude?"

Henry shook his head, "Them fellers been tellin' me that now that LeRoy's about—his own relation—Mr. Taylor will be turning me out. He won't need me anymore. What's rightfully mine for working so hard will go to LeRoy when Mr. Taylor passes. This is my home, Nadine. I just can't go back to the poor farm. It's a terrible place." Nadine saw this grown man's eyes, whom she had seen little emotion in before, mist over.

Nadine folded her hands in her lap as she listened. "What fellows said this?"

"Them whites that live behind here in those shacks." He pointed beyond the railroad tracks.

"Those ruffians are just teasing you, Henry. They're trying to make you jealous. Besides, LeRoy is only supposed to be here long enough to get back on his feet. He'll leave then. There'll be the five of us again—Mom and Pop, Frances, you and me."

Henry's hands began to relax, and he looked up, "Sure do hope so. I sure do." He wiped his nose on the back of his hand.

"Just don't pay any mind to those ruffians, causing trouble. You hear? They're jealous of you and want to make you jealous of LeRoy." Nadine continued trying to soothe this side of Henry she had never seen before.

"Yessum. I feel better talking to you, but I still don't like LeRoy." Henry shook his fingers in her face.

"Well, I best be going. Frances won't go to sleep until I knock on the wall to let her know that I'm in bed." Nadine smiled at the comfortable ritual that she and Frances went through at bedtime. She buttoned her coat and said goodnight and Merry Christmas to Henry and then Dutch who was still gnawing on the ham bone. She stepped into the cold night and walked toward the house with lights glowing in the kitchen and the master bedroom.

*   *   *

Decoration Day was approaching which always excited Mom Taylor. It was a time to remember loved ones who had "passed," she would say as well as to see relatives and friends not seen in years. She began preparation several weeks in advance, or several years in fact, if you counted the planting of her prized rose bushes.

This Decoration Day she decided Nadine was to wear a white organdy dress, so she ordered the material, and got out her Singer sewing machine and began the labor of love. Everyone dressed up to go to the cemetery because there was preaching accompanied by a choir. Plus, Mom wanted Nadine to look especially nice because there would be Millers there. She wanted them to be assured that Nadine was being well cared for. So after making the dress, it would be starched, just so, and Nadine's hair would be combed into long curls with a ribbon to match her dress.

The day before the holiday, Nadine was dispatched to gather wild fern, daisies, and sweet smelling honeysuckle. Nadine's sources were the green meadow where the cows pastured, the woods and hillsides. She knew to keep an eye out for snakes. Mom also warned her not to get her feet wet in Tackett's Creek which meandered through their property. "There's nothing worse than a summer cold," she always said.

Nadine found some honeysuckle growing close to Henry's place. She was down on her hands and knees behind his house when she heard a low throaty growl. Peeping around the corner, she saw LeRoy walk by. Dutch was lying on the porch not moving but giving LeRoy warning. *He must be of the same opinion as his master*, decided Nadine.

The flowers Nadine gathered and the roses and peonies that grew in the yard were placed in a washtub of water to keep fresh.

The evening before going to the cemetery, Mom began sorting and arranging the flowers. "Let's see, yes this bunch is for my mom.

She liked white roses. That's where I got the start for these roses, off her and Pop's property. Nadine, I wish you had known her. She was so much fun, happy go lucky, always telling jokes."

Nadine listened, sometimes wondering if Mom were talking to herself instead of her. She spoke so quietly and reverently, almost like saying a prayer. After arranging a bunch, she would look at it from all angles, adjusting where need be. Satisfied, she would go through the same ritual again. "This is for Pop.

I'll put in his favorite red roses. Now Pop was a good man and a hard worker. Quiet like, he let Mom do most of the talking."

If Pop Taylor were around, he would smile and say, "That sounds like us you're talking about, Mrs. Taylor."

Around 7:00 a.m. on Decoration Day, Mom was in a flurry inspecting Nadine's dress, which had so much starch it almost stuck straight out, and getting the bunches of flowers together and rounding up Henry who was taking them to the cemetery. "Nadine, quit scratching at your dress collar like that. You're going to make your neck all red. You know you have to look your best."

"But the collar is itching," Nadine whined as she continued to scratch.

"Now, I wish Henry would come on." Mom slid her gold watch out of her breast pocket to check the time. "He knows the preaching begins at nine."

Red pulled the spring wagon over the rough mud road, leading to Teays Hill Cemetery. "This horse sure goes slow when he's leaving the house but gallops at full neck speed going home," Mom said impatiently.

"Mrs. Taylor, Red ain't going to be able to get up that rutted road, going up the hill. We'll have to walk." Henry said, taking his hat off and scratching his head.

"I'm tired and thirsty," Nadine fussed as she wiggled in the stiff dress. "I'm not dressed for hiking."

"We're almost to the top."

As they crested the hill, Nadine saw the mound where the preacher gave his sermon and the choir sang. There were hard back chairs, making a semi circle around it. "Henry, go over and save seats for Nadine and me." Mom fanned herself with her handkerchief.

"Yessum," Henry was glad to sit a spell after carrying the washtub with water and flowers up the hill, stopping every time Mrs. Taylor saw an acquaintance to gossip with, proudly showing off Nadine.

"Now let's get busy putting the flowers on the graves," Mom took Nadine's hand to lead her from plot to plot. Mom got down on her knees to place each bouquet. Sometimes a tear would roll down her cheek, and she blotted it away with her handkerchief.

Nadine thought the cemetery was the prettiest place in St. Albans. From this vantage point, Coal River could be seen merging into the Kanawha, forming a valley with green mountains bordering both sides. Even though there were lots of people here today, the cemetery was quiet, for they spoke in hushed voices as they went about their work. Birds' singing filtered through the trees.

After leaving the Allen plot, Mom led Nadine to where her mother, Hazel, was buried beside her Aunt Vonzine Rimmer. There Nadine knelt, placing a bouquet on each, inhaling the sweet honeysuckle as she did. It felt strange to her, placing flowers on graves of two women—one she could hardly remember and one she never knew. Yet there was a connection and a desire to do so. It just seemed right. Mrs. Taylor watched Nadine, and again thought how grateful she was to these two. One bore Nadine. The other entrusted Nadine to her.

Walking toward the mound for the Decoration Day Service, Nadine stopped abruptly, looking skyward at the tallest concrete monument in the cemetery. Then she looked down at its concrete base which covered an entire lot and read: "I FORBID ANYONE BURYING ON THIS LOT, John R. Teass." This warning was written in copper letters embedded in the concrete. The monument had a deep zigzagged crack across its base. John R. Teass, Nadine remembered the man with the large gold watch and heavy gold watch chain who was stingy in buying apples from Buddy and her.

"Seems he wanted to be alone in death as well as life." Mom said quietly. "See that crack? Lightning struck this monument. Maybe a symbol of God's justice. You can't take material possessions with you."

The only thing that enabled Nadine to endure the long sermon on "The Shortness of Time and The Reality and Nearness of Eternity" while sitting on a hard seat in a scratchy dress was the thought of going to Uncle Sam's after the service. Uncle Sam was Mom's brother, who rented one of Mom's houses on Smokey Road. Aunt Grace, his wife, was a wonderful cook, and she had a doll with curly hair that Nadine played with when they visited. Best of all was the vanilla ice cream that Uncle Sam always made on Decoration Day.

*   *   *

"That was a mighty fine supper, Mrs. Taylor," Pop said as he went to the stove to get Frances' plate.

"I think you just out-did yourself," agreed LeRoy, smiling his charming smile. Wiping his mouth on the back of his hand, he reached for his third piece of fried chicken. "Nadine, hand me some of those delicious mashed potatoes there." While Nadine complied, she watched Mrs. Taylor beam at all the compliments. As Pop walked toward the stairs, Mrs. Taylor cut LeRoy a piece of apple pie and began clearing the table. After gobbling his pie, LeRoy leaned back, picking at his teeth with a toothpick.

Nadine grabbed the water bucket and ran out to the well to fetch water to wash the dishes. Mom had just warned her not to splash water onto the newly mopped linoleum when there were a series of loud thumping sounds and a soft thud followed by another loud thump.

Nadine instantly put the pail down and followed LeRoy and Mom to the stairs. "Oh my God," screamed Mom in disbelief, "No, no, no." Nadine saw Mom kneeling and LeRoy leaning over the spreading pool of blood that oozed from Pop's head. Pop did not move, not even a twitch.

It was LeRoy who took control, "Nadine, fetch Henry, and we'll put Mr. Taylor to bed. Then I'll get Dr. Wilson, quick."

LeRoy did not have to utter the last direction. Mom continued kneeling there. Her body gently rocking back and forth.

"Dear Lord, no." Henry repeated over and over as he followed Nadine back to the house. Dutch's low foreboding baying at the full moon sent chills up Nadine's spine. Her tears blurred her vision, making her stumble along the way.

Henry stood over Mr. Taylor with his mouth opening and shutting and no sound coming out. LeRoy explained exactly how to lift him into his bed.

Frances stood at the top of the stairs, wringing her hands.

"What wrong with Poppy?"

Nadine had the presence of mind to answer, "It's okay, Frances, Pop just slipped. Finish your supper now."

Henry gently helped LeRoy lift Pop as his warm blood spreading now onto Henry's shirt and trousers.

Dr. Wilson was there in no time. He bent over and called, "Mr. Taylor." There was no response. He felt his pulse. Then he fished out a mirror from his warm leather bag and placed it in front of Mr. Taylor's mouth and nose. There was no vapor. He looked into Pop's eyes. There was no dilation. Besides the blood, he noted cerebral spinal flood visible in one ear. He then closed Mr. Taylor's eyes and covered him with a blanket.

Mom sat with a look of disbelief. Nadine walked over and hugged her pop's still warm body. She then stood beside Mom, trying to wipe Mom's tears away with her bare fingertips.

Dr. Wilson stood, bag in hand, as he had done numerous times in his career, yet never knowing the right words. He cleared his throat. "Seems he died instantly, no suffering." Then he patted Mrs. Taylor and Nadine on the shoulder. I'll leave this powder. Take it and get some rest."

He stepped into the hall where LeRoy waited to explain his theory on how Mr. Taylor had fallen. Henry was pacing up and back in the hall, mumbling. LeRoy stopped in the middle of his sentence, "Henry go now. You've done all you can. Go back to your cabin." Henry, as if in a daze, turned and left.

LeRoy resumed, "It looks like Mr. Taylor was coming down the stairs from taking Frances' supper to her, got his foot caught in the carpet that had pulled loose, lost his footing, fell and hit his head on the ball at the end of the banister here," he pointed.

"Seems plausible," Wilson agreed, shrugging into his coat. "Mr. Taylor was a mighty fine gentleman. I certainly hate this."

He shook his head and walked out the door.

Going up the stairs to her bedroom, Nadine glanced back into the master bedroom where Mrs. Taylor sat blinking back tears.

LeRoy sprinkled Doc Wilson's medicine into a glass of water for Mom.

Nadine knocked on the wall to reassure Frances. Then she buried her head in her arms, crying herself to sleep.

The next morning she awoke, hoping that her memories of last night were a nightmare. She could smell smoke coming from outside, and she went to the window, shielding her eyes from the bright sunlight as she looked out.

LeRoy was burning something. Nadine recognized the dark blood stained carpet. Dutch barked as the orange and red flames shot skyward. Suddenly LeRoy turned and kicked the dog. Instantly, upon hearing Dutch's whimper and whine, Henry's front door flung open. Henry was in LeRoy's face, yelling. LeRoy roughly elbowed Henry out of his way and turned toward the house while Henry still yelled.

LeRoy abruptly turned before entering, and said, "Shut up, don't you have any respect for the grieving?"

Nadine's stomach convulsed at the ugly scene, and she balled her hands into fists. She hoped Mom didn't witness the scene. Indeed, the wake and the funeral passed in a blur.

Only one sound remained with Nadine. The low moan which came from deep within Mom's body as Mr. Taylor's body was lowered into the grave. It was the sound Melinda used to describe as her mom's reaction when her husband was shot and killed by the Ku Klux Klan.

It had been a different time, place and circumstance, yet this wail of the deeply bereaved echoes throughout the ages.

Since Nadine missed several days of school, she looked for Charles to help her catch up with her class work, but Lillian said he was home sick. The next morning she waited again, but both he and Lillian were absent.

Right before school was dismissed, the classroom door slowly opened, and Mr. Blair the school principal stood framed in the doorway. He cleared his throat as he walked to Miss Woods, their seventh grade teacher's desk. Turning his back to the class, he whispered something to Miss Wood. "Oh no," she responded as she pulled her handkerchief from her front dress pocket and dabbed her eyes. She stood and then leaned against her desk to steady herself.

"I will handle it," said Mr. Blair, taking her elbow and guiding her from the room.

Returning, he stood in front of the class, cleared his throat again, and took off his glasses, wiping them with his handkerchief. Silence enveloped the class. "Boys and girls, I have some bad news to share. As you know, Charles Miller has been absent from school for a few days with what Dr. Wilson believed to be the flu." He began to stutter, "The flu, yes, the flu." Then blurted out, "I just received word that he died this afternoon."

Initially the silence deepened. Then came utterances of disbelief and tears. The sounds became louder. Nobody their age could die. Unless of course, there was a flu epidemic or accident. This was not the case this time. Disbelief was the emotion now voiced.

Nadine did not move. Sweet Charles, her friend, her cousin, her tutor, could not be dead. She glanced at his desk in front of hers with its contents still in place. Her eyes moved to the coat closet where his red plaid cap still hung, left from the last day he came to school. Death was hateful. It came so suddenly with no warning, first for Pop and now Charles. Nadine felt as if she were going to choke as her throat constricted. *It can't be true, it can't be*, she thought.

"School will be dismissed for the rest of the day. It is almost three anyway," Mr. Blair announced amid all the sobs and highly excited voices.

Nadine ran from the room, bumping into Buddy as she bounded down the stairs. Hand in hand, they walked past Lillian and Charles' house. On the front door, hung a black wreath like an oversized period.

Saying goodbye to Buddy, Nadine ran down Smokey Road, not running up the stairs to the house but to the barn. She had to be alone. Mom had told her not to go into the hayloft where she might fall through, but that is exactly where she went. Rolling over in the hay onto her stomach, her body convulsed and tears flowed. After her emotions had crested, she grew quiet. Her mind went back to another day as she breathed in the sweet smell of hay and heard Prince and Red in their separate stalls munching hay.

It was last May around six in the morning at Pop's Poca farm. She and Pop, along with the other workers, were cutting and bailing hay. She sat astride Prince waiting for her job of binding the bales to begin. As Pop lifted his pitchfork up from gathering the hay into bunches, she caught sight of a snake pierced by one of the prongs writhing in pain and struggling to free itself. Nadine remembered the lack of fear she experienced because she knew Pop was her protector and would never allow harm to come to her. For the first time, it sank in that Pop, her protector, was gone and now Charles— forever. She lay there for a long time.

Realizing that Mom would be worrying about her, she finally pushed herself upon her knees to climb down out of the hayloft.

As she did, she felt the boards give way, and suddenly she was lying in the horse's trough with her knee bleeding. Mom would get to say once again, "I told you so. Didn't I tell you that hayloft would collapse if you went up in it?"

Crawling out of the trough she headed for the house. As she flung the front door open, LeRoy was exiting the master bedroom.

He turned and placed his finger over his lips, signaling Nadine to be quiet. "Mrs. Taylor is resting and can't be disturbed," he said, turning abruptly and walking away. Nadine had to tend to her own wounds.

*   *   *

Pop had been dead for over a year. Mom became more and more of a recluse, staying in her room and sleeping a lot. When she did join Nadine and LeRoy for dinner or did a few necessary chores around the house, she moved like a zombie, speaking little. Nadine hoped she would soon snap out of this state. Nadine knew that the formal mourning period was a year, and indeed Mom still wore a lot of black.

LeRoy had taken over the operation of the house, resulting in he and Henry arguing frequently. Nadine often awoke to their raised voices. When she went down for breakfast she would see LeRoy fly into the kitchen with the veins in his neck protruding from the encounter. He totally ignored Nadine. To him, she was an invisible being. Henry became more sullen, mumbling a lot to himself. LeRoy hated Dutch and the feeling was mutual as shown by Dutch's low throaty growls whenever LeRoy was in the vicinity.

Frances was affected by Mom's despondent mood more than Nadine. Nadine was out and about. Frances depended on her sister to keep her hands busy with mending. It made her feel like she made a contribution to the family. Now Mom didn't seem to take an interest in the running of the house. Nadine often heard Frances singing in a low soulful tone, "I took the gold from your hair and put the gray there." Nadine hated that song.

*   *   *

Nadine was now in the eighth grade. She knew that for many this was the last grade for attending public school. Few went on to high school. An eighth grade education for completing necessary tasks to support ones self, especially for young ladies who were expected to get married and rear families, was considered enough. Nadine wanted a family of her own, the security of her very own home, and most of all to love and be loved. However she planned to continue on into high school.

Buddy knew she herself wanted to go to high school. She talked about it all the time. Getting married and having children was not her prime interest. She worried about Nadine though. She had heard concern in her mother's voice when she talked to Aunt Ada or Aunt Effie about Nadine's future. They recognized the change in Liz since Mr. Taylor's death and were indeed surprised at her docile attitude.

She had always been a strong independent woman. What was happening? It was a godsend, they said, that LeRoy was there to hold the family together. Even though anyone could see the property was beginning to look shabby, but one man could only do so much. Liz always took such an interest in her flowers, lawn and kitchen garden. All were now overgrown with weeds. Henry was becoming a nuisance, walking the streets mumbling to himself about LeRoy's trying to take over the family and money.

Buddy took the responsibility of trying to keep Nadine out of the gloomy atmosphere that had settled over the Taylor home. However, she would have to admit that Nadine remained her impetuous self, never complaining. "You know the Ku Klux Klan are parading down Main Street this afternoon. Let's go watch," Buddy suggested to Nadine.

"Don't know if I want to. They give me the creeps." Nadine shuttered as if a chill shot through her.

"Don't be silly, they are just neighborhood men wearing white sheets and hoods over their heads. I think it is the grown-ups way of playing Halloween." Buddy answered placing her hands on her hips.

Nadine shook her head, "They do bad things to people."

"They just put bundles of switches on individual's porches or burn crosses in their yards as a warning to quit beating their children and wife, to quit running around on their wife, or for staying drunk and not supporting their families. It certainly got Mr. Dicken's attention when he was going out on Mrs. Dickens. Everybody in town knew about it but her," Buddy said with a shrug.

"Buddy, how can you say that is all they do? I told you about my friend Sassy's grandfather being shot on his very own front porch in front of his family because he was a white man living with a Negro who bore his children. Who made those men judge and jury?" Nadine's frown wrinkles deepened at recalling the incident that was so painful for Sassy to talk about.

"That was a long time ago, not now. Quit being so serious."

"Oh, okay."

The two met on West Main. Nadine was wearing her shiny satin bloomers pulled down below her skirt. She thought they were too pretty to hide up under her skirt; even though Mom told her it wasn't lady like. The other girls began doing it also. So what the heck.

She and Buddy stopped at Effie Wickline's bakery to buy an oatmeal cookie each and then ran along to get a seat on the curb to watch the parade. "We'll look at the member's shoes to see if we recognize them. Membership is to be such a big secret you know." Nadine said as she took small bites from her cookie to make it last.

People lined both sides of the street as the somber hooded men shuffled by. Some of the onlookers cheered as others jeered. In the front row of marchers on Buddy and Nadine's side of the street, Nadine spied a man about 5'6" with a distinct limp. One that couldn't be mistaken. Nadine's eyes widened, and she nudged Buddy. "Do you recognize that limp?" she whispered.

Buddy turned and looked at Nadine as she nodded her head in disbelief and in fear of uttering the name.

"That is Police Chief Thatcher!" Nadine said out loud as she jumped up and began running along beside of him yelling, "Hello there Police Chief Thatcher, Hello there Police Chief Thatcher."

Other children, including Buddy, took up the chant, forming a small parade of their own, following him along as he tried in vain to push them away. Their parents and other grown-ups, after the first wave of shock passed, began to snicker.

*   *   *

It was Sunday and one of those days that invites you to come out and enjoy the weather. Nadine ate breakfast and carried Frances' to her. She then walked out on the second floor porch to see if she needed a sweater. The days had been getting cooler. However, the sun shone on the river like gold sequins sprinkled on it's surface. Nadine breathed in the fragrance of honeysuckle which hung heavy in the air and listened to the songs of birds reverberating from tree to tree.

Briskly walking down Smokey Road was a solitary figure, but there was no doubt in Nadine's mind that it was Mrs. Howe. Nadine could set her watch by Mrs. Howe passing by every Sunday morning headed toward the First Baptist Church to teach the I.E. Handley Bible Class. You could also tell the season by her attire. In the summer she wore a straw hat and in the winter a felt one. Nadine threw up her hand and yelled, "Hello Mrs. Howe."

This Sunday, Mrs. Howe did not just wave back but motioned to Nadine. Nadine bounded down the stairs and out the door. As she approached Mrs. Howe, she admired her floral print dress and the cameo pin clasped at its neck. "You certainly look pretty today, Mrs. Howe. You headed to church?"

"This is the Lord's day! Do you go to church?"

"Just when the Circuit Preacher comes and Mom takes me. She packs a lunch, but the benches sure get hard, sitting all day."

"Why don't you get ready and go with me today. You'll be in Sunday School with young people your own age. Your cousin Lillian comes every Sunday. It only lasts an hour." Mrs. Howe tilted her head, "If you don't like it, you don't have to stay for church. I'll sit on the porch and wait for you to dress." She looked at her watch. "We have some time before the bell rings."

Nadine squinted her eyes in thought. It would be fun to be with Lillian. "I'll just be a minute," she said, running into the house.

Not only was Lillian in Sunday School but also Buddy. Their teacher, Mrs. Reynolds, did not turn red in the face with veins popping out in her neck, yell, nor beat her fist on the podium like the circuit minister. In fact, it was down right pleasant, singing and learning about Jesus. She already knew God cared for her. After all, he sent an angel to watch over her and to pray for her. So, it was not hard for Lillian to persuade Nadine to stay for church. "It only lasts an hour," she cajoled.

As the choir took their seats, Nadine saw her cousin Esther and Nadine's Uncle Frank's daughter Mollie. Nadine thought she might join the choir. After all, she and Frances had been singing hymns for a long time. Plus, she loved those flowing white robes with the burgundy trim.

Everything went fine until Deacon Burns got up to pray, and his false teeth kept juggling around in his mouth until Nadine, Lillian and Buddy thought he might bite his tongue off. Nadine began shaking, not wanting to laugh out loud. This made Buddy and Lillian giggle just looking at Nadine turning red in the face, trying not to make a sound.

"Stop! You are going to make me pee in my pants," Buddy said, holding her nose and mouth squelching her laughter.

Suddenly a snort like a horse escaped her lips, and the congregation turned to stare at its source. Nadine and Lillian managed to straighten their faces just in time to turn and look at Buddy also. As soon as everyone shifted their attention back to the deacon, Buddy whispered, "I'm going to get you two for that."

Returning from church, Nadine started up the stairs to tell Frances about her experience at the First Baptist, when she heard, "Nadine?" coming from the master bedroom. The door was half open, so she went in. Mom was seated in her rocking chair beside the window. "Did you have a good time at church?"

"I sure did. I think I might like to join the choir." She didn't mention Esther and Mollie because she worried that Mom might interpret her talking about relatives as a desire to be with them rather than her. She didn't mention Buddy making the horse sound or her laughing at the deacon either.

Mom, with her finger, flipped a white powdery substance from the nightstand beside of her chair. "It was nice of Mrs. Howe to take you. She is a wonderful Christian example. Who was your Sunday School teacher?"

"Mrs. Reynolds," Nadine didn't compare her with the circuit preacher to Mom as she had in her own mind.

"You'll learn a lot from her too. Mom then motioned to the dressing table. "Would you care to brush my hair?"

Nadine loved doing that, so she reached for the brush on the dressing table and began combing out the tangles, noting the numerous gray strands now in Mom's hair. But, it was still thick.

"I don't know what has come over me since Mr. Taylor's death," she breathed deeply, "I just can't seem to get my wits about me." Nadine couldn't tell if she spoke to her or herself, so she didn't reply.

"Nadine what do you want to do with your life now that you have graduated from the eighth grade?"

"Someday I want to marry and have a family, but I still want." Mom interrupted her before she could say, "to go to high school."

"You know one of the main reasons that Mr. Taylor and I sold our farms and moved to St. Albans was so you could get a better education. I think you have." Folding her hands in her lap she continued. "However, with things as they are now, I think you can accomplish your goals with an eighth grade certificate."

Nadine started to object, but Mom broke in again. "So, I asked Effie if she could use you in the bakery. She said she couldn't right now because business is slow and won't pick up again until Thanksgiving and Christmas." Mom pulled out her handkerchief and blew her nose. "Effie knew that Mr. Stone had lost a clerk in his store, and you can have a position there."

Nadine felt her fingers tighten around the brush. She pursed her lips to speak, but did not. Mom had always been so good to her, raising her as her own. How could she be a burden now when she was having such a difficult time just functioning herself? However, the thought ran through her head that LeRoy had a hand in this decision. He turned on his charm with Mom and just as quickly turned it off with Frances, Nadine and most certainly Henry.

There was silence broken by Mom's blowing her nose again.

"You will begin working a week from tomorrow."

"That sounds exciting," Nadine managed to force out. "I'll go by this week and speak to Mr. Stone and of course thank Effie for her finding me a job." She could tell by the look on Mom's face that she was pleased with Nadine's receptiveness to this idea.

Nadine kept brushing, trying to think of the positive aspects. It would be a new experience, she would meet new people and have money of her own. She remembered, with a smile, getting paid for finding chicken eggs laid among the bushes and in the yard at the farm. That seemed long long ago. It had made her feel grown-up, earning money for the chicken eggs, and this would too. Anxiety returned, however, when she thought of telling Buddy that she wouldn't be joining her in high school.

*　　*　　*

Stones sold just about everything except groceries. She was quick to catch on. Having been raised on a farm and on the river, she knew a lot about planting, seeds, tools, fishing, and animal husbandry. What she didn't know about planting, she searched out in the *Farmers Almanac* which had been Mom and Pop's "Bible" for farming. After supper, she went to her room and read the Almanac, so she could answer farmers' questions. They learned to respect her knowledge. She also discovered she had an artistic knack in the way she displayed merchandise to catch the customers' eye. The front window was the most fun to decorate.

At Christmas, she made a make believe fireplace out of discarded boxes that she painted brick red. Then she sneaked a pair of Pop's long red underwear and a pair of his rubber high top galoshes. She stuffed the red underwear until it looked fat and placed the galoshes where the feet should be. The finished product was a look alike Santa down on his knees looking up the chimney with only his shoulders and below exposed. The children gathered around the window and looked at Santa with glee. Even the adults liked the window display. Of course Mr. Stone was pleased with the attention his store was getting which increased business. Gradually he gave Nadine more and more responsibility. Every once in a while he took a day off, leaving her in charge.

On one of these days Mr. Turley, a raw boned man with a ruddy complexion from working outside, came in to get supplies. With everything bagged up and paid for, he started out the door, and then with a snap of his fingers, turned, "I plumb forgot. I meant to pick up some Spanish Fly."

Nadine didn't have the slightest idea what Spanish Fly was, but her pride would not allow her to admit ignorance. She decided it must be some type of fishing lure. In box after box she hunted for the label. Time went by, "Its got to be here someplace, I'm sure," she apologized. Looking up she saw a mischievous smile on Mr. Turley's face. "That's okay. I'll pick it up next week when I'm back in town," he said backing out the door.

"Mean time, I'll keep looking here among the fishing tackle. If I don't find it, I'll certainly order it."

"Right," he tipped his hat with a sparkle in his eyes.

The next day, Mr. Stone, looking over his spectacles, inquired, as he always did, "How did everything go, Nadine?"

"Fine, except a customer was wanting Spanish Fly. I looked all through the fishing tackle to no avail."

Mr. Stone flushed said, "Who ordered that?"

"Mr. Turley was in from up on Brown's Creek. I must have spent a half hour looking while he stood there smiling. At least he didn't get mad," she shrugged.

Mr. Stone, still flushed said, "Indeed he shouldn't. He was having some fun with you, and I don't appreciate his lack of respect."

"What are you talking about?" Nadine's eyebrows raised.

"Spanish Fly ain't fishing tackle, and he darn well knew it."

"What is it then?"

"Well its for horses, cattle and such."

"Horses and cattle," she repeated. "You mean like feed?"

"No, not exactly."

"What for then?"

He averted her stare, "Well uh, yes," he stuttered, starting toward the back of the store.

Following him, she said, "He'll be back next Saturday. I need to know what it is for to find it."

"It's, well it's to make animals horny, some believe." He bit his lips. Why on earth had he said that?

"Horny?" Nadine repeated never having heard the word. Cows have horns but horses?

"Yes, yes, oh well, for breeding purposes," Mr. Stone tried to erase his previous statement. "And Mr. Turley must have gotten a kick out of your spending a half hour looking in the fishing tackle. I just don't appreciate that one little bit."

Nadine got busy dusting to avoid showing her embarrassment. After all, Mom said young ladies never talked about such topics in mixed company, and in fact very little at all, except for birthing babies and then only with women.

*   *   *

The clouds rolled over the sun and there was a softly falling snow as Nadine walked home from work. She wrapped her scarf tighter around her neck and jabbed her hands deep into her coat pockets to ward off the cold. It was past supper. She walked fast, so Frances wouldn't have to eat too late, and the food would still be warm. As her mind was going over the things she had to do at work the next day, she automatically turned off Smoky Road onto the walk leading to her home.

Right before reaching the front porch, the cold seemed to intensify, and she felt something lightly touch her ankle as it passed. She looked over her shoulder, catching a glimpse of a young woman wearing what appeared to be an 1860s-style dress with a hoop skirt. The top was indigo blue and the bottom was a blue, green and black plaid. She wore no coat or hat, and her honey colored hair hung loosely around her shoulders.

Hanging her coat and scarf on the hall tree, the only sound Nadine heard in the house was the ticking of the grandfather clock. She walked past the master bedroom where Mom was rocking and looking out the window. The light in the room was the dim light coming through the window. Nadine went in and gave Mom a hug, feeling her warm body against hers. "Did you have a good day, Mom?"

"Yes, I love watching the snow fall. They say no two snow flakes are exactly alike; you know." Mom nodded her head, agreeing with her own words. "Oh, well, you better take Frances her supper. She does look forward to your time together when you relate your day at work. It's getting harder for me to make it up and down those stairs, and you know how men are. When LeRoy takes it up, he just sits it down and leaves."

Nadine started out the door but stopped abruptly. "Did you enjoy your company today?"

"I didn't have any company today," she answered with a start.

"But a young lady dressed in an old fashioned dress passed me when I was coming in just now. I thought," Nadine began but did not continue, noticing Mom's frown wrinkles deepen as she twisted a loose thread on her shawl. Recognizing that Nadine watched her, she shrugged her shoulders as if to say, I don't know what you are talking about.

After visiting with Frances, Nadine walked out on the upstairs porch to throw leftover bread crumbs onto the front walk, so the birds could see them. She heard the crunch of snow beneath her feet and felt the wind on her cheeks. *Frances eats less and less*, she thought. Maybe she misses Mom's cooking. I certainly do. Frances now walked with a shuffle and stooped shoulders. Hard to believe she and Mom were both in their seventies. Nadine felt a catch in her throat at this thought? It was growing dark and colder. Nadine turned quickly to go inside as a chill ran through her, making her shiver. It was then that she caught sight of her set of footprints in the snow coming in but none leading out from the house. That night, she awakened with the image of her single set of footprints outlined by the snow. She reasoned that the wind must have covered the other set. But then Mom said she had no company.

Nadine got up and went to the porch again, looking out at eye level at the black lacy tree limbs and then down. Now there were no prints. A hoot owl hooted, but Dutch did not bark, because Henry now kept him inside for fear that LeRoy might harm him. She gathered her blanket about her and ran back to her bed. Warmth returned, sleep came, but it was a troubled sleep.

About two weeks later and an hour later in the day, Nadine hurried from work down Smoky Road. Thanksgiving had just passed. Again she was planning in her head. This time, her thoughts were on an original idea for decorating the store for Christmas. Nadine's decorations had become so popular that the townsfolk made a point of taking out-of-town visitors to see what she had put in the windows now.

Walking down the front walk to her home, a movement at the upstairs window caught her attention. There silhouetted in the window, peeping between the lace curtain was the young woman with honey blonde hair. This time she wore an old fashioned white dress. Their eyes fastened, and she did not look away but looked directly into Nadine's eyes. *She looks so sad*, Nadine thought as she quickened her steps, running into the house and up the stairs. When she reached the window, the hall was empty, but a chill lingered.

Something prohibited Nadine from mentioning this to anyone. Mom had became so tense when she mentioned it the last time, Frances wouldn't know what she was talking about; nor Henry who was so angry with LeRoy that he stayed in an agitated state. LeRoy would love to think she was losing her mind. He had already convinced the neighbors that Henry was losing it. Now he could add her to his list. So even though shaken by the experiences, she went about her nightly routine, waiting for someone else to mention something.

*   *   *

Nadine heard the stairs creak as someone came up them, but she was reading and didn't check to see who it was. There was a tap on her bedroom door. Opening it, she was surprised to find Mom because she didn't come upstairs often anymore. "One of the "itis" boys is bothering me today," she would say. She made reference to arthritis, bronchitis, and bursitis, but in her case arthritis.

"We need to talk awhile," Mom began after they seated themselves on the bed. She pushed a strand of hair off of Nadine's forehead then took both of Nadine's hands into her own. She swallowed then spoke, "I'm worried about your coming in from work so late in the evening. It's sometimes dark when you get home."

"Well, I have to close the store, and the days are shorter."

"I know, I know," Mom nodded her head. "Then you have prayer meeting on Wednesdays and choir on Thursdays." Mom patted her hand.

Nadine had no idea where this conversation was going. "I'm not afraid to walk in the dark if that's what worries you."

"That is part of it, I guess. Your lack of fear and cautiousness comes from being young. There is harm that can come to a young girl, walking alone in the dark; you know?"

Nadine's voice went up an octave. "Here in St. Albans? Never."

"You walk across the railroad bridge, coming over Coal River.

Do you know that is where a past owner of this very house, John Hansford, was hit by a train? He managed to drag himself into this house, dying in the downstairs hall."

"Yes, Pop told me, but I figure he must have been drunk to stumble out in front of a train on the bridge or deaf, not hearing the train's whistle. I can hear and I don't drink," Nadine said emphatically crossing her arms.

"Now don't get snippy with me or disrespectful of the dead," warned Mom. "LeRoy tells me that hobos are sleeping up under the railroad bridge lately."

"I know that. They bathe and wash their clothes in the river and cook up the best smelling stew." She was dying to say it sure smells better than what LeRoy cooks, but she minded her tongue since she'd already been warned not to be snippy. "Lillian's dad, Charley Miller, gives them soup bones and such from his meat market."

Mom leaned closer, "How do you know all this?"

"Lillian told me about the meat."

"And," Mom turned Nadine's chin, so they were looking in each others eyes.

"And, I talk to them sometimes. They wouldn't harm a fly."

Nadine bit her lip, waiting for Mom to give the actual reason for her coming to her room.

There was a long pause as Mom had a flash back to the first time she had seen Nadine at age four, seated by her Aunt Vonzine on the train, taking her to the Davis Child Shelter. She had fallen in love with the little girl with long auburn curls and green eyes flecked with gold, holding the white muff. Her eyes misted at the thought of how much she had grown to love her, and what she must do and say next. Everything is passing, for everything there is a season and that season has passed, she thought with regret.

Clasping her fingers together, she spoke what she had come to say, "LeRoy and I are concerned about your safety. So I have made arrangements for you to board with your dad's brother Frank and his wife Amanda. You've met their daughter Molly in choir, no doubt."

Nadine's heart beat in her throat. She couldn't believe her ears. She wanted to scream. LeRoy doesn't give a snip about me. He just wants me out of the way, but she said nothing.

Mom felt guilty because she saw tears in Nadine's eyes, yet she knew she was doing the right thing for safety. Nadine was the only person who brought life into the house. It was going to be lonely and lifeless now. She swallowed hard.

"But I'll miss you, Frances, Henry and Dutch." She didn't mention LeRoy whom she disliked and distrusted. Maybe she was just jealous of him?

Mom patted the blanket, "We'll miss you too, but you can phone me. I have a phone by my bed, and you can visit on the weekends."

Nadine could not answer. The hurt, anger and disbelief knotted in her stomach. Only a deep sigh escaped her lips.

Mom hugged Nadine quickly, turned and switched off the bedroom light, so Nadine could not see the emotion in her face, nor could she in Nadine's. "You better get to bed child. You have to work tomorrow. We'll pack your things Saturday." Her voice cracked at these words. She walked out and closed the door.

Nadine put her hands behind her head and gazed at the ceiling, listening to the creak of the stairs as Mom descended at a slow pace, step by step. Frances' knock came on the wall, and Nadine reciprocated. The only sound now was the tick of the hall clock. *What will happen to Frances? She'll be even more isolated*, Nadine worried.

*   *   *

Buddy missed Nadine's living across the river from her, and she knew Aunt Liz missed her too. Buddy dropped by sometimes after school. More and more frequently, LeRoy met her at the door to say that Aunt Liz was sleeping and could not be disturbed.

However, one day as she and Aunt Liz passed the time of day, Buddy heard someone on the other side of the wall where the fireplace was, raking the coals and making a loud clatter. Darkness was falling, and with the only light coming from outside, shadows began to intrude upon the room where they sat. At first Buddy ignored the sound as did Aunt Liz. Then she saw LeRoy on the front porch, yet the clanking continued.

"Is that Henry, Aunt Liz?"

"No," she responded with a blank stare as she nervously reached up to massage her temples. "No, no, Henry doesn't live here anymore. LeRoy sent him away; you know."

Buddy, with a start at these words ceased speaking for a moment to gather her thoughts. "What do you mean LeRoy sent him away? Where?"

Aunt Liz whet her lips before speaking, "Henry became down right abusive to LeRoy and finally physically attacked him. On top of that, LeRoy had complaints of Henry's making a nuisance in the neighborhood, walking the streets mumbling to himself. People were afraid of him." Liz paused then continued. "LeRoy feared he would do me harm next."

Buddy leaned over into Aunt Liz's face, "But where is he? Where did LeRoy send him?"

"He made arrangements for Henry at the mental hospital at Weston."

"Does Nadine know?"

"No, I haven't had a chance to tell her."

Again there was a loud clatter in the fireplace. "Do you have company, Aunt Liz?"

"You!"

"No, beside me. Who is making the noise?"

Liz massaged her temples again and began to rock, averting Buddy's eyes. "Oh, that is the woman who comes in and fusses at me all the time."

"Fusses at you?"

"Yes," Aunt Liz nodded.

"Who is she?"

Liz shrugged her shoulder and flung up her hands as if to say, "I don't know."

There was a tap at the door, and before anyone could answer, LeRoy stepped in. "Mrs. Taylor, you look so tired and weary."

Liz nodded.

LeRoy turned to Buddy, "It's coming on dark. It's not safe for young ladies to be walking alone this late in the evening."

"I'm just leaving." Buddy walked over and hugged Aunt Liz.

Liz patted her shoulder, "Come back soon. The days are long without Nadine."

LeRoy began turning the covers down on her bed.

Buddy walked out into the hall. When she heard LeRoy's cajoling tone directed at Aunt Liz, she stepped into the kitchen. It was empty.

I can't believe they've institutionalized poor Henry. Nadine needs to be told. She'll be so upset. I can't tell her over the phone. And, I have to tell her about Aunt Liz's saying there is a woman who quarrels with her, Buddy thought as she attempted to shake off the feeling of uneasiness. She also tried to think of an adult whom she could trust to share her concerns with. Who might know what was going on at Aunt Liz's? Aunt Ada was her answer. *She knows everything that is happening.*

*   *   *

Aunt Ada had squeezed lemons for her delicious tangy lemonade and was chipping ice to put in glasses for Nadine, Buddy and herself when the doorbell rang. Wiping her hands on her white apron, she opened the door for the two girls. She was flattered when young ladies came to call. It made her feel young again. Besides, the young knew gossip that her older friends did not. After hugging them both, she suggested that they all sit on the porch, and she would bring out the lemonade.

After a few minutes of conversation about the weather and how Nadine liked her new living arrangements, Buddy steered the conversation to her latest visit with Aunt Liz. While I was there, "I kept hearing movement around the fireplace."

"What kind of noise?" Nadine put her lemonade down.

"Clanking as if someone was building or banking a fire."

"Must have been LeRoy," Nadine suggested.

"No, he was on the front porch. I could see him."

"Henry doesn't come into the main house much, but it could have been him," Nadine said.

Buddy shot Ada a look, and they both understood not to broach that subject yet. "No, after pressing Aunt Liz, she said there was a woman who comes in and quarrels with her." Buddy rushed on, "After LeRoy practically asked me to leave, and I knew he was occupied with Aunt Liz, I tiptoed into the kitchen and there was no one there."

"LeRoy is down right rude," Nadine interjected.

"Now don't be hard on LeRoy," said Aunt Ada. "We're fortunate that he cares for Liz. Poor thing never has snapped back from Mr. Taylor's accident. I guess it's her age. None of us are getting any younger." Her glance down at her hands' protruding blue veins confirmed this.

Nadine rolled her eyes at Buddy because they both disliked LeRoy. However, she made no comment. LeRoy seemed to have mesmerized all of the adults, except Henry of course.

Nadine's thoughts drifted back to the first spooky occurrence in the house that she witnessed. "Buddy, do you remember one night when you stayed over, and the light in the upstairs hall came off and on?"

"Yes, I joked that it must be your angel."

"Well, other spooky things happened around the house."

Ada tilted her head and listened but said nothing.

Buddy felt a tingle up her spine, and she moved to the edge of her seat. Nadine related her encounter with the young woman dressed in the style of the 1860s on the sidewalk and then her watching Nadine from the upstairs window.

"What did she look like besides her dress?"

"She is thin with honey blond hair, flowing loosely around her shoulders." Nadine stopped and then added, "She looked real sad."

"And she touched you? Oh, my gosh!" Buddy did an exaggerated shiver.

"Her hoop skirt just brushed my ankle!"

"I think it must be the same person, or ghost?" Buddy self corrected.

Nadine and Buddy turned to Ada, "Do you believe in ghosts?"

Ada flushed because it was not an accepted idea by many, but it was a direct question which could not be avoided. "Often when there has been an untimely death, sightings of ghosts have been reported, and by very respected people, I might add." Her voice raised, "Heaven only knows there certainly have been untimely deaths in Liz's house."

"Really?" Buddy's eyes opened wider.

"Indeed there is a blood stain in the entry hall. Some say a Civil War soldier died there. John Hansford was hit by a train and died in the same spot as the blood stain. Then your Pop," Ada turned to Nadine. She started to continue but abruptly stopped.

"Those were all men. Nadine says that this was a young woman."

"Yes, yes, I've heard about the young woman also, roaming about the house."

"Who is she?"

Ada took a sip of her lemonade. "Some say it is a past owner's daughter."

"Did she have an untimely death also?" Nadine wondered why Ada did not include her in the list.

"I guess you could say that. It was during the Civil War." Ada stopped to gather her thoughts. "She was a beautiful young woman, fair with complexion as smooth as a white rose petal. They say she was as pretty inside as out, always kind. The slaves loved her as did everybody. Well, it seems she was engaged to be married to a Confederate soldier who was killed in battle."

"Did she marry anybody else?" Nadine asked anxious to get all the details and relieved that she was not the only one to see this young woman.

"No, no, she went into seclusion and deep depression. Just withdrew from the world, staying in her room, refusing food."

"I bet it was the front bedroom where she stands and watches through the window," Nadine said.

"Now that you mention it, I believe it was." Ada nodded her head and took another sip of lemonade before continuing. "Well, anyway, she just pined away, dying of a broken heart so they say."

"No wonder she looked sad," interjected Buddy.

"Um, and I bet that white dress that she wore the last time that I saw her was to be her wedding dress."

Ada leaned over, placing her finger to her lips. "Now I'll have to swear you two to secrecy about this story and the ghost and all."

"Why, I know she is there. I saw her with my very own eyes." Nadine motioned toward her eyes. "Evidently others have too."

"I saw the lights going off and on for no apparent reason and heard the noise in the kitchen fireplace. That's for sure," seconded Buddy.

"That might be," agreed Ada, "but some won't believe in ghosts, thinking you are hallucinating, or your imagination is out of control. Also, Liz might need to sell the house someday. Some people would hesitate to buy a haunted house. So cross your heart." Ada made the symbol of the cross on her chest.

"Cross our hearts and hope to die," Buddy and Nadine chanted in unison.

Nadine smiled to herself, after doing the pledge, remembering that was what they did as children. Here was a grown woman joining in. Aunt Ada had always been fun. Nadine recalled that it was Aunt Ada who taught her to peel a potato without breaking the peel and to toss it over her shoulder. The alphabet letter that the peel formed was the first or last initial of the person you would marry. I'll have to try that, thought Nadine with anticipation.

"You girls stay here while I freshen up your lemonade. Your ice has melted." She turned to Nadine. "I have something else to discuss." In a few minutes, she was back with refills. This time she did not sit but stood by the porch banister. Absent-mindedly she plucked off a dried bloom from a geranium growing nearby. Then she turned again, facing Nadine.

Buddy began to fidget realizing what was to follow. She wished she could leave, but she was Nadine's friend. She must stay.

"When did you last talk to Liz, Nadine?"

"Oh, a couple of nights ago but not for long. Something seemed to occupy her mind, or she was tired or something. Come to think of it, it seems like I did all the talking to keep the conversation going. By the time I close the store and eat supper, it's near her bedtime." Nadine felt guilty at the fact that she had not visited for over two weeks.

"Aunt Liz does seem to be going to bed earlier and earlier."

Buddy offered in defense of Nadine. "Besides it is so gloomy there anymore." she added.

"I believe she's depressed. That will make one feel tired," agreed Ada. She bit her bottom lip and got to her point. "Nadine, nothing stays the same. I often wonder how people get bored because life's situations keep changing. Just aging, can bring change and death."

"You don't have to explain that to me, Aunt Ada. I am a walking example of how situations change lives. I never imagined I'd be living with my Uncle Frank and Aunt Mandy."

"I know, Child. You have definitely been shuffled about in your life. Yes," she nodded emphatically, "you are indeed a survivor, adjusting to what life has thrown at you." Aunt Ada fingered the dead geranium bloom that she held. The dried brown petals floated to the porch floor. "Well, when you visit your mom, Henry won't be there."

Nadine bolted from her chair, knocking over her glass of lemonade. "Where is he?"

Ada, now facing Nadine at eye level, did not attempt to clean up the liquid which slowly spread outward across the porch. "He has been institutionalized."

"Institutionalized," Nadine mouthed. Then she blurted out, "Not the poor farm, please no, he hated it."

"No, the mental institution at Weston."

Buddy sat motionless and saddened, witnessing her dear friend's mental anguish.

Nadine stepped back. She turned pale and her lip trembled as her hand kept wiping at her eyes and nose. "Why, why?" Then Nadine's thoughts turned to LeRoy. "LeRoy did it; didn't he? He hated Henry and wanted him out of the way." Her hands now wadded into fists as she cried out, "And, how could Mom allow this to happen to poor old Henry? I just don't understand. How could anyone be so cruel?"

"Stop it, Nadine. Just quiet down and get hold of yourself."

Ada took Nadine by the elbow and seated her in the swing. Nadine just sat there limp as a rag doll, feeling so helpless.

"Liz spoke to me about this. She is as upset as you are. Even more, she had to make the decision. Henry just lost it after Mr. Taylor died. The neighbors were afraid of him, and he physically attacked LeRoy. You can't have a man like that wandering the streets."

"Henry had reason to attack him. Henry feared being turned out, and LeRoy taunted him about it. Besides he kicked Dutch, and Henry was not going to allow that. Nobody knows. I lived there. I saw. Is everybody blind? He's evil."

"Nonsense Nadine. I've never heard such foolishness," Ada's voice raised.

Nadine remained quiet for a moment then looked at Buddy and mouthed the word, "evil."

"Nadine, here take a sip of my lemonade and swallow slowly."

Ada smoothed Nadine's hair, trying to calm her as they swung gently. Nadine began sobbing.

"Don't come down so hard on LeRoy. He just came to the family at an inopportune time for himself but to our advantage because he cares for Liz. Try to look at it from his point of view. He has his hands full with Frances, a seventy some year old woman with a mind of a child; Henry, a simple minded old man; and Liz, old herself and depressed. I don't know why he just doesn't pack up and leave. Then look at what a fix we would be in."

Nadine's face reddend, "You forgot to add orphan to your list of dependents upon Mom and LeRoy, but he got rid of me first."

Ada's chin jerked forward, "Nadine, how could you think such a thing? The Taylor's love you as if you were their own." Ada shook her finger at Nadine. "Well, if Liz were selfish, she would keep you there to help with Frances. She is thinking of you and your safety, Child."

And LeRoy is thinking of the money, Nadine thought but didn't say. "Henry might be simpleminded as you say, but he is loyal, honest, hard working, and he was fine before LeRoy came."

*   *   *

When Nadine called Mom in the evenings, LeRoy answered, "I'm sorry she is sleeping and cannot be disturbed." This was his pat answer, making her more determined to see Mom. On Sunday afternoon, she made a visit. She glanced at the front bedroom window as she went up the walk to see if the ghost of the young woman was watching her. She saw no one but did notice the lace curtain appear to be pulled apart and quickly pulled together again.

As she entered the hall, Leroy was coming from Mom's room. "Well Nadine, fancy seeing you here," he said nervously, having been caught off guard. "I am afraid you've come at a bad time. Mrs. Taylor is taking her afternoon nap."

"Then I'll just go visit Frances." She refused to be sent away. Starting up the steps, she glanced back into Mom's room.

She was shocked to see that the chubbiness was gone from Mom's face, making her cheekbones appear sharp and her nose more prominent. Her hair now almost white flared out around her head like a halo on the pillow. There was something missing in the room, but Nadine did not stop to figure it out because she felt Leroy's gaze upon her as she hurried on up the stairs.

She tapped on Frances' door and then stepped in. Frances jumped from her chair beside the window and ran to fling her arms about Nadine's neck. "Oh, Nadine, I'm happy to see you. Come sit a spell." She motioned to the other chair in the room.

Nadine did so as she took inventory of the room, noting Frances' half eaten breakfast was still on the nightstand. Mom no longer plaited her hair for her. Frances attempted it, missing strands which hung loosely in her face. Her dress needed to be laundered also. Frances looked a mess.

"Get a comb Frances and let me braid your hair." Frances quickly complied, as always, wanting to please. She sat with her bony hands folded in her lap.

"Tell me about your new life," coaxed Frances.

"First Frances, I noticed you ate only half of your breakfast."

"LeRoy can't cook. The food is awful." She shook her head in disgust.

Nadine fished down in her purse and pulled out the bag of chocolates that she bought Frances. "I hesitate to give these to you since you haven't eaten all of your breakfast. Where is your lunch plate?"

"Sometimes LeRoy forgets meals, but that's okay because they're bad, bad, bad." Frances sat, eyeing the chocolates.

When Nadine gave them to her, she began cramming them into her mouth until her cheeks looked like a squirrel with jaws full of acorns. "Stop, Frances. Eat one at a time, or you'll choke." Frances began chewing slowly as requested, licking off the excess chocolate from her fingers. "Okay, Frances, that is better."

Nadine talked as she braided Frances' hair. "To answer your question, Frances, Aunt Mandy is a heavy set woman and wears glasses. She is a wonderful cook." Nadine felt guilty as soon as that was out of her mouth, since LeRoy was such a poor one.

"Anyway, she is very good to me. She also takes in other boarders. There are two engineers who are planning the bridge which will cross the Kanawha River, connecting Nitro and St. Albans." Nadine stopped braiding to think about that. "Can you imagine a bridge and no more ferry?"

"How about Aunt Mandy's husband?"

"He's my dad's brother. He's blind. He used to be a painter; you know. His being blind is why they take in boarders.

He mostly stays in his room except when he comes to the table to eat. Then there is their daughter, Molly. She's so pretty, but she works on that a lot." Nadine hesitated and then continued, "It pays off. She has all kinds of beaus."

"Do you have a beau?"

"Not yet." Nadine giggled. "The preacher made a joke about that, saying he saw me, looking down a manhole for a man."

Frances turned her head, "Is that true?"

"Turn back around, so your braids will be even. No, he was just kidding, silly. On second thought, I do have a young man who pays me a lot of attention." She handed Frances a mirror, so she could see her improved appearance.

Frances stroked her braids. Seeing her reflection, a big smile crept over her face. Then she turned to Nadine. "What's the boy's name?"

"Henry, but I don't think he is suitable."

"Why not?"

"When he visits Aunt Mandy, he brings me an O'Henry candy bar."

"What's wrong with that?"

Nadine walked to the closet to select a clean dress for Frances. "I think he is self-centered." There was a pause as she tried to decide between the red dress or plaid. "I think by him always bringing an O'Henry shows he's self-centered. Ruth is my middle name. Why doesn't he bring a Baby Ruth? Which dress do you want?"

"The red," Frances pointed.

"Okay, now you get washed up, and I'll take your dirty dress home to wash and iron." Nadine folded it and put it in a bag.

When Frances was squeaky clean, she looked much better, but even the braids and red dress did not conceal her frailty. Nadine gave Frances a kiss as she was leaving.

"You come back soon?"

"I will, I have your dress, remember?" Turning to close Frances' door, she saw Frances still standing with outstretched arms. Nadine smiled and gave a wave goodbye.

Going downstairs, she saw LeRoy posted at Mom's door like a guard. It then hit Nadine what was missing from Mom's room. "LeRoy, where is the telephone that was in Mom's room?"

"I had it moved to my room, so it wouldn't disturb Mrs. Taylor."

"But she enjoyed me calling as well as Ada and Effie and her other friends."

His eyebrows arched and his jaw tightened. "Talking wears her out. Every time she tried to take a nap the phone rang."

"I think she naps too much. She needs to get up and move to exercise her muscles, or she'll become a blob of jelly," Nadine flushed as she spoke.

"Have you gotten a medical degree so soon after leaving this house?" The veins in his temples began to protrude.

Ignoring his last statement, Nadine decided while she was having her say that she would mention Frances' plight. "Frances says you forget to bring meals to her."

"She doesn't eat what I bring. Are you her doctor too? It is easy for you to come once or twice a month and start criticizing. Besides Frances is old and has a mind of a child. You can't believe everything she says."

Guilt seized Nadine. She pursed her lips to defend herself but thought better and left the house.

*   *   *

Following her visit home, Nadine stayed busy in an attempt to ward off thoughts of Frances. But when she least expected it, the image of Frances standing in her dreary bedroom with her arms outstretched, invaded Nadine's mind. More than once she envisioned Frances' gobbling the chocolates, and awakened in the night hearing Frances' words. "Sometimes LeRoy forgets meals, but that's okay because they're bad, bad, bad."

Three days later Nadine was restocking shelves when she heard the phone ring and Mr. Stone answer, "Just a minute, Ada, I'll get her. Nadine, it's Ada here?"

Nadine answered and something in Ada's voice warned of bad news. "Nadine, I wanted to be the one to tell you that Frances passed away during the night." Nadine said nothing and heard only her heart thumping in her chest. "Nadine, are you there?"

"Yes," she said softly.

"We must have a bad connection. I can hardly hear you, Child. Anyway, Liz asked if you, LeRoy and I would make the funeral arrangements." Ada heard a sound like a catch in Nadine's throat. "Nadine, Frances is in heaven with the Lord and is better off."

Nadine swallowed to moisten her throat, "How did she die?"

LeRoy said when he took her breakfast this morning that he found her dead. She must have passed in her sleep very peacefully. She was nearing eighty you know. She went to sleep and woke up in heaven. That's how we all hope to go."

Nadine closed her eyes and the image of Frances in her red dress, outstretched arms and white braids hanging down her back came into her mind once again. "Well, I guess LeRoy will be happy."

"What do you mean, Nadine?"

"He won't have to climb those steps with her meals."

"Nadine now don't be throwing off on LeRoy. I know you're upset because you loved Frances as we all did, but LeRoy is young and not related by blood. He is good to stay and care for Liz at all." Ada's voice became firm as did all adults when they defended LeRoy.

Nadine felt numb and didn't want to hear about LeRoy's sacrifices, so they made arrangements to meet at the funeral home.

Nadine got there first and waited on the porch. She had to smile, watching Ada coming up the sidewalk. Spying a blade of grass pushing its way through a crack in the walk, Ada leaned over to pluck it up and cast it aside. *Ada takes care of everybody's property it seems*, Nadine thought.

They both waited on LeRoy who pulled up in a cab. He got out and then stuck his head through the open cab window to arrange to be picked up later.

Nadine said quietly, "He must have money to burn, riding in a cab this short distance."

Ada gave Nadine a look of warning. "Well, hello LeRoy," she said, waving her white gloved hand in the air.

"Well Miss Ada, you look especially nice today, but then you always do." He lifted her hand and gave it a gentle brush of his lips. Ada smiled all over herself, receiving the attention of this young handsome man. She almost forgot why they were there until LeRoy glanced at his watch.

"We best be about our business. I can't leave Mrs. Taylor too long." He then remembered to nod at Nadine.

As the plans proceeded, LeRoy raised several objections to Nadine's suggestions. "Costs need to be kept down, he argued."

Ada, under his spell, nodded her head.

This infuriated Nadine. She felt ashamed arguing over money when it came to poor Frances' funeral. LeRoy reminded her of Judas, who Mrs. Reynolds said, quarreled about wasting ointment on Jesus' feet instead of giving money from its sale to the poor when he himself was a thief.

Frances was buried in the Allen plot in Teays Hill Cemetery. As Nadine hung her best dress that she had worn to the funeral in her closet, Frances' freshly laundered dress came into view. Nadine pulled it to her face for comfort and let her tears flow into its fabric. Aunt Mandy stuck her head around the door frame, "Are you all right, Nadine?"

"Yes, thank you," but she did not turn to face her aunt.

*   *   *

Nadine, from the musty smelling stockroom, heard the bell when the door opened and shut, and then garden tools being moved about. Resenting being interrupted from inventorying, which Mr. Stone needed finished by the end of the day, she pushed a strand of hair off of her forehead and walked toward the front counter. From this vantage point, she saw a young man about her age. He was intent upon examining the tools, not turning to look at her.

She was struck by how neatly he was groomed with his sandy colored hair slicked straight back. He wore a white starched shirt and tie with a pullover sweater and freshly pressed dress trousers. Plus his fingernails were clean. He certainly didn't look like the other young men who shopped here.

He turned abruptly in her direction, catching her staring at him. She quickly shifted her gaze to the counter top, feeling a blush come to her face. "May I help you?"

"Are these the best tools you have?"

When she looked up to answer, "Yes," he looked at her with a clear open gaze. She noted his soft brown eyes. He smiled as their eyes met.

Nadine managed to say, "I haven't seen you around here before."

"No, I usually shop in Hurricane. My dad and mom own a farm about five miles from there." He ran the palm of his hand across the edge of the hoe. "Just thought I might get a better deal here."

"My brother lives in Putnam County, Winfield that is." Nadine could still feel her face redden. *That's the problem of being a redhead*, she thought. *The blush always shows.* Trying to conceal her nervousness, she rattled on, "His name is Carl Miller. Do you know him?"

"Indeed I do." His smile broadened making creases around his eyes. "I guess you could say we're pretty good friends. Being Winfield is the county seat, Pop and I go there on business ever so often. Never knew Carl had a sister, but I can see a definite family resemblance."

The thought that he didn't know Carl even had a sister brought a sting to her heart, but that he recognized that they looked alike made the sting fade quickly.

As Nadine made change from his purchases, her hand brushed his. She felt warmth but also calluses from hard work.

The bell rang as he left the store, but almost immediately,sounded again. The young man stuck his head through the open door, "By the way, my name is Vinson Erwin. I didn't catch yours."

"Nadine, Nadine Miller," she answered, hearing her voice crack.

*   *   *

Early the next morning, Nadine heard Aunt Mandy in the kitchen, scurrying around. It was the first Saturday that Nadine had off in over a month, and she hoped to sleep in, but the smell of fresh coffee brewing could not be resisted. Swinging her legs over the edge of the bed, she slipped her feet into her slippers and pulled her robe around her.

Aunt Mandy began apologizing as soon as she looked up and saw Nadine yawning. "I'm sorry to be up and about so early on your day off, but I have to prepare food for today's croquet game.

Molly invited some of her young friends over, remember?" Aunt Mandy took her glasses off and cleaned them on the edge of her floral dress. "What can I fix you for breakfast?"

"Don't worry, I can get it myself." Nadine buttered two slices of bread, lit the oven and placed the buttered slices in to toast as she went to the refrigerator to get the dark red homemade apple butter. She breathed deeply to smell the blend of cinnamon and cloves as she removed the lid.

Eating her toast and apple butter, Nadine caught sight of Molly through the window, setting up the croquet set on the wide flat side yard. "As soon as I finish eating, I'll help you with those cucumber sandwiches, Aunt Mandy."

Esther was the first guest to arrive. She wore her black hair in a short, fashionable bob. Now that they were older, Nadine and Esther's age difference didn't seem to make much difference. They had become closer, singing in the church choir.

Pulling Nadine to the side, Esther whispered, "Did you know your father remarried?"

Nadine shook her head.

"Well, after I don't know how many years, he has." She rushed on as other guests began to arrive. "Anyway, Uncle Phil is bringing his new wife Essie to St. Albans to meet his family. He'll be staying at our house. He wants to meet you, Nadine."

Nadine did not speak. Her first emotion was elation, but then panic swept through her, fearing her father's rejection. In all the years he hadn't even tried to make contact.

Esther touched Nadine's shoulder, "Nadine, I thought you would be happy. Say something."

"I've dreamed of meeting my father. Now that it is a realization, I'm scared."

Esther placed her hands on her hips, "What on earth of?"

Nadine stared at the floor, "What if I'm not good enough?"

"He left you, Nadine. You didn't leave him. The question is, is he good enough?" Esther patted Nadine's shoulder again.

"Now let's enjoy the party." She took Nadine's elbow and pulled her onto the porch.

The grass had just been mowed for the party. Nadine breathed in its sweet smell and was drawn into the activity by the excited voices and the sound of wood hitting wood as the mallets made contact with the balls.

Buddy was the last to arrive. Her breath was heavy from running most of the way in an attempt not to be late. Aunt Mandy was quick to notice and offered her ice tea with a slice of lemon.

Nadine walked up beside her. "It's about time you got here. Where have you been?"

"I'll tell you later. Let's get into the game." She placed her glass on the table laden with fried chicken, finger sandwiches and Aunt Mandy's famous coconut cake. Wiping her hands on her skirt, she joined the game.

"Buddy, I've got some exciting news to tell you after the party. I guess it will wait." As the party proceeded, Nadine appreciated Aunt Mandy and Molly's inviting her friend. Buddy fit right in and was in fact an accomplished croquet player.

Following the party, Buddy and Nadine helped scrape plates of their few remaining morsels of food and folded the tables and chairs borrowed from the funeral home, leaning them against the porch to be picked up later. Molly and Esther were busy putting the game away when Aunt Mandy said, "I'll clean up the rest. Go on and have fun," shooing them with her dishcloth. "It won't take me any time to do up these dishes." Further persuasion was unnecessary.

"I'll walk you halfway home, Buddy. I've got news." Nadine gave Buddy's hand a squeeze.

"Okay, okay, let's hear it."

"My very own father is coming back to St. Albans to visit his family, staying at Uncle Lucian's and Aunt Emma's. You know, Esther's dad and mom. And guess what! He wants to meet me. Can you believe it?"

Buddy's reaction surprised Nadine. "I've never understood why you've been anxious to meet a man who abandoned you. I can remember your going to the showboat with the sole hope that your dad would be a member of the band, and how disappointed you were when he wasn't." They had stopped walking and faced each other.

"It's because he left when my mother died giving birth to me. I need to know why. Does he hate and blame me?"

Buddy saw desperation in Nadine's eyes as she said these words. "Well, he'd have to be stupid to think it was your fault," she said in a protective tone.

Nadine's voice lowered to just an octave above a whisper.

"Buddy I also feel disconnected, not knowing my father. A part of my life is missing. I see other kids with their dads and I'm envious."

"I don't have a father either," Buddy shook her head.

"But he died. He didn't voluntarily walk away. When I see a man my father's age, I wonder, could it be?"

"Well then I'm happy for you Nadine. If that is what you want, and it is to come to pass." Buddy gave an exaggerated nod as they began to walk again.

"Now what is your news, Buddy?" Buddy did not respond, thinking how inappropriate the timing was for what she had to say.

"Well, spill it."

Buddy blurted out, "Aunt Liz fell and broke her hip. That is why I was late. LeRoy called Aunt Ada early this morning. She called me. We went together. Dr. Wilson had already come and gone. He sedated her, so she wouldn't feel any pain." Buddy looked away, not wanting to see the hurt in Nadine's eyes.

"Oh no, how, where did she fall, when?" The questions came tumbling out as pools of tears formed in Nadine's eyes. "Poor, poor, Mom." They ceased walking again.

This time Buddy took both of Nadine's hands into hers. "She fell down the stairs."

"The hall stairs where Pop fell?"

"No the front porch stairs, and it was early this morning. The how, I don't know. Seems, when LeRoy took her breakfast, she was not in bed, and he went looking for her. After he'd gone all through the house, he said he heard a soft whimper from outside.

He ran to the front porch and saw her sprawled in front of the steps on the lawn."

"Oh my gosh," Nadine began to feel queasy. "Wonder how long she was there alone and in pain?"

Buddy shook her head. "You know she has been so inactive, spending most of her days in her room and even in bed, that her muscles are probably weakened."

Nadine's mind traveled back in time and focused on Mom's flicking particles of white powder from her nightstand as she visited one time. "Buddy, I think LeRoy keeps Mom sedated. That's why she is so inactive."

"But Aunt Ada says she is depressed, and that's how it affects her, making her sleep to avoid life. Besides if he is, Dr. Wilson would have to be prescribing it. You would have to be there to see how truly upset LeRoy was. He was just beside himself, so attentive."

Then the inevitable question came, "Why was Mom on the front porch early in the morning when she had been sticking so close to her room?"

Buddy shrugged, "It's such a beautiful day. Maybe she just couldn't resist."

Nadine did not ask anymore questions. It seemed as if LeRoy had won even Buddy over to his defense. Perhaps, she thought, Mom was slipping out early in the morning, trying to escape LeRoy, or perhaps the ghost which quarreled with Mom. Nadine pictured the house in her mind. It did not look scary; unless you knew what might be happening there.

"You've already walked me more than half way home, Nadine."

Nadine crossed her arms in front of her. "I know. I just thought since I was this close to Mom's I'd walk on over to check on her."

"She'll be glad to see you if she is awake. Dr. Wilson set her hip you know. She might still be sleeping."

"What's new about that?" Nadine's voice was cutting.

"Don't be curt, Nadine, it's completely out of character for you."

"I'm sorry. I just feel out of control in Mom's situation. We never get to talk. Either she's asleep, or LeRoy is hovering about."

Buddy shrugged, "He's trying to protect her. You of all people should appreciate that."

Nadine rolled her eyes as if to say here we go again. Inwardly she thought that Buddy sounded like Aunt Ada. This made Nadine feel more helpless. "Well, maybe I'd like to protect her too."

"Who from?"

Nadine ignored the question, and they walked in silence until they came to the Coal River Bridge where they parted. Turning to wave goodbye,

Nadine began the familiar walk down Smokey Road.

Every once in awhile someone, sitting on the porch, threw up a hand in greeting. She waved back. Some would yell, "Hi there Nadine."

She felt an inward warmth spread through her. She was comfortable in these surroundings. She had missed looking out at the river every morning. It was a "sparkler today" as Pop always said when the sun made gold patterns on the river's surface. She walked along, looking at the river which mirrored the overhanging trees, making it seem like a world of make believe. Hard to believe, she thought, how my world has been turned upside down since Pop's death.

As she turned and started up the walk to Mom's, she automatically looked up at the upstairs window to see if the young woman's ghost watched. She was not there, nor did the lace curtain move, but Nadine thought she saw a shadow pass by the window. It's only the sun, she assured herself.

Raising her hand to knock on the door, she had second thoughts. She reached for the doorknob instead, turned it, and then slipped into the hall. The house was quiet except for the tick of the grandfather clock whose black metal hands were a stark contrast against the clock's white face. Hoping to steal a few moments alone with Mom, she cautiously approached Mom's half closed bedroom door to listen for LeRoy's moving about inside. She heard only Mom's deep slow breathing. She stepped in. A floor board gave a loud snap against her weight. She stopped abruptly. Mom did not stir. Nadine tiptoed to stand beside her. She looked at the harsh lines in her face. Lines that had not been present until after Pop's death. Nadine remembered the night she had fallen on the glass jar, breaking it and nearly cutting her thumb. Mom had comforted her, swinging in the swing, holding the white cloth tightly around her thumb to stop the bleeding, and singing the hymn, There Were Ninety and Nine. . . She could hear the words in her head. She wished she could somehow comfort Mom. It seemed to be her turn, she thought as she sat on the edge of Mom's bed, holding Mom's hand.

She doesn't know I'm here, Nadine decided after awhile, so she slowly got up to leave, hoping to escape without encountering LeRoy. "Ice, ice my mouth is dry," Mom spoke without opening her eyes.

Nadine turned back, but Mom did not move. Nadine's eye caught the half melted cup of ice on the bedside table. With her fingers, she scooped up a few pieces to rub across Mom's lips. Mom's tongue licked away the wetness, taking a piece of ice into her mouth. She patted Nadine's hand. "You sweet, sweet girl. I always loved you most."

Suddenly LeRoy came through the door and with but a few strides stood at Nadine's elbow. Glaring at her, he jerked the remaining pieces of ice from her fingers. "What are you doing, Dr. Nadine, trying to choke her to death on chunks of ice. Can't you see she is unconscious."

"She is thirsty," Nadine snapped back. She wanted to say, *Are you going to let her lie here and die of thirst?* But she didn't want to start an argument here in Mom's room.

Instead she gave Mom's hand a squeeze, and Mom squeezed back.

Suddenly, Mom said, "Mr. Taylor is buried in Poca beside his first wife. He wanted it that way. Frances, where Frances is!"

LeRoy roughly took Nadine's elbow and guided her toward the door. "Stop, she's talking."

"She's out of her head. She doesn't know what she's talking about. Now let her rest."

Nadine did not resist until they were in the hall where she jerked away from LeRoy. "How did you get in? I didn't hear you knock."

"I didn't knock. The door was unlocked, and I came in. Why should I have to knock?"

LeRoy hiked up his trousers and fumbled at his top shirt button. "I guess it was my oversight in not locking the door. Mrs. Taylor might get out and fall down the steps again."

Nadine knew that he was saying from now on when she came, she would have to knock. He was going to make sure all the doors were locked.

"What did Dr. Wilson say to do beside sedate her?" Nadine's eyes narrowed.

"I'm to keep turning her, so she won't get bed sores and keep her propped up to ease her breathing and guard against congestion. So don't you worry. Everything is taken care of."

"Well you've put my mind at ease," she didn't care if he heard the edge on her voice.

He stood at the door until she stepped from the porch. She then heard the click of the bolt on the door when she hurried down the front steps, thinking she wanted to stand in the middle of Smokey Road and scream at the top of her lungs. But then LeRoy would have her declared insane as he had Henry.

Nadine walked toward Aunt Mandy's. The leaves began rustling as a light breeze stirred and the clouds moved over the sun, turning the river into a slate gray. Crossing the bridge, instead of continuing down Main, she turned toward Aunt Ada's. She had some questions to ask.

Walking, she pondered Mom's words, "Mr. Taylor is buried in Poca beside his first wife. He wanted it that way, where Frances is." She must have meant that she would be buried in the Allen plot where Frances was buried, not beside Pop.

Nadine recalled Mr. Taylor's telling her about the Battle of Scary. On the night before the battle, he wrote a letter to the young woman who was to be his first wife, proposing marriage. Nadine knew LeRoy was Mr. Taylor's cousin by marriage.

*   *   *

At the Taylor house, LeRoy entered Mrs. Taylor's room with her supper tray as Mom began to stir from sleep. Forcing her eyes open, she felt drowsy.

"See what I've brought you to eat." LeRoy set the tray on the night stand and fluffed her pillows, so she could sit up to eat. "I've brought you a baked sweet potato with brown sugar and butter, your favorite food."

Mom reluctantly took a few bites, but she felt tired, her hip pained her, and her pupils were dilated, causing the light to hurt her eyes. "Was Nadine here, LeRoy? I seem to remember her being in the room."

"You must have dreamed it. Dr. Wilson sedated you. You've been sleeping all day."

Mom put her plate aside. The smell of the potato made her nauseous. "What did Dr. Wilson give me for pain?"

"Aren't you going to eat some more. That's not enough to keep a bird alive." LeRoy scooped up a spoonful of potato and held it to her mouth. She pushed it away.

"The medication, LeRoy, what is in it?"

LeRoy shrugged, "I'm not a pharmacist, Mrs. Taylor. It might contain a little something for the pain. He picked up the tray and began toward the door.

"Did you call Nadine as I asked?"

LeRoy turned a half circle to face Mom. "Mrs. Taylor, don't I do everything you ask?"

"Well?" furrows formed in her forehead.

"Well, she can't come today." When he felt his face flush, he started toward the door again.

"LeRoy, I wish you had left the phone in my room, so I wouldn't have to bother you about making calls."

LeRoy, stepped out into the hall, "I really don't mind."

Mom's eyelids began to feel heavy. "But LeRoy I want the phone in. . ."

"Just trust me Mrs. Taylor, I'll take care of everything. That's why I'm here." He then abruptly turned and stepped back into her room. "Oh, I forgot. If you hear a knock on the door, it will be Dr. Wilson, coming to check on you and change your medication. I believe you need something more for the pain." She did not respond, having drifted off again. The only sound coming from her room was a raspy cough and a wheeze when she breathed.

*   *   *

Nadine knocked on Ada's door. She heard quick footsteps in response to the knock, and the door flung open, "Well, Nadine, I do declare. I was just thinking about you. Come on in." Ada stepped aside to let Nadine in, swatting away a fly, "I guess you've been to see Liz. She really had a hard fall. I told Buddy to tell you. Here, sit a spell," she pointed to the rocker. I'll get you some ice tea. Ada hurried into the kitchen, continuing to talk, raising her voice to be heard from the kitchen. "How is Liz? Resting I hope."

"She was sleeping."

Ada came back with two glasses of tea with a spring of green mint on each, sitting them on a doily, so not to mar the furniture. "That's good. She isn't in pain then. Now to what do I owe this rare visit." She sat down in the other rocker.

Nadine sipped her sweetened tea and licked her lips before speaking. "You remember Buddy's saying once when she visited Mom that she heard noises come from the fireplace. She asked Mom if she had company?"

"Yes, and Liz said it was a woman who came in and fussed with her," Ada finished Buddy's conversation which Nadine alluded to.

"Well, I've been thinking, could the ghost have pushed Mom down the front steps?" Nadine leaned forward to look directly into Ada's eyes. "Maybe the ghost was angry—she fussed at Mom."

"That's out of character for the ghosts I've heard tell of, to be violent," Ada responded thoughtfully. "They may act in a way to bring attention to something that you are doing that they don't approve of but not become violent." She shook her head to emphasize that thought. "Besides," she continued with a stern look, "I told you and Buddy that the discussion of the ghost was not to go beyond these four walls, remember?" She shook her finger to emphasize that agreement.

"I just don't understand why she was out on the porch going down the steps, when she stays so closely to her room."

Ada reached over and patted Nadine's hand. "Now quit fretting about that. Maybe she was feeling better and wanted fresh air. We'll ask her when she's up to it. Meanwhile, I hope she doesn't get pneumonia."

"Pneumonia? Why do you mention that?"

A worried expression crept across Ada's face. "Often when an older person breaks a bone and is confined to bed, he or she gets pneumonia."

Their conversation ceased for a minute, then Nadine spoke. "Pop told me about his fighting in the Battle of Scary, and his writing a letter to his fiancee, his first wife. That's the first time I knew he had another wife."

Ada narrowed her eyes as her thoughts turned to the past. "Yes, both he and Liz had been married before, and their spouses died. You knew he had his farm at Poca and Liz had one at Goff Mountain where you first came to live, remember?"

Nadine nodded her head. How could she forget? She straightened up and continued, "When we moved, I was helping to put away things, and I came across a beautiful white christening gown. I asked Mom if I could put it on my doll. She became very firm, saying that it belonged to Mr. Taylor, and he wanted to keep it. She wrapped it in tissue paper and carefully placed it in the dresser drawer."

Ada took a drink of tea. "That belonged to his baby. That is how his wife died, in childbirth."

"Did the infant die?"

"Yes, a little girl, I believe."

"That must be why he was so good to me."

"Indeed, you were the apple of his eye. Now I hesitate to rush you off, but darkness is coming, and you are walking, alone."

Ada put her arm around Nadine's shoulders as they walked out onto the porch, "Ada, why was Pop buried beside his first wife instead of Mom?"

Ada pushed her spectacles up on her nose, "I believe he told LeRoy that was his desire."

"He told LeRoy and not Mom?"

"That's how I remember it."

"Do you think that could be one reason Mom is so depressed?"

"What do you mean, Child?"

"It's like being rejected or saying, 'you aren't as important as my first wife'."

Ada gripped the banister till her knuckles turned white. She nodded, "I guess, I'd never thought about it. Liz has too much pride to mention such feelings—jealousy I guess or hurt, but don't you fret. It is none of our doings."

"No it's LeRoy's," Nadine said emphatically.

"Nadine hush your mouth. I've told you before. Don't be having and saying bad thoughts about LeRoy. He's over there right now nursing Liz when most young handsome men his age are out having a good time. He has no help except for Sally who comes now and again to take care of Liz's personal needs. Don't bite the hand that feeds you, so to speak. We are dependent upon LeRoy. Don't forget that."

Nadine certainly did not agree, but leaned over and hugged Ada goodbye.

Ada kissed Nadine on the cheek, "Don't stay away so long the next time." She waved goodbye.

"Keep me advised of Mom's health," Nadine yelled back as she walked down the road, noticing that the lightning bugs had begun flashing their yellow light, punctuating the darkness.

*   *   *

Nearing Aunt Mandy's, Nadine began running. As she entered the yard and stepped on the front porch, she noticed an unfamiliar black 1928 Ford. Aunt Mandy saw her coming and opened the door.

"You have a special guest. He's been waiting awhile, and we've been chatting." Nadine stopped to catch her breath, tuck her white cotton blouse into her skirt and run her fingers through her short curls.

"Who is it?" she whispered to Aunt Mandy.

"It's a surprise." Aunt Mandy walked into the living room in front of Nadine.

As Nadine entered, a young man with auburn hair and green eyes with gold flecks, which matched hers, stood up and flashed a broad smile. "Carl, oh it's been so long." She, without hesitation, flung her arms around him. Unlike their first meeting, he reciprocated. He now was a man, no longer shy around girls. "Let me look at you. Carl, you've grown so tall. Look at your brown tweed sport coat." She swept her hand over its collar. "That car out front can't be yours?"

"It is, and it's a dandy." Carl shoved his hands into his trouser pockets and subconsciously jingled his loose coins, "When are you going to grow? How tall are you, 5'1"?" Carl asked teasingly.

"5'2", Nadine corrected with a smile.

"What did you do to buy that car?"

Aunt Mandy, still standing, interrupted, "You two have a lot of catching up to do. Sit down and make yourselves comfortable. I have some fresh coconut cake left from the party today. I'll get you two a piece."

"That sounds great," Carl answered, seating himself again.

As Aunt Mandy cut big chunks of cake, she couldn't keep from marveling at how much Nadine and Carl looked alike. They were the "spitting image" of their dad.

"Well, Carl, catch me up on what you've been up to. I know you went to Berea to college. Did you like it?"

"Loved it. I was on the debate team. We did well for ourselves."

Aunt Mandy served the cake with two glasses of cold milk, then excused herself.

Carl bit into the cake, "This is delicious. Does she cook like this all the time?"

"She's a wonderful cook and such a caring person. I'm lucky to board here. Now, tell me more about Berea."

Carl wiped his mouth and continued, "I began to attend there when I was in the eighth grade and just graduated. There were lots of school requirements. We had to have a job. I worked in the print shop and waited tables at the Boone Tavern. We also had to attend chapel and wear uniforms.

I really got tired of those uniforms." He took another bite of cake.

Nadine waited for him to finish chewing, thinking how much she would have enjoyed college.

"I also met a lot of nice people—life long friends. After chapel on Sundays, a professor and his wife might invite a student to dinner. Boy, was that a welcome relief from cafeteria food."

"What are your plans now?"

"I intended to go to Toledo, Ohio and work in a printing office, but those plans have changed." He knitted his brow. "Maybe another day. You

CARL MILLER

know, Uncle John's newspaper office burned to the ground, and he didn't have insurance. He and Aunt Noni are old and need me to help in rebuilding the business. After all, they took me to raise. I owe them. Plus, living with them allowed me to buy a car. It's not brand new, but it chugs along."

"Did you know Daddy remarried and will be visiting his family here in St. Albans soon?"

Carl flicked a few cake crumbs from his jacket before answering, "He wrote Uncle John and said he'd also be visiting Winfield, so I'll see him there, I guess." Carl did not wish to get emotional about meeting his father for the first time since age four, so he abruptly changed the subject. "I've got a friend pestering me to set up a blind date with you. He's really a nice guy. How about it?"

"I don't know." Nadine questioned, "Who is he, and how does a friend of yours know me?"

"Wait now, I said it is a blind date. If I answer all your questions, it won't be blind." Carl had picked up his cap in preparation to leave and was turning it around nervously in his hand. "You have to take my guarantee on his good character.

Anyway, I thought we might double date."

"Who are you taking?"

"Your friend Rachel."

"Where will we go?"

"Since I have a car, we can drive to Charleston to take in a picture show. How does that sound?"

"Great," Nadine trusted Carl's judgement, but she felt better that Rachel was going.

*   *   *

The day of Nadine's blind date, she was busy decorating the front store window for the Fourth of July, carefully arranging the American flag as a backdrop for the display when she noticed a cab being parked, and then Sam the cabdriver walk toward the store. The bell rang as he entered. He was a slight man with a balding head, wearing overalls. He had driven her home on rainy and snowy evenings when the store closed late. "Hi, Sam, what do you need today?"

He shifted his wad of tobacco from one side of his jaw to the other.

PHIL MILLER

"Truth is I didn't come to buy, Missy." He looked as if he were hesitant to speak.

"Oh, just to chat?"

"I guess you might say that."

"You been fishing lately above the falls?"

"Not that kind of chattin', Nadine. I came to tell you something, and I hope you don't think I'm butt'n into your family matters. I don't mean to be gossiping."

"I know that, Sam."

"Well anyway, as a cabdriver here abouts, I know and see a lot." He stopped, opened the front door, spit the amber contents of his mouth out on the sidewalk and closed the door.

"I guess you do," Nadine agreed.

"If I see something that might harm somebody I've taken a likin' to, I sometimes speak up."

He had captured Nadine's attention, "Yes?"

"As I say, I don't mean to be carrying tales, but since you left the Taylor's and Mrs. Taylor's been down, LeRoy has been havin' me drive him to the bank. He says he's doin' business for Mrs. Taylor." Sam squinted his eyes. "Seems since she broke her hip, he calls me more and more. I'm a thinkin' he's got himself appointed power of attorney and is bleedin' her bank account dry."

An alert button went off in Nadine's head, and she felt heat moving up her neck to her hair roots. "What makes you say that, Sam?"

"Well, he's sneaky the way he comes out, gettin' in the back seat and slippin' a wad of money out of his pocket to count. He thinks no one sees, but you'd be surprised what I can see in my rear view mirror." He gave his head a quick nod, "I can smell too, and I've been smellin' alcohol on his breath more and more lately."

Nadine did not wish to display the feelings she had inside. Nor did she wish to make Sam feel like a traitor in sharing this confidence. She just wanted to get to the phone to call Ada. "Sam, I appreciate your coming to me. It does sound curious, and I'll certainly check into it. It's good to have a friend like you." She managed to smile.

"Yes, I'm just keepin' an eye out for you and Mrs. Taylor. You've been awful nice to me, and that LeRoy, I can't say the same for him." He cleared his throat. "Well, I best be going. I can't make any money in here gabbin'." He bowed his head and left.

Nadine went straight to the phone and called Ada. After hearing what Nadine reported, Ada's reply was casual and critical but only of Sam. "Nadine how did you think the house was being run. Of course, LeRoy uses Liz's money. He doesn't have any of his own, and even if he did, he wouldn't be paying Liz's bills with it. It is true that he has power of attorney. He has to have if we expect him to run the house and other rental property Liz owns.

"What about the alcohol?"

"He might take a nip every once in a while. He probably has to in order to keep his sanity, staying in that big gloomy house with Liz half out of her head. Besides, you can't believe what a gossip like Sam says."

"The house was full of life, bright and happy before LeRoy. Now you're saying Mom's half out of her head. If she is, it's because LeRoy keeps her doped, and Sam is my friend, not a gossip." Nadine felt her voice break on her last sentence.

Ada ignored Nadine's negativity toward LeRoy, believing they had covered that ground before. "Listen to yourself, Nadine. How can you call somebody a friend who has upset you so? Now just calm down, hear?"

Nadine wanted to slam the phone down, but maybe Ada was right about her becoming overly excited over the obvious, paying bills and all. She'd never thought of the mechanics before.

Hearing sadness in Nadine's voice and sensing the quietness of unspoken thoughts, Ada added, "Sometimes ignorance is bliss. Just don't worry. You'll put wrinkles in that young beautiful face."

"Whatever you say Aunt Ada," she whispered, hanging up the phone, feeling helpless once again. However, she refused to let LeRoy put a dark blot on her evening, so she turned her mind onto what she would wear and say. To think, she was double dating with her very own brother, Rachel and whom ever?

*   *   *

Closing the store a little early, she walked briskly, breathing in the fragrances of summer, a mix of honeysuckle, roses and freshly mowed grass. She went straight to her room, opening the closet to select an outfit. After much thought, she pulled out her dark blue dress with the white organdy collar which tied in a bow at the neck. She decided the dark blue was slenderizing.

Getting ready much too early for the date, every time she heard a car drive by, she peeked out the window. Then she returned to the mirror to redo her hair. *Maybe this dress is too drab. I'll change*, she thought and then rethought, knowing she would have to completely redo her hair.

There was a knock on the door. "Please, Aunt Mandy, get the door." She said to herself, *I don't want to appear too anxious. They'll think I've never had a date before.*

Thankfully she heard Aunt Mandy's quick steps going toward the door. Then she heard three voices greeting Aunt Mandy. One was Carl's and then Rachel and the third sounded slightly familiar. Where had she heard that voice before? Just as Nadine slipped inside the room, she heard the third party say to Aunt Mandy, "I hope you don't mind, but our strawberries are in, so I picked you a basket." He had his back to Nadine, but she could see the delicious looking, big, red strawberries as he extended his arm and hand.

"Well thank you. How thoughtful you are." Aunt Mandy reached and took them. As she did, Nadine cleared her throat to announce her presence. All eyes turned in her direction, but Nadine's eyes were captured by the young man's soft, friendly, brown eyes. That gentle kind face was indeed familiar. "Vinson Erwin!"

"You remember my name. That's a good beginning," he said with a twinkle in his eyes. "I'll leave you young people alone. I need to clean these berries for the strawberry pie that I'll bake, thanks to Vinson." Turning to walk out of the room, Aunt Mandy softly whispered as she passed Nadine who stood at the edge of the room, "Grab this one. He's a winner and practical. A basket of strawberries beats an O'Henry candy bar." Nadine's face blushed, hoping the others did not hear.

Also smelling the strawberries reminded Nadine that she hadn't eaten. She hoped her stomach didn't start growling. As Vinson helped her into the car's back seat, his closeness, clean cut appearance and the smell of his after shave made Nadine's heart flutter.

*   *   *

The following weekend, Nadine and Vinson went out together, but this time not on a double date. They went swimming at Lower Falls Beach on Coal River a few miles from St. Albans. Vinson took her hand in his. They walked along the crowded beach with their hands swinging together like two children.

Nadine found Vinson easy to talk to. She told him about her mother's death, her father's flight, how the decision to give her to Mrs. Taylor was made on the train, and how her life changed, following Pop's death and Mom's illness. She could have talked on because Vinson was a good listener.

After swimming in the clear icy river, they stretched out side by side on a towel with their bodies still wet. It was Vinson's turn to share his family. "I have one brother and three sisters. I'm next to the youngest, and the only one still living at home. My younger sister Ima is not married either, but she lives with my oldest sister, Ochal and her husband and children in

NADINE & VINSON

Huntington, and Ima works."

"It must be wonderful coming from a big family." Nadine mused. "I have Carl, but we weren't raised together as you know."

She raised up on her elbow. "I do think as they say, 'blood is thicker than water,' because we have so much in common."

"I've never seen a brother and sister who look so much alike," Vinson said reaching up to push a red lock of hair off Nadine's forehead.

"Besides working at the store, what do you do with your time?"

"Oh I do a lot of church work. I'm in the choir and teach a Sunday School class of fifth graders." She didn't bother telling him about the preacher's saying that he saw her down on her knees in the street, not praying but

NADINE & VINSON

looking in the manhole for a man. But she did think of it, and it made her smile. Vinson loved to see her smile. Her whole face lit up. "I also fish. I'd love to have a rowboat of my own, so I could put out a trot line."

There was a lull in the conversation and Vinson broke the silence. "We live across the street from Adda Baptist Church. My Mom's pop gave the land to build the church on. Mom and Pop are over there all the time."

"Pop, being a deacon, made grape juice for communion at our house. It was ready to take to church. My buddy and I, I guess we were twelve, sneaked some and made homemade wine. We crawled up under the porch to drink it, and got so drunk that we couldn't crawl out. Pop found us and what a whipping we got over that."

Nadine laughed, visualizing two skinny little boys, down on all fours, bumping into each other, looking like spiders, so disoriented they couldn't go in the direction they wanted. "Has the depression affected your life on the farm?"

"Not so much us. Pop is able to keep the taxes paid, and we raise our own food. But we sure don't have any luxuries. They had been bought from our cash crop, tobacco."

"I've not been directly affected yet. Except I took a pay cut, so I could keep my job. Business is down at the store."

To change the mood, Vinson began laughing.

"What's so funny?"

"You're breaking out in freckles."

"That's one of the many pitfalls of being a redhead, so we better get out of the sun."

As they packed their blanket, towels and thermos, Vinson leaned over and with his finger drew a heart in the sand, writing "Vinson +." Nadine reciprocated by tracing "Nadine". They smiled unembarrassed and arm in arm walked toward the car, both feeling something stir inside.

That night, as Nadine was going to sleep, she thought, *Vinson, as Aunt Mandy recognized, has a practical solidness about him; the characteristic I desire in a husband.*

*   *   *

Nadine and Vinson enjoyed many of the same things. Even when Nadine didn't like something that Vinson enjoyed, she was wise enough to pretend she did. If he wanted to go fishing at 6:00 a.m. when there was still a chill in the air and the fog hovered over the river, Nadine was there by his side.

Nadine usually initiated their date plans, always keeping in mind Vinson's preference. "Let's catch a streetcar and go uptown to a movie, *The Call of the Wild* is playing" or "We're having a special program at church Sunday, come on up, and Aunt Mandy will fix you another lemon pie that you like so well," she would say.

One Sunday, as the offering plate at church was passed, she got a glimpse into Vinson's frugal nature. When he dropped a dollar bill into the offering plate, before he could pull out change, the usher quickly passed it on. Vinson's eyes widened, and he whispered, "I didn't get my change."

"We don't make change out of the offering plate," she whispered back, hoping no one overheard.

"Well, we do at Adda Baptist," he said emphatically. As their relationship deepened, so did the great depression which strangled many lives and the nation's economy.

*   *   *

Vinson's brown eyes gazed into Nadine's green ones as she once again spoke of her past and of her goals of finding security and a family of her own. Because she was confiding her innermost thoughts to Vinson, she did not notice his eyes begin to evade her's and that finally he shifted them onto the checked tablecloth. They were at Wren's Nest Restaurant situated on Coal River Road where they had gone for dessert. He then shifted his attention to the green river as it moved toward its mouth to join the Kanawha River and eventually the Mississippi.

He breathed deeply, letting his breath out slowly. He could not offer this security she frequently spoke about. He didn't have a real job but only worked on his pop's hillside farm. Watching the river flowing westward, his mind cleared as he realized that his answer to his cousin Hobart would be, "Yes." Vinson received Hobart's letter a week ago, asking him to join Hobart in Detroit where he promised Vinson a job in a laundry. This was not much of a job, but it was more than he had here.

After looking for a job for months, there were none to be had. The depression continued. He saw the gaunt hopeless faces of people, with sunken eyes and sharp cheek bones from hunger, wandering the roads, homeless and jobless. Sometimes the stream of ragged migrants wandered as families. Sometimes men rode the rails alone, jumping off when their bellies cramped with hunger to knock on doors, hoping for a handout—to beg food.

Pop had taken in neighbors and extended family after they had lost their farms due to unpaid taxes and mortgages. Pop could only put food into so many mouths. Pop was having a time of it. He needed some help. Now Nadine was talking of desired security which she of all people deserved. If he had reservations about joining Hobart, the doubt was erased.

Perhaps he could send money home to aid Pop. Maybe he could put aside some and propose to Nadine. But no, his meager salary would not allow any extra. He might as well not make any promises or commitments that he could not keep. The truth is harsh. Vinson bit his lip as he tried to decide how to tell Nadine that he would be leaving. This would be their last time together. He didn't want to belabor their parting.

*   *   *

Vinson listened to the chatter around him and the rattle of loose windows as his train headed toward Detroit. This was his first trip on a train. It required a contribution of several family members to afford his ticket: Pop; Ochal and her husband; Earl, his brother; and Mom had even dug into her egg money in order to pay his fare.

He was thankful to have a passenger's seat. He knew trains pulling boxcars contained ragged passengers who had hopped the cars, not knowing or caring where they were going, just going. When the train stopped and the boxcar door slid open, they squinted into the sunlight, waiting for the pupils of their eyes to dilate and adjust to the light, in order to gaze out over an unfamiliar landscape.

At home he had also watched as trains carrying coal slowed down on an incline, and men, women, and children hopped the coal cars to throw coal off into waiting hands.

He got to know some of the homeless, standing in lines with them in front of factories. Word would spread that perhaps the Nickel Plant might be hiring, and men lined up at the plant's entrance. Some camped all night in order to be first in line to get a job. Someone from inside the plant would walk the line, sizing up the men and tapping maybe five to be hired that day.

Often the line was reduced in number when men passed out from hunger. Awful to say, but this brought relief because it increased the chance for the next fellow to be hired. Often getting hired did not solve the problem because the company sometimes did not have money to meet the payroll. These were hard times. He knew he was fortunate to be a paying passenger, riding toward a promised job and to a place where he and Hobart planned to room together, splitting the costs.

Vinson watched the landscape roll by. It had been an unusually dry summer. When fields of corn dried up, the farmers cut it down. As they did, they too cut away their hope of escaping the fate of the bands of homeless, drifting from place to place, seeking jobs.

He leaned his forehead against the window and looked at the forest where the dry brown leaves drooped toward the earth, seeking moisture, but there was none. A single match tossed, and the forest would erupt into a wall of flames.

Vinson reached into his trouser pockets, pulling out folded paper and pen. He had to write Nadine because he had not told her his plans. He had not been able to hurt someone face to face who suffered loss many times before. He had let their last evening evaporate in sweetness and no sad good-byes. As he wrote, the black words glared back at him.

Dearest Nadine:

While writing this letter, I am on a train going to Detroit. My cousin Hobart has a job there for me. I feel I must go. I know this comes as a shock. I hope you don't think I am a coward in not telling you my plans in person. Our last date was perfect, and I didn't want to ruin the memory.

I tried to get work at home, but with the depression deepening, I couldn't. I have nothing to offer you. You want financial security, a home and children. I can't provide that. I too have obligations to my parents. Now, I'll be able to work and send them money.

Fondly,
Vinson

He wanted to sign, "Love, Vinson," but he felt he must let go. Even though, it hurt. Before he changed his mind about adding a promise for the future, he sealed the envelope and placed a three cent stamp on it.

*   *   *

Nadine was busy working when she heard the store door open and shut. She looked up to see Aunt Mandy waving an envelope. "Here is what you've been waiting on, Child. It's a letter from Vinson. I can tell by the handwriting. I'm on my way to the grocery store, so I can't stay." Aunt Mandy laid the letter on the counter and was out the door with a flick of her hand. "I'll see you at supper."

Nadine picked up the letter. As she hurriedly unsealed the envelope, she noted an unfamiliar postmark which sparked her curiosity. *Maybe Vinson gave the letter to someone else to mail*, she thought. The same black marks which glared at Vinson now glared back at her. She felt faint and leaned against the counter. She heard Mr. Stone coming from the stockroom. She dared not let their eyes meet as he walked in her direction, wiping his hands on his apron which had written across the front, "In America We Are Building Not Destroying—George Weimer and Son's Building Materials."

The word "Destroying" leaped out at her. Vinson was destroying their relationship. "No, it can't be true," she whispered to herself. "What did I do wrong?"

"What did you say, Nadine?"

"Oh, nothing. I was just reciting a little poem to myself, Mr. Stone."

"You look pale. Are you ill?"

Nadine felt beads of perspiration breaking out on her forehead. "Well, to tell the truth, I don't feel well today. Do you think I might have the day off since we are not busy?"

"Business has quieted down even more than usual since the Fourth. This depression is beginning to hit everywhere. Go on!"

Nadine pulled her purse from under the counter and made her exit as gracefully as possible, not wanting Mr. Stone to see her eyes. She needed fresh air and to be alone. "See you tomorrow," she managed to say over her shoulder as she closed the store door behind her. She breathed deeply. Deep breathing helped relieve her stress.

Mrs. Reynolds yelled across the street, "This is another hot one today."

Nadine could tell Mrs. Reynolds was about to cross the street to chat a few minutes, so she kept up her quick pace, "It certainly is," she waved. Nadine just wanted to get back to the house before Aunt Mandy.

NADINE

Finally inside, she was grateful for the dimness of her room. She slid Vinson's letter out of her pocket and reread it. She felt a choking sensation in her throat as she read the lines, "I have nothing to offer you." As her hands began to tremble, she laid the letter on the table before her and read the words again and again. It was his writing. It was true. He was gone. The reason was there—her need for security. Why hadn't she kept this need to herself? She chased him away. How could she stand it?

The telephone's ring startled her, and she jumped. It rang again. I can't answer it. Another ring brought the thought, *it might be Vinson.* She ran into the hall almost tripping over her purse that she had dropped as she had entered her room. "Nadine," the voice on the other end said. It was Aunt Ada. "Are you all right? I called the store and Mr. Stone said you had gone home, not feeling well?"

"I'm feeling better, thanks." Nadine thought, *there is something wrong.* She heard it in Aunt Ada's tone of voice—a higher pitch. Nadine gripped the phone tighter, waiting.

Then in a whisper—almost a gasp—the words came, "Liz passed away this morning," Ada's voice broke. She forced herself to go on to get it all out as if it would relieve the pain. "LeRoy called about eight. He took Liz's breakfast in and could not arouse her. I rushed over. She had a peaceful expression on her face, bless her heart. Doc Wilson has come and gone." Nadine made no response. "Nadine," Ada repeated with panic in her voice. "Do you understand? Liz is dead."

There was a pause then, "Yes."

"Nadine, I need you to help with the funeral arrangements. LeRoy is so distraught, I don't think he'll be able to do much. After all, it is he who has been under the strain of twenty-four hour care for Liz."

Nadine recoiled at the mention of LeRoy's name. Her mind raced back to the first conversation that Mr. and Mrs. Taylor had over LeRoy. She had asked Pop how well he knew LeRoy, adding Mr. Stark down in Winfield allowed a stranger in. Now Mr. Stark is dead—-murdered. Ada would vehemently reject this line of thinking, so Nadine held her tongue concerning LeRoy. "When?"

"Come at one."

"I'll be there." Nadine placed the receiver in its cradle and walked back into her darkened room. She laid down and pulled her knees up into a fetal position. She then encircled herself with her arms. No tears came to relieve the terrible tension, just numbness. *Why is life so hard? If it could only be like it was before Pop died*, were the thoughts flowing through her mind over and over.

The house was quiet. She felt the noon heat closing in. She untangled herself and sat up in the bed and began rocking herself.

The rocking reminded her of Mom's swinging her that night she fell on the glass jar, chasing lightning bugs, and cutting her thumb.

Then the memory of Frances' singing crowded into her mind. "I stole the gold from your hair and put the silver that is there… I don't know any way I could ever repay you for my cradle days."

Nadine had this terrible need for Vinson, and he was gone. Mom was gone. She was abandoned again. Nadine anticipated the sweet talcum scent that came in troubled times to bring relief, but it did not come. She lost track of time as her thoughts darted from one memory to another.

Looking at the clock, she was shocked how swiftly time had passed and remembered her appointment with Aunt Ada. She looked up at her angel picture that she had brought from Mom's. She then had the urge to read her Bible. She flipped on the light and picked up her Bible. It fell open to Joshua 1:5, "No one will be able to stand against you all the days of your life. As I was with Moses, so I will be with you; I will never leave you nor forsake you." The sweet talcum fragrance was no longer needed for comfort. She had God's word. Tears finally flowed and the tension subsided. She was not alone.

*   *   *

Nadine looked about the church sanctuary at familiar faces. LeRoy was properly dressed in a tailored black suit. He was handsome; none could argue that with high cheekbones and his black hair slicked back. His fingers smooth, his nails neatly manicured, exhibited no hard work. Nadine thought, *One's eyes are the window to the soul*. His dark eyes were small, deep set and cold.

Aunt Ada had grown old. Nadine had not noticed before. She no longer had her erect posture but was stooped. Her blue eyes showed grief. Effie had facial features testifying to her relationship to both Mom and Ada. Mom's brother and his family were there. Cousins from Virginia, whom Nadine had never met, had come. Nadine was pleased to see Carl. Buddy, seated between her Mom and Nadine, patted Nadine's hand, as the preacher gave the eulogy.

Preacher Bailey concluded Mom Taylor's funeral by comparing her to the woman described in Proverbs 31: "She opens her arms to the poor and extends her hand to the needy…She is clothed with strength and dignity; she can laugh at the days to come. She speaks with wisdom and faithful instruction on her tongue. She watches over the affairs of her household and does not eat the bread of idleness. Her children arise and call her blessed... Charm is deceptive and beauty fleeting; but a woman who fears the Lord is to be praised. . . ." *What a perfect description of Mom*, Nadine thought.

As the procession followed Mom's casket, being carried to the Allen plot in Teays Hill Cemetery, Nadine noticed once again James Teass' oversized monument with its copper inscription embedded in concrete "I Forbid Anyone Burying On This Lot." *He lived alone and wanted to be alone throughout eternity, but I don't*, thought Nadine. She remembered also Mom's observation of these words, "You can't take your money with you."

No one uttered a sound as they encircled the open grave and the preacher said his last words. Nadine's tongue was dry. She felt perspiration trickle down her blouse and tears run down her cheeks. Turning to leave, she noticed a black woman standing off to the side, holding a child on her hip and another child stood beside her, clinging to her skirt. As the mourners thinned out, the woman walked toward Nadine.

"Nadine, remember me?"

Nadine searched her facial features for a clue. The mischievous eyes were the give away, "Sassy!" The two walked rapidly toward each other to embrace, as the two children looked on in astonishment. "It's been so long."

"I saw where Miz Taylor passed. So I get myself over here to pay my respects. She was a fine fine lady. Yes, she was." Sassy nodded her head and dabbed her eyes. "She be a strong lady just like the preacher say. She sure was."

Nadine's emotions swept over her. Seeing Sassy brought back many memories of long ago. They seemed almost unreal. Sassy wrapped her free arm around Nadine's shoulders. "Now now, you be strong Miss Nadine. You're goin' to have your hands full with that big house and all."

Nadine nodded. "What beautiful children." She ran her hand over the oldest one's hair and smiled into her brown eyes. "I swan she is a mirror image of you."

Sassy smiled proudly. "I hope she ain't as mean. You and me we had some times." Sassy gestured toward Nadine.

Nadine laughed, and it felt so good. "We sure did. It's a wonder we didn't get ourselves killed. Remember spying on the Gypsy camp?"

"Yes'um." Sassy mopped her forehead as the heat bore down. "You got any young'ns?"

"Not yet," Nadine shifted her eyes to the ground.

"Well, when you give birth, just call, and I'll come and help. I'm good with young'ns."

"How is Melinda?"

Sassy's smile evaporated. "She passed two years ago."

"I'm so sorry."

Sassy saw an older man, wearing glasses moving in their direction. "There's a man been waiting to speak to you. I best be on my way." They embraced. Then Sassy walked over the hill toward the road.

"Nadine," came a deep voice. "I need to speak to you." It was Attorney Reed.

"Yes," Nadine turned to face him.

"I regret bringing the will up at this time, but seems Mrs. Taylor's relatives from Virginia are anxious to catch their train and want to be present for the reading of the will." He cleared his throat. "I know there will be a gathering at Mrs. Taylor's and the neighbors and church have brought in food, but could you come to my office around four?"

"Yes, of course." A will? Nadine had never thought of a will.

*   *   *

Attorney Reed pushed his rimless glasses upon his nose, opened his desk drawer, pulled out the will and began reading. "Last will and testament of Elizabeth Allen Goff Taylor, October 11, 1929." He stopped and looked over his glasses as he heard the relatives from Virginia fidgeting about. Noting their non-verbal expression for expedience, he said, "I'll not read every word but will summarize Liz's desire."

"Upon the payment of LeRoy Richards for nursing fees and other outstanding debts, taxes, etc., I Elizabeth Allen Goff Taylor, being of sound mind bequest to my niece and namesake Elizabeth Taylor (Buddy) my gold watch and chain. The remainder of my estate, property and current bank account, I bequest to Nadine Ruth Miller."

Ada and Effie nodded in agreement, but the cousins from Virginia were outraged. "Its not right, ignoring blood relatives, leaving us out of the will to give everything to a child of questionable parentage. She's not even been adopted," said the thin lipped lady with salt and pepper hair.

"You'll be hearing from our lawyer, Mr. Reed," said the cousin's husband who began pulling on his suit jacket in preparation to exit the office.

His wife, following him, looked over her shoulder and gave Nadine a look of disgust, "Well, I never!"

The lady's sister jumped up and shook her fingers in Nadine's face. "You better not be spending that money yet, for we're contesting the will. Liz had to be out of her mind." With those parting words, she slammed the door behind her so hard that the glass in the door rattled.

Nadine felt blood rush to her face as the painful words "of questionable parentage" reverberated in her mind.

Attorney Reed again adjusted his spectacles. "Well this could be a drawn out process. I can see that. Meanwhile, Nadine, I'll check on the bank account, taxes, outstanding debts, etc. Nadine, we'll discuss this at another time."

Nadine shifted her eyes to LeRoy for he had not said a word. She was amazed that he too did not contest. He made no eye contact with anyone but stared out the window, showing signs of boredom by frequently pulling out his pocket watch to check the time. Contrary to usual, he did not paw and gush over Aunt Ada and Effie.

*   *   *

"Attorney Reed is absolutely right Nadine. Don't count your chickens before they hatch," Aunt Mandy warned as she spooned another portion of her fresh green beans and a slice of a big juicy yellow tomato onto Nadine's plate. "Eat your vegetables, they're good for you. You're looking down right peeked," She said, wiping her mouth on her napkin.

"I'm not counting on anything, don't worry." Nadine was having a difficult time swallowing. She didn't care about the inheritance but about not hearing from Vinson.

Several weeks later Attorney Reed called Nadine to his office. As she sat in his outer office waiting, she saw him through his office door, which was ajar. He repeatedly pushed his glasses up on his nose as he read awhile and then wrote awhile. He was surrounded by books. In fact, his office smelled of books and dust. It must be wonderful to be so learned, Nadine thought, wishing that she could have finished high school and gone to college as Carl had.

The only sound in the outer office was Mrs. Picken's typing and turning pages as she completed one and went to the next. It seemed whenever Nadine's mind was not absorbed in work, her thoughts drifted to Vinson.

This always brought pain. She had a difficult time even concentrating during conversations, so she was glad Mrs. Pickens was busy because if not the tall, thin, properly dressed secretary would be chattering on about all the town gossip. She knew everything before anybody else, working in a lawyer's office. In fact, the ladies in town loved to schedule into the hairdresser when she did, to be the first to hear about who was getting a divorce or about the latest crime. If they couldn't get an appointment at that time, the next best thing was to get the same operator, Frances, who embellished the gossip as her cutting shears clipped away.

Nadine heard Mr. Reed cough which signaled Mrs. Pickens to look briefly and motion with a quick nod of her head. Mrs. Pickens didn't miss a beat on her typewriter in this process. Nadine in compliance to the chain of command walked in.

Attorney Reed stood, extending his hand for a warm handshake.

Nadine in compliance, extended her white gloved hand. He then motioned Nadine to sit down. He did likewise, leaning back in his chair and placing his hands across his ample belly. "You doing okay, Nadine?" he inquired, studying her non-verbal communication and listening to the tone of her voice as his profession had trained him to do. This was not just any client; this was Nadine. He knew her history. He had known the Taylors as well as the Millers. He and her uncle, Dr. Dan Miller, had gone to school together. It was a loss to the town when Dan died. He had never married. He had been the first doctor, here about, to use cold to treat Typhoid Fever patients. Nadine had gotten a lot of raw deals in her young life, being passed from one family member to another and finally out of the family completely. Nadine indeed had been a survivor, not letting all of this dampen her spirit. She was a hard worker and even made it look like fun, enjoying and joking with Mr. Stone's customers.

His thoughts were broken into. "I'm doing fine, Sir," her lips said, but her eyes didn't agree.

"Always remember, Nadine, after the dark comes light."

"Yes sir. I will. Mom always said that very thing."

The attorney now leaned across his desk and with concern showing in his eyes said, "I'm sorry to say that your seemingly good fortune of inheriting the Taylor estate has pretty well evaporated."

Nadine swallowed but didn't reply.

"Seems Liz's bank account is drained pretty much dry. That which is left has to be used to pay back taxes on property which have not been paid for several years. Then the property must be sold to pay LeRoy Richard's nursing bill which is a lien upon the estate. Next, because you were never legally adopted and none of the estate went to Liz's family members in Virginia, they will probably have a claim. Your portion will not amount to much."

That is why LeRoy was bored at the reading of the will. He knew what the outcome would be. Most of the money was in his pocket. The remainder he would get from the enormous bill he filed against the estate. He had not paid the property taxes but pocketed the money. Now everything had to be sold. He saw to it that I would inherit nothing. Anger shot through Nadine like an electric shock.

When he entered the Taylor home, evil walked by his side. First, Pop fell down the stairs and died; there was the animosity between Henry and LeRoy, ending in Henry's being sent to Weston; she had been sent to live with Aunt Mandy; Frances, due to neglect, died. Finally, LeRoy held the reins, isolating Mom by removing the phone from her room, discouraging people from visiting, and sedating her; Mom's fall followed by more sedation and her giving him power of attorney. He got it all.

Henry might have been simpleminded, but he, unlike Aunt Ada and ultimately even Buddy, saw through LeRoy. Henry knew he was vile. "Vengeance is mine saith the Lord," flashed across Nadine's mind. She must cling to this, for nobody would believe what she knew in her heart——too many coincidences. Cling as she may to this passage of scripture, the anger returned when she let her guard down. At night, she awoke in a cold sweat, feeling her nail prints in the palms of her hands and the soreness of her jaws from gritting her teeth.

During the day, she maintained a smile on her face and a warm greeting for everyone. She thought of herself as a clown with a tear rolling down her cheek. The tear was internal and no one saw it.

Whom could she share her suspicions without being told she was prejudiced or over reacting? She decided on Aunt Mandy.

With the screen door open in the kitchen, the pleasant sounds of the early fall evening drifted in. Aunt Mandy had a pile of ironing sprinkled and wrapped in towels. Her days of cooking and laundering for boarders seemed to never cease. Nadine sat down in an oak kitchen table chair and picked up a biscuit with sweet strawberry jam before speaking. Then she poured out her concerns about LeRoy. To her surprise, Aunt Mandy was nodding in agreement as she put sharp creases in trousers.

When Nadine had finished, Aunt Mandy leaned the iron on its rest, poured a cup of coffee and sat herself directly across from Nadine, placing her hand on Nadine's. "What you are saying is no surprise to me, for I've observed LeRoy's actions myself from a distance, not up close like you. Others too have commented on the abrupt change at the Taylors' upon Mr. Taylor's fall and death.

"You can often tell the attitude of the inhabitants of a house by the upkeep on the outside. LeRoy let the lawn and house go to pot so to speak. Cab drivers spoke of his frequent trips to the bank and his drunkenness. LeRoy might have wooed some such as Effie, Ada and Buddy into an unconscious state, but as the cliché goes, 'You can fool some people some of the time, but you can't fool all the people all of the time.'" Aunt Mandy absentmindedly moved biscuit crumbs across the blue and white checked oil cloth tablecloth as she spoke. "But what you know, and what you can prove are two different things."

"But," Nadine began, and Aunt Mandy reached across the table and placed her finger across Nadine's lips. "Now hear me out. We have no proof, just intuition, so there is nothing you can do. If you let yourself dwell on it, you will become bitter. You're allowing LeRoy to cast his evil spell over your sweet disposition. Stop!" Aunt Mandy lifted her finger and pointed it at Nadine. "Give it time. In the long run crime does not go unpunished."

Nadine swallowed. At least Aunt Mandy pointed out that there were others with her own mind set, concerning LeRoy. Aunt Mandy had repeated what Nadine knew—-suspicion without facts got nowhere.

Aunt Mandy stood up, taking her post behind the ironing board. "Did you know Phil, your dad, will be in St. Albans this Friday? Now think on something pleasant for a change." With that she shook a wrinkled pillowcase until it made a snapping sound and placed the hot iron on it to expertly smooth out the wrinkles.

*　　*　　*

Wednesday evening, following prayer meeting, Esther stepped beside Nadine as they walked down the church steps and down the walk. Esther's voice rose to a loud whisper, "Can you come to my house for dinner Friday evening?" Even though Esther was her first cousin, she, like Molly, had jet black hair which she wore in a stylish bob with a spit curl in the middle of her forehead. She did have green eyes as Nadine and was about the same height. If nothing else distinguished them as cousins their Miller nose did.

"I don't have plans for Friday. That sounds nice."

"Your dad and Essie, his new wife, will be staying at our house, so it will be a good opportunity to meet him."

Nadine paused, and Esther noted a frown on Nadine's face. "What if I'm not what he expects?"

"What do you mean?"

"I mean what if I don't measure up to his expectation of a daughter," and she raced on, "What if he leaves me again, after I grow to love him."

"I thought you wanted to meet your father. You've talked of it for years," Esther said matter-of-factly.

"Oh, I do. I really do. Not knowing my father makes me feel disconnected. You know as if a part of my life is missing."

"Nadine, Uncle Phil is my favorite uncle. He is a good man and fun to be with. He won't be disappointed in you. No one could be." Esther placed her hand on Nadine's shoulder as she spoke and then pulled Nadine toward her in a hug. "Now, I'll count on your being there at six."

"Thanks Esther, I'll be there." Nadine felt reassured at Esther's words.

Thursday night Nadine could not get to sleep. The moonlight filled her room, and she could hear the branches of the forsythia bush brushing against her window pane. Thoughts flooded her mind. The same ones that she had pondered many times. *Why had her dad abandoned her and Carl: lack of responsibility, anger at God for taking his young wife, grief, fear of raising children as a single father?* Perhaps all of these as a collage formed the truth?

Friday, Nadine dressed fastidiously in a pale blue dotted Swiss dress to go to Uncle Lucian, Aunt Emma and Esther's to meet her dad and stepmother. *Stepmother*, in thinking about her father, she had not given her any thought. She had to impress them both. She knew wives had great influence over their husbands when it came to children, especially stepchildren. Nadine felt her stomach knot as she combed some curls around her face and fastened her gold cross around her neck.

* * *

As Nadine stepped onto Uncle Lucian's front porch, she heard a low whine followed by a thump, thump, thump. A dog, black as a lump of coal, was wagging his tail as he lay on the porch floor. With a leap, he bounded toward her, knocking her backwards and licking her face. "Dutch," Nadine exclaimed bending down to pat his head. She remembered Esther saying, "He came to our house when Henry left. We began feeding him, and he stayed. He has become my dad's dog. He wouldn't let any harm come to Dutch."

It made sense that Dutch would be a man's dog, always being around Henry, Nadine thought. *Henry would be pleased to know Dutch has a good home.* Nadine smoothed the prickly hair on Dutch's head. In response, he wagged his tail and his red tongue hung out of his mouth, as if he were smiling. *He remembers*, she thought.

Nadine saw the screen door open. The doorway framed a man who looked much like Carl but older and heavier. A tingle spread through her. She, much as Dutch had done minutes earlier, bounded toward the door. It seemed as if her legs would not carry her fast enough, but the distance was shortened by his fast long strides in her direction. His arms were outstretched and tears unashamedly flowed down his face, "Nadine, Nadine, at last," his voice trembled as their bodies intertwined, their tears mingled, and it seemed as if their hearts beat in sync.

Finally, he stepped back to study her face. "You and Carl have such a strong resemblance to each other with my auburn hair and Hazel's green eyes. You don't know how I've longed for this moment, Nadine."

She reached out toward him, "Me too," she cried. "But, why were you not here for me all along?" she blurted. Her hand went to her mouth from whence her words had shot out with a will of their own. *What if I've made him angry?* she feared.

"You don't know how much I wanted to be here for you. I worked with a traveling band in the beginning. I couldn't drag an infant and a three year old with me from one horse town to another. I knew Mrs. Dunlap, your grandmother, would take excellent care of you until I could gain some economic security." He stopped to mop his wet face with his handkerchief. "Then, you see there weren't phones then, and mail was uncertain, especially for a traveler such as me." He reached down and tipped Nadine's face up, so their eyes met. "By the time I learned of your Grandmother Dunlap's death, you were placed with the Taylor's. They could certainly offer more financial security than I."

"But you never let them adopt me?"

"No, no, I could never bring myself to do that. Please don't feel contempt for me. I beg you." His eyes were imploring. "Can we not begin a new life, no longer having a void in our hearts for each other?"

Nadine's response surprised her. "But you've been away so long."

"Yes Child, I waited for Mrs. Taylor's death. I promised her in the letter, refusing to let her adopt you that I would never interfere in her upbringing of you. The waiting was very very hard. Can you understand? It was because I loved you that I dare not interfere. I wanted the best for you, not for myself."

Nadine found it unbelievable that as she had feared rejection from her father, so he did of her.

"Can you forgive me? Can we be a family? I have felt so alone. Do you understand that Nadine?"

"Yes, I understand loneliness."

He continued. "You are my precious child whom I love." How she had longed for those words.

His voice broke into her thoughts once again, "I'm here for you now to be your father, but I can't undo the past. I know you may view me as a coward but please try to understand."

"I missed the security of having a father."

"I know, I know. May I begin now being your father? That is my question?" She gripped his hand, smiled and nodded. He hugged her again. "Now you must meet Essie my wife, so we can become a family."

Essie was anxiously waiting in the living room, watching through the screen door. "Essie, I want you to meet my daughter Nadine." Nadine quickly recognized that her dad certainly had not married Essie for her looks. She was heavy with her brown hair cut short, almost masculine. She had clear blue eyes which reminded Nadine of Mrs. Taylor's. Essie's eyes were full of love for her husband and her embrace exhibited warmth toward Nadine.

After all, this was Phil's child. His separation from Nadine had put stress on him. Anything to lessen the stress, Essie favored. Besides, Nadine was a perky little thing. *She couldn't have many of Hazel's features because she looked too much like Phil*, Essie thought.

Nadine's father and Essie unfolded their plans for Nadine, dealing with their move to St. Albans. Phil had taken his brother John's offer to open a small print shop to do job printing. John knew there was a market for this but had no time for it himself while printing the weekly *Putnam Democrat* newspaper in Winfield. They had rented a small house on Smoky Road from Mr. Lawrence.

* * *

Nadine and Carl were frequent visitors to their father's small cottage. In fact, their father began a small orchestra for the young people. Grace Lawrence played first violin and Nadine second. Grace later became a member of the Charleston Symphony Orchestra. Herb Bryant, a young attorney, played the saxophone, and Carl the clarinet. Carl always joked, that when they were invited some place to perform, by the time they got tuned up, the audience had gone home.

Meanwhile the town was a buzz about LeRoy's flamboyant life style since Mrs. Taylor's death. He continued living in the Taylor's house while it was on the market. It had been neglected since Pop's death. Ivy had encompassed the exterior. High weeds and overgrown shrubs made the house almost disappear from sight. When LeRoy bought a brand new Ford automobile, the children along Smoky Road were directed by their parents to get off the road when they saw him coming. He had a heavy foot, and they knew his taste for alcohol had not slackened since coming into his small fortune. Even though, he now sported expensive clothes, he appeared unkept with his fine suits and shirts, looking as if he slept in them.

* * *

Vinson flipped his coat collar up and tightened the knit wool scarf around his neck that Nadine had knitted. Winters were bitter cold in Detroit with the wind whipping across Lake Erie and the Detroit River, carrying droplets of ice which bit into his skin like pin pricks. As he walked briskly toward the laundry, where he worked, he noted the ugly graffiti smeared on buildings' walls and glanced at the snow banks blackened by passing cars which expelled carbon monoxide. This poisonous gas hovered between the tall buildings which lined both sides of the streets like walls. Strangers hurried by, avoiding eye contact with approaching pedestrians. The honking of car horns was abrasive to his ears.

Vinson mentally transported himself from this unpleasant setting to his home in West Virginia. He stood on his parents' front porch where the pure white undisturbed blanket of snow could be seen stretching across the yard and fields until it slowly angled up into the rolling hillside. He breathed in the pungent smell of pine as the boughs of the evergreens drooped toward the ground under the weight of snow. If he were very quiet, he could hear the sound of Cow Creek as it began to thaw and see little bubbles appearing right below the creeks surface of ice. As the sun melted this layer of ice, leaving a thin white lacy crust along the edge of its banks, the sound of the swift stream could be heard once again. From inside the house, came the smell of home smoked ham frying, biscuits baking and fresh coffee brewing. Cooking up this breakfast was Mom. She expertly maneuvered about the kitchen, dressed in her crisp feed sack dress. He could hear her call "Vinson, breakfast is ready. Come and get it while it's hot."

His thoughts then turned toward Nadine with her auburn hair shining like copper in the sunlight, her quick warm smile lighting up her freckled face, and her never ending plans for a fun evening: sleigh riding, ice skating, going to a movie, visiting friends. Then regret swept over him about his leaving her, sending only a letter of explanation. As he opened the door to the laundry, he heard the loud hissing of steam from the presses. He was back in Detroit.

One evening as he walked down the hall of the boarding house, where he and Hobart shared a room, the landlady waved him down. "Got a letter today," she said, fishing into her deep apron pockets to pull out a white envelope. "Looks like a woman's writing to me."

Vinson, always anxious for mail, grabbed it from her outstretched hand. "Thank you, Ma'am."

"Yep," she said with a nod, "Now be careful not to track water down the hall. Somebody might slip and fall. You hear?"

"Yes, Ma'am," Vinson responded over his shoulder, moving quickly toward his room while tearing open the envelope as he walked. He recognized his sister Ochel's handwriting.

Dear Vinson:

I hope you and Hobart are getting along well in Detroit. I know it must be cold there because we're having a colder than usual winter here. Everybody is in good health. Our spirits have been lifted since Roosevelt's election. The hundred day bank holiday began moving the nation in the right direction. Now there is hope even though there is still lots of unemployment. Uncle Pearl Erwin's boys are working for the WPA which is helping Pearl. He was really having a tough time. The bank was about to foreclose on his loan.

Some of the plants here abouts are doing a little hiring. They'll need coal to operate, so mining should pick up. It will take time to pull out of this economic mess, but as I said there is a glimmer of light. By the way, I hear that in about a month, DuPont at Belle is going to do some hiring. Mom and Pop sure would like to see you come home. They send their love.

Your Sis,
Ochel

Vinson stared at the squiggly marks of the letter for a minute before folding it. His eyes drifted around the sparsely furnished room equipped with a small heating plate for warming food, a bed, table, and two chairs. The one window afforded little light, and dark was coming on. He brushed his hand down over his mouth. It had cost more to live here than he had anticipated. He had sent very little money home. He might just have saved enough for a train ticket home though. If only, he could get a job at DuPont or if worse came to worse, the WPA. He slipped the letter under his pillow.

*   *   *

A group of onlookers stood gaping at the half submerged car being pulled up from the bleak February waters of Coal River.

Police walked about with pencils and tablets in hand, jotting down information. Nadine heard comments fly among the neighbors. "I just don't understand how he failed to make the curve. He has driven this road a hundred times," said one.

"The road was wet from the rain," interjected another.

"He'd probably been drinking again," a woman added as she tightened her scarf over her head to ward off the cold.

A man beside her said, "But still he should know this road like the back of his hand as many times as he drove it."

A fleshly woman still in her thick robe pushed her way toward one of the cops. Nadine recognized her as one of Mom's newer tenants. Her voice rose above the others, "I seen the whole thing; I did. It was down right eerie." A policeman turned toward her. "I was closing my bedroom window to keep the rain out." She pointed a finger with a dirty jagged nail toward her house, "When I seen it."

"What exactly did you see?" probed the cop.

Everyone's attention turned in her direction, and all discussion ceased. Noting she had everyone's attention, she lowered her voice. "As the fast moving car approached the curve, its yellow headlights flashed onto a short haired black dog. I swear, instead of trying to avoid the dog, the driver seemed dead set on running it down." She stopped to take a breath. "The dog ran across the road, there-abouts," she made another gesture toward the river side of the road, "trying to escape the on coming wheels. The dog didn't bark or nothing." Her eyes widened as she vividly recalled the incident. "He, LeRoy that is, swerved to the opposite side of the road in pursuit of the poor animal. That was when the car went into a skid on the wet pavement, flipping top side into the river."

"Was LeRoy in the car when it submerged?"

"Yes, sir."

Somebody in the crowd spoke up, "He was probably too drunk, if he were in his usual shape, to get out."

Once the car was pulled from the water, this conjecture proved true, for there was LeRoy blue from the cold with a horrified expression on his face, with his eyes wide open and his mouth gaping. Beside him was a half empty pint of whiskey.

Nadine turned her head at the sight of LeRoy being lifted from the car. *Dutch, it was Dutch. LeRoy always hated Dutch. He was the only black dog along Smoky Road. Thank goodness Dutch escaped.* She felt neither sorrow nor glee, only numbness over LeRoy's death. She knew he was an evil person. The image of his standing guard over Mrs. Taylor as the expression in her eyes seemed to be telling of LeRoy's neglect flashed through Nadine's mind. She also remembered the plate with a crusty egg yolk setting on Frances' bed stand with a fly buzzing about.

*   *   *

Nadine was intense as she wrote out an order to the store's wholesaler. Dropping her pencil, she leaned over to hunt it. At that moment, the bell on the front door rang. Quickly straightening up, her eyes met his. It seemed as if their eyes interlocked. Try as she may, she could not look away. "Nadine, I waited until Mr. Stone left the store. I wanted to talk to you alone."

Unable to shift her gaze, she began to roll her pencil between her thumb and forefinger. "Vinson, its been so long," were her only words.

"I know. I am ashamed that I didn't say a proper goodbye our last evening, but it was so perfect that I couldn't ruin it. Please forgive me."

"A lot has happened since you left," she said, hoping the flutter in her heart would stay there and her voice remain calm.

"Yes, when I got home, Carl told me about Mrs. Taylor. I'm so sorry and then LeRoy." Vinson stepped in her direction, but Nadine stepped back. He wanted to rush forward and take her in his arms, but he dare not. This was not the time.

"So you've been home long enough to talk to Carl?" The words caught in her throat, and she coughed.

Vinson lowered his eyes, "Yes, I had some things to get settled before I came to see you." He looked up and saw that Nadine was blushing. "Nadine, I made a reservation for two at Wren's Nest for this evening. We have a lot of catching up to do."

Nadine's eyes narrowed. "I believe we can do all our talking right here." Her mouth was saying words that contradicted what her heart said. *He deeply hurt me, and he can't just come strolling in and expect to pick up where we left off.*

"Ok, if that is how you want it." He crossed his arms.

Nadine wondered if she had offended him to the point that he would turn and walk out.

"We'll just talk here, then." Vinson responded, shoving his hands deep into his trouser pockets.

He's just as handsome as ever, hoping her face did not betray her. "Are you in town visiting?"

Encouraged by her question, even though it was asked in an icy tone, he took another step in her direction. This time she stood her ground.

"No, I'm here to stay," he said softly.

"Didn't you like the big city?" Her chin jutted forward.

"No, I can't say that I did. I missed my family, but mostly I missed you." This time it was he who blushed. He looked away and then back at her. He forced himself to complete his mission. "Nadine," he said, looking directly into her eyes. "I left because I had no job, and I couldn't offer you the security you deserve."

Nadine felt she was hearing her own words coming back to her, "security, family."

Vinson continued, "Sis wrote me about DuPont hiring, so I caught the next train home and guess what?"

"You have a job here?" Nadine couldn't contain herself. She clapped her hands in glee as a smile warmed her face and eyes.

Vinson dared now to move still closer. As he did, he pulled a small box from his pocket, flipping it open. The overhead light hit its contents just right to show its rainbow of colors. "Since I have a job, Pop lent me money to buy this diamond ring. He felt his nerve waning, but he managed to ask, "Nadine will you marry me?" Suddenly his mouth felt dry and he swallowed.

Nadine did not say a word as she extended her left hand to allow him to slip the ring onto her finger. "It is so beautiful. I've never had anything like this, ever." She held it up to make it sparkle. She was in disbelief that this could be happening. If only she could freeze this moment in time.

"But, will you marry me?"

"Of course I will. I love you. Vinson, you are my love and my security. This ring is the only concrete proof that this happened, or tomorrow when the morning light comes I'd think I had been dreaming."

*　　*　　*

Nadine felt the warmth of a tiny squirming body in her arms. She gently pulled back the blanket and peeked at her first child, a baby girl. "I'll always be here for you, little one," she whispered. She leaned over to nuzzle closer as the baby's high pitched cry penetrated the quiet Hamrick and Bailey Clinic on Main Street. This high pitched cry set off another set of lungs which sounded like a bull frog.

Nadine looked over at Parthena Hutchinson her roommate and only other patient in the small clinic. Parthena radiantly looked down at her first born, David.

Someday I'll have a boy too, Nadine thought.

That thought was interrupted by, "I understand I have a niece." Carl peeked around the door and then stepped into the room. "The nurse said that it was visiting hours," he added suddenly feeling a little uncomfortable standing in a hospital room with two new mothers. He wanted assurance that it was okay.

Nadine propped herself up to hand her baby girl to her Uncle Carl. Carl tried not to look awkward holding a tiny baby. Looking down at her he said, "I think she knows me. Look at her smiling. What did you name her?"

"Patricia. You know my birthday is St. Patrick's Day, and Vinson's pet name for me is Pat. I think Patricia is just the right name, don't you?"

"Sounds right to me," he said, looking at the five pound bundle. "I thought proud Poppa would be here."

"You know Vinson. He's taking advantage of the last of the daylight to clear the lot we're building on. He goes straight there every day after work."

Carl handed Patricia back to Nadine when the baby started crying. "Yep, Vince takes this family thing seriously all right."

Clearing some magazines off the bedside chair, he sat down. Dr. Hamrick's wife, who was the hospital's only nurse, walked in and with one jerk pulled the white curtain around Parthena's bed to afford privacy. Without a word she turned about and walked out.

Nadine became serious, "Carl, just think I have a husband with a good job, a healthy baby and soon a home. I think an angel must watch over me."

"God is good," Carl agreed. "But he sure takes us through some rough knocks."

"But He is by our side even in the rough times," Nadine said thoughtfully, "or one of His angels," she added.

At her last statement Carl glanced up with a knowing look but only responded by a nod.

"Mrs. Taylor had a saying, 'After the darkness comes light.'"

Now, I know this is true and must remember it for the hard times to come."

REFERENCES

Call, Patricia E. Personal interview with Cunningham, Lillian, Telephone interview—July, 2000.

Call, Patricia E. Personal Interview with Townson, Jesse Orthmeyer, June 12, 2002.

Cook, Jack and Joe Philpott. Audio taped interview of Nadine Erwin & Molly Philpott, March 17, 1982.

Davisson, Russell L., Editor. *A Century With St. Albans, West Virginia.* St. Albans, WV: Harless Printing Co. Inc, 1963.

Derks, Sarah A. "1918 Flu & Midcentury Polio Epidemics Took Their Toll." Memphis: *Commercial Appeal*, July 4, 1999.

Graley, Carol Sue, Chairperson for the St. Albans History Book et.al. *St. Albans History 1872-1993.* St. Albans, WV: Walsworth, 1993.

Harris, Vernon B. *Great Kanawha.* Charleston, WV: Jarrett Printing Co., 1994.

Hereford, A.D., and H.P. *Early History of St. Albans.* St. Albans: Dawson Printing, 1950.

Lowry, Terry. *The Battle of Scary Creek.* Charleston, WV: Pictorial Histories Publishing Co., 1982.

Wintz, William D., Editor. *Recollections & Reflections of Mollie Hansford, 1828—1900.*

Wintz, Bill. "Echoes From The Past: Show Boat Era" by Jerome Collins. St. Albans, WV: *Community News*, September 16, 1997.

Wintz, Bill. "Echoes From The Past: Murder on the Street Car" by Rufus Clendennen. St. Albans, WV: *Community News*, September 2, 1997.

Wintz, Bill. "Echoes From The Past: The Zany French Yankee During The Civil War" from *Military Reminiscences of the Civil War*, p. 70, St. Albans, *Community News*.

ABOUT THE AUTHOR

Patricia Erwin Call has an earned doctorate from West Virginia University. She was a tenured Professor at West Virginia State University, and taught at West Virginia Institute of Technology, University of Memphis, and retired from Marshall University. She was Research Director for the West Virginia Post-Secondary Commission and taught school at the elementary through secondary levels.

She has been published frequently in juried educational journals, historical magazines, and prize winning collections. Her first published book is the humorous *Nadine and Vinson*.

Nadine: After the Darkness Comes Light is her first foray into a more serious vein.